"When Wayne asked me to read his latest book, I didn't think I had the time, but he was relentless. But once I starting reading I just couldn't stop. I only wish he'd written it sooner. Chock full of heartfelt personal anecdotes that entertain as well as inspire, the book provides a powerful motivational pep talk as only Wayne Allyn Root can deliver it."

—Peter Schiff, author of the *New York Times* bestseller *The Real Crash*, president of Euro Pacific Capital, and chairman of Schiff Gold

"I was a college football Coach of the Year, then a 2-time AFC Coach of the Year in the NFL. I can tell you *The Power of Relentless* is the same playbook I used to win football games at the highest level and mold young men into champions. When you read this book you will become closer to success in your chosen field of endeavor."

—Ron Meyer, two-time AFC Coach of Year (New England Patriots, Indianapolis Colts)

"Wayne Root is truly relentless. No matter your field of endeavor—business, sales, picking winners on Wall Street—it's always dependent on your being relentless in the face of challenge, adversity, obstacles. Wayne understands success is about cracking the door open one inch, pursuing your dreams relentlessly, refusing to accept defeat, then banging the door down. Bravo."

—John Mauldin, chairman of Mauldin Companies, editor of *Thoughts from the Frontline*, and *New York Times* bestselling author of *End Game*

"The Canadian physician Dr. Marion Hilliard wrote that he 'would never wish anyone a life of prosperity and security. These are bound to betray.' Instead he wished 'for adventure, struggle, and challenge.' Wayne Root's *The Power of Relentless* is a wonderful account of his own failures and successes, poignantly narrated. What caught my fancy is that *The Power of Relentless* is not just a book about monetary success but about contentment, peace of mind, generosity, health, and friendship—all qualities which remind us that a truly rich man is one whose children run into his arms when his hands are empty."

—Marc Faber, founder of Marc Faber Limited, financial commentator on CNBC, and author of *The Gloom, Boom & Doom Report*

"As a serial entrepreneur, I have been up and down the success ladder more than once. My family mantra is, 'The harder I fall, the higher I bounce.' You have to be 'Relentless' to bounce in business. Fortunately, at the age of fifty-five, I once more bounced 'relentlessly.' Our kiosk company has sold over one and a half billion dollars of products in the specialty retail industry. They say defeat is not an option. At least it is not a desirable one. Wayne Root in the epitome of being 'RELENTLESS.' His drive is inspirational, and his advice is germane to your business and your personal success."

—Max James, founder and executive chairman of American Kiosk Management, member of the Specialty Retail Hall of Fame, Air Force Academy Distinguished Graduate Award winner, Founders Board Director of the Air Force Academy Endowment Foundation, and philanthropist, founder and chairman of the Camp Soaring Eagle Foundation

"I've known Wayne since we were both seven years old. I've had a front row seat to his passion, relentless drive, and success. Study him and learn from him. *The Power of Relentless* works."

—Peter H. Diamandis, founder and Chairman of XPRIZE and Singularity University and *New York Times* bestselling author of *Abundance* and *Bold*

"*The Power of Relentless* is the bible of the new digital age and a powerful new way to achieve the highest levels of personal, professional, and financial success. My path to success started by reading every major success book. This book goes beyond anything I've ever read. Wayne Root will leave a legacy that will inspire readers to realize their dreams for generations to come."

—Joseph Sugarman, founder and chairman of BluBlocker Sunglasses and marketing, branding, and copywriting legend

"Wayne Root is on the money with *The Power of Relentless*. This book describes exactly the principles I utilized to start a small company in a basement and achieve hyper-growth into the largest online vitamin retailer in the world, winning the INC 500 Hall of Fame award for the fastest growing company in America, followed by a NASDAQ IPO and its recent sale to a Fortune 100 company. Wayne combines a relentless pit bull mindset with the perfect balance of body, mind, spirit, and nutrition. He's got the winning formula."

—Wayne Gorsek, founder and chairman of DrVita.com, entrepreneur, and philanthropist

"There never would have been a bestselling book or mega hit movie called *The Wolf of Wall Street* if I wasn't relentless. I was relentlessly hungry. I was relentlessly driven. I was relentlessly intense. I was relentlessly aggressive. I built an empire. Now I've come back bigger than ever. *The Power of Relentless* works. Just be sure and put ethics and integrity first."

—Jordan Belfort, the real-life "Wolf of Wall Street," *New York Times* bestselling author, international business speaker, and sales legend

"Energy, passion, intensity, and unbridled enthusiasm are the keys to Wayne's incredible life. I'm proud to place this dog-eared book on my nightstand as a daily reminder that being RELENTLESS is the key to opportunity, success, wealth, and ultimately happiness."

—Phil Gordon, professional poker player, entrepreneur, philanthropist, star of *Celebrity Poker Showdown* on Bravo, and CEO and founder of Chatbox.com

"The Power of Relentless is the answer to what you do when life smashes you in the face. Wayne Root shows you how to fight back and throw a knockout punch."

—David Bego, founder and CEO of The EMS Group, Executive Management Services, Inc., a nationwide commercial cleaning and facility services company and author of *The Devil at Our Doorstep*

"As the founding editor of *Ms. Fitness* magazine, I can honestly say that the twelve-step program found in *The Power of Relentless* is a boot camp to success, fitness, and power in ALL areas of life. Wayne Root has taken the concept of mind/body to a powerful level while organically tossing in what most have missed: that financial fitness is a vital part of the picture to having the life of your dreams."

—Greta Blackburn, editor of *Ms. Fitness* magazine and co-author of *The Immortality Edge*

"No guts, no glory. Without question, author Wayne Root is the most relentless person I have ever known. Which is why it's no surprise that, in his fabulous new book *The Power of Relentless* he does such a great job of teaching the reader how to get whatever he or she wants out of life. No doubt about it, Wayne has chutzpah!"

—Robert Ringer, No. 1 *New York Times* bestselling author of *Winning Through Intimidation* and *Looking Out for Number One*

"*The Power of Relentless* should be required reading in every business school in America—you can literally feel Wayne Root's passion, high-octane energy, and relentless spirit jump out of the pages of this book. I am left speechless!"

—Ronald L. Loveless, former assistant to the president of Walmart and former senior vice president and general manger of Sam's Club

The Power of Relentless

THE
POWER
OF
RELENTLESS

7 Secrets to Achieving Mega-Success,
Financial Freedom, and the
Life of Your Dreams

WAYNE ALLYN ROOT

REGNERY
PUBLISHING
A Division of Salem Media Group

Regnery® is a registered trademark of Salem Communications Holding Corporation

Library of Congress Cataloging-in-Publication Data

Root, Wayne Allyn.
  The power of relentless : 7 secrets to achieving mega-success, financial freedom, and the life of your dreams / by Wayne Allyn Root.
      pages cm
  Summary: "Wayne Allyn Root, the "Capitalist Evangelist" of Las Vegas, explains how he relentlessly pursued success in this motivational and inspirational guide for hopeful entrepreneurs and capitalists"-- Provided by publisher.
  ISBN 978-1-62157-410-1 (hardback)
  1. Success in business. 2. Success. 3. Determination (Personality trait) I. Title.
  HF5386.R56 2015
  650.1--dc23
                                        2015018807
Published in the United States by
Regnery Publishing
A Division of Salem Media Group
300 New Jersey Ave NW
Washington, DC 20001
www.Regnery.com

Manufactured in the United States of America

10 9 8 7 6 5 4 3 2 1

Books are available in quantity for promotional or premium use. For information on discounts and terms, please visit our website: www.Regnery.com.

Distributed to the trade by
Perseus Distribution
250 West 57th Street
New York, NY 10107

"Never give in—never, never, never, never, in nothing great or small, large or petty, never give in except to convictions of honour and good sense. Never yield to force; never yield to the apparently overwhelming might of the enemy."

—Sir Winston Churchill

Contents

Foreword

RELENTLESS. That is the only way to describe Wayne Root.

I have been Wayne's friend, mentor, and business partner for over thirty years. As such I can take credit for some part of Wayne's enormous success, as well as a few of his failures. But, his relentless, never-say-die attitude? No, that's something he taught me!

I first met "Mr. Relentless" in 1983. Wayne had just graduated from Columbia University, where, as I'm sure many of you know, he was a classmate of future president Barack Obama (but that's a whole 'nother story). My wife and I had recently sold our apparel company in San Francisco and moved to New York to run her Seventh Avenue design company. As a quick background, I'm a Nebraska farm boy with an MBA from Stanford who spent a career involved with twenty-some startup and turnaround companies—some successful, some I couldn't save.

I've threatened for many years to write my own book titled *The Care and Feeding of Genius for Fun and Profit*. Wayne certainly qualifies as one of those special geniuses I've been fortunate to have met, mentored, and partnered with. Wayne's genius is his ability to read people; envision and, more importantly, grasp opportunity; maintain an incredible level of energy and enthusiasm; have the courage to risk everything again and again on an idea; and his unrelenting willingness to do the hard work and yes, be RELENTLESS in his pursuit of extraordinary success.

You're in the right place. Wayne isn't Warren Buffett or Donald Trump. He's not a billionaire mogul. But he has to be one of the most successful small businessmen in America and certainly THE most high-profile one.

Wayne is a one-man army running a self-created media empire. There's not much for anyone who isn't a billionaire to learn from billionaires. But there is much for everyone to learn from "Mr. Relentless." Wayne has made countless miracles happen with just an idea, a game plan, and a faith that never allows him to give up or give in. It's actually remarkable, bordering on miraculous.

At the time we met, Wayne was selling commercial real estate. In addition to some other high-end properties, he had a famous Manhattan nightclub for sale. For some unknown reason a mutual friend thought I might be interested in buying the nightclub and introduced us. Now, let me tell you, Nebraska farm boys who become Stanford MBAs do not buy nightclubs. It was so far out of my wheelhouse that when Wayne said he'd pick me up at 11:00 to see the club I responded (actual quote), "I didn't know they were open in the day time." Wayne of course meant 11:00 p.m., when the place just started getting going.

I might not have been interested in the nightclub, but from our first meeting I was definitely interested in Wayne as an entrepreneur. Here was a young man from the Bronx borderline, a blue collar S.O.B. (son of a butcher) turned Ivy League whiz kid, whose upbringing was totally different from mine. I was fascinated. At the time we met he was wearing Armani suits, driving an exotic sports car, living on the Upper East Side of Manhattan, and dating Wilhelmina models; and he was a bundle of unharnessed energy. From my perspective it looked like his life was already pretty darn good. Even then, Wayne had great ambition, vision, and chutzpah (he aimed for the sky). But Wayne was smart enough to know how little he actually knew, and how much more he had to learn to get where he wanted to go. He was hungry. Actually *STARVING!*

One night we were having dinner at a Chinese restaurant in Manhattan after looking at real estate. Wayne looked across the table and confessed, "Doug, I know you're from a tiny, one-horse, no-stoplight Nebraska farm town. You've clearly done well for yourself. Well, I'm an S.O.B. (son of a butcher) struggling to achieve some mighty big goals. I need your help to move to the next level. I think meeting you was fate. What advice do you have that can help me become a *real* success?"

I hesitated for a minute, considering "Do I really want to commit myself to this?" before telling him, "Wayne, one of the things I have learned is that the way you turn dreams into reality is to have a plan. So, dream with me. What would you love to do with your life?"

"That's easy," he quickly responded. "I love sports and have a gift for betting on sporting events and beating the odds. I also have a gift for gab and was born to be on television. I should be my generation's 'Jimmy The Greek.' The Greek is getting old and will retire soon, someone will replace him . . . why not me?" (Note: At the time Jimmy "The Greek" Snyder was a big name in television and the most famous Vegas oddsmaker in the world.) But Wayne didn't stop there. "After I become a media star and 'The King of Vegas' I want to go into politics."

I'll admit my jaw dropped a little. First, if guys with my background don't buy nightclubs, we also don't tend to dream about becoming media celebrities and Vegas oddsmakers either. And then, there was an idea I had never heard of, mixing gambling and politics. This kid's dream was crazy. But I'd come this far, and if that was this brash young man's dream, then my job was to help him make it come true. And, as I had just told him, step one is a plan. As in all great entrepreneurial stories, we sketched out that plan on the back of a napkin right there in that Chinese restaurant.

My first son had just been born, and I was taking the year off playing "Mr. Mom." The plan we came up with was that we would write a press release and blast it out to get the media's attention. I told Wayne about the movie *The Hustler* (starring Jackie Gleason and Paul Newman), where a young upstart pool shark wants to challenge and beat the "old guy." We decided to use a similar pitch, "Wayne Root challenges Jimmy 'The Greek' to a duel for $1 million." Of course Wayne didn't have $1 million. But that never stopped (or slowed) Wayne.

We drafted a press release and sent it to two hundred newspapers, radio, and TV stations with me listed as Wayne's agent and contact. Actually, I should say I helped draft the news release, and Wayne did all the work of finding the addresses and sending it out. I wrote the "newsy" part of the press release. Wayne wrote the part with the brash challenge.

As a quick aside, over the years, as a person known to be an entrepreneur and willing mentor, I've gladly met with dozens of people looking to start their own business. They invariably come "seeking advice." Unfortunately, what they are really seeking is someone to do the work for them. That wasn't Wayne … not by a long shot. What has made Wayne so wonderful to mentor and partner with over the years is that a few days after asking my advice, he'd always come back with "Ok, I did all that, now what?" He absorbed ideas and wisdom like a sponge and always wanted more.

I must admit I gave our plan little chance for success and was not surprised when we got exactly ZERO responses.

"Ok, what do I do now?" Wayne asked. "Send out another two hundred," I responded. When that second two hundred had the same result, I mentally gave up. But not "Mr. Relentless." He sent out another several hundred … and then sent a slightly revised press release to another several hundred … and another several hundred.

The result? We got one yes. A small newspaper ran a story about Wayne's challenge. I thought to myself, "So what? What do we do with this small story?" Wayne saw the bigger picture. Even then he understood that once a door is opened a crack, you've got to bang the door down. He made a copy of that one insignificant story and sent it out to hundreds of media—*again*. Once again we got one yes, one single response. Actually I should write that yes as "YES!" because it was the most important yes of Wayne's young life. In baseball 1 for 400 gets you sent to the minors, or retired forever. But to "Mr. Relentless" this was a victory. And Wayne was right!

This one single call changed Wayne's life (as well as my own). The call was from Vic Ziegler, Sports Editor of the *New York Daily News*, at the time the most-read newspaper in America. Vic said he liked Wayne's challenge and wanted to interview Wayne. Two weeks later a full-page story appeared in the *New York Daily News*, read by millions of New Yorkers, with the headline: "The Kid Wants The Greek." It branded Wayne as a Wild West gunslinger with brass balls in the media capital of the world.

Soon, the media came calling from all over America. They even interviewed "Jimmy The Greek." The Greek's quote: "You tell Wayne Root that in every city, town, and village in America there are a thousand guys who want to be Jimmy The Greek. Get in line."

From there it was history. Four years later Wayne, without ever having been in front of a TV camera (but with an incredible manager) got hired as a sports anchor on Financial News Network, now CNBC. He was a star from the moment he sat in front of the camera. The kid who had never been on television was quickly hosting five shows on national TV. *FIVE*. To my knowledge nothing like this has ever happened in TV history and probably never will again.

Now, I won't tell you it was an easy journey. Wayne's journey was so difficult few would have ever stayed committed. But then that's why Wayne is special. Wayne's power of RELENTLESS is what separates dreams from reality, dreamers from successes. Few understand that a relentless mindset is the secret to success.

As Wayne's manager at the time, I can attest to the fact that he received more rejections and outright "NOs" than any man should ever be forced to suffer in a lifetime—literally thousands of rejections. Were all the rejections hard to hear? Absolutely! But did they stop Wayne? Not a chance. They actually inspired him. The man is ... well, he's *relentless*.

One of those wonderful twists and turns in life happened when, during his second week at FNN, Wayne was called into his boss's office and asked to co-host a new show. His co-host? Jimmy "The Greek" Snyder. Wayne's commitment, faith, and relentless, never-say-die attitude had moved him to "the head of the line." Soon Wayne had a book deal, a magazine column, and a radio show and was interviewing the biggest stars in sports, from famous NFL owners Jerry Jones of the Dallas Cowboys and Al Davis of the Raiders, to managers and coaches like Bill Walsh of the San Francisco 49ers and Tommy Lasorda of the Dodgers, to star athletes like Joe Montana, Brian "The Boz" Bosworth, Magic Johnson, Larry Bird, and Steve Garvey, to Olympic champions Mark Spitz, Janet Evans, and Bruce Jenner.

Wayne left FNN when he leveraged his position as Network Oddsmaker and NFL analyst into the world's greatest job as a professional sports handicapper. It earned him a mansion overlooking the Pacific Ocean in Malibu, California. For a decade Wayne's job, on Tuesdays during the seventeen weeks of football season, was to drive down the hill from his Malibu mansion to LAX airport, catch a flight to Las Vegas, be picked up by a limo and dropped off at a suite at the Rio Resort, film a TV show the next day, fly home, and tell his wife, "Honey, don't bother me, I have to watch football, it's my job."

Eventually Wayne even wound up being awarded a 180-pound granite star on the Las Vegas Walk of Stars, as one of only sixty legends so honored in the history of Las Vegas. The day it was installed was named "Wayne Root Day" in the state of Nevada, with the Governor introducing Wayne at the ceremony. This "Power of RELENTLESS!" thing is pretty amazing!

Every guy in America would have given his left arm for Wayne's life. But for Wayne ... it wasn't enough.

During that time, I was off running multiple companies, living my life, and raising my family. But we stayed in touch weekly, and often daily, sharing experiences and advice. Wayne is godfather to my sons. One day in 1995, Wayne called, told me he had been thinking about his life, thought he had more to offer than just picking sports winners, and decided he wanted to be a motivational speaker like Tony Robbins. I told him that plan was easy: "Write the book."

A month later he came to me with the draft of the book. Yes, I said one month later. *Just like that.*

When I asked Wayne how he had the energy to knock out a book in such a short time he replied:

"Doug, when I set my mind to it, there is nothing I can't accomplish. You know I don't smoke or drink, have never touched a drug, eat healthy, and take mega-vitamins. I'm a fitness fanatic, pray, and meditate. When the pressure is on or things are going badly, most people turn to negative addictions: drinking, smoking, drugs, unhealthy food, overeating. Not me. I just become more and more addicted to those positive, healthy habits that I know are good for my mind, body, spirit, and soul. I am relentless about my positive habits."

Wayne calls them "Positive Addictions," and if there is one thing you simply must learn from this book, it is how to integrate Wayne's "Positive Addictions" into your personal life.

By the way, you're about to read Wayne's tenth book! The guy is ... well, he's RELENTLESS!

A few years later Wayne started pursuing me to join him in starting a new company, similar to the one he was working for in the sports-hand-icapping industry.

"I'm making a lot of money," he said. "But the company's owner is making a heck of a lot more and he is in control of my life. I understand the media and how to attract millions of customers to buy my advice, you know how to run a company ... let's start and build a business together."

I had just had a start-up that I tried to help get off the ground fail and was involved with saving another one. I told him, "Wayne, start-ups are just too hard. I've only got the time and energy to do one more before I retire and it's going to be internet-related because that's where they're passing the bowl of cherries on Wall Street."

For the next couple of years Wayne kept after me ... *relentlessly!* I kept saying no. But for Wayne, "no" is just the start of a negotiation. Finally I gave in and we launched a sports-handicapping business in Las Vegas producing television and radio shows and operating a one-hundred-employee call center.

Over the next ten years, in addition to Wayne, who was always the star, we had a stable of well-known sports luminaries and NFL superstars as handicappers, including Hall of Famer John Riggins, New York Giants Super Bowl champion Phil McConkey, Hall of Famer Dan Hampton, and Hall of Famer Randy White, along with two-time AFC coach of the year Ron Meyer. After a ten-year run it was time for me to retire and play golf, so we sold the company to a publicly traded British firm. Wayne will tell you the details of that story. It's amazing. A testament to the power of RELENTLESS!

I must admit I was not surprised when Wayne told me in 2008 that he wanted to run for the presidential nomination of the Libertarian Party. I was well aware that even with all his other endeavors, politics had always been his passion and first love. A lifelong Reagan conservative, Wayne had recently turned to the Libertarian Party, telling me he had not left the Republican Party, but rather "the party left me." Now he wanted to be on their presidential ticket. Crazy, right? Impossible, right? Delusional, right? Not with "Mr. Relentless." No dream is too big when it's Wayne you're talking about. *Anything is possible.*

As with everything he does, Wayne went after his goal relentlessly. Even though he laid considerable groundwork, including traveling the country meeting Libertarian leaders and delegates in every state, it became clear that as a "newly minted" Libertarian he was fighting an uphill battle. Wayne was competing with a United States senator, a congressman, and lifelong activists, leaders, and legendary authors from within the party. Every expert said he had no chance at the convention. But Wayne moves mountains, *relentlessly*. With his normal never-say-die attitude and never-ending enthusiasm Wayne beat out a veteran U.S. senator, almost beat a four-term congressman who led the impeachment of President Bill Clinton, and was voted by the delegates, whom he'd won over by now, as the vice presidential nominee. Crazy, right?

I'd met this young man some twenty-five years before and had told him "dreams become goals with a plan." Now he was on a presidential ticket, just as he had aimed for. Why? Because he was relentless in pursuing his dream. I couldn't have been more proud when the next morning I watched him on Fox News discussing his plans for saving the U.S. economy. All I could think was, "WOW. There's Mr. Relentless."

Later that night in Wayne's campaign suite, after countless television interviews, we were reviewing the events of the day. Wayne commented to me, "I know we have little chance to actually win the election, but what if we do?"

"That's easy," I replied. "I'm Ambassador to France. And you're in deep trouble." Wayne smiled that Wayne Root smile. It's a smile that makes you think anything is possible.

Now, from "Mr. Relentless" himself, Wayne Allyn Root, a man who has taken himself from humble beginnings as a blue-collar S.O.B. (son of a butcher) to a well-respected businessman, vice presidential candidate, political pundit, bestselling author, and national media personality, you are about to have the great pleasure of reading "The Power of RELENTLESS!"

In it you will also learn how to apply Wayne's "Positive Addictions" to your life so you too have the energy and mindset to make all your crazy, impossible dreams come true! Trust me, you are in the right place. Opportunity is knocking, all you need to do is let it in.

Sit back, buckle up, and hang on. You are about to take one hell of a ride.

Douglas R. Miller
Texas, U.S.A.
Spring 2015

Introduction

Think and Grow Relentless

·····································

"Everyone has a plan, until they get punched in the face."
—Mike Tyson

I wrote this book as "Part Deux" to follow what I consider to be three of the greatest books on success and wealth ever created: *Think and Grow Rich*, *The Power of Positive Thinking*, and *The Secret*. These three books changed and improved countless lives. Including mine.

The takeaway from all three is that you have to master your mind to become successful and attract the things you want in life. In the forward to *Think and Grow Rich*, Clement Stone, a billionaire business mogul of his day, promises that changing your thinking will lead to miracles. I agree wholeheartedly. How sad and tragic that the magic of positive thinking is not taught in every school and college in the world.

But ...

I'm going to let you in on a priceless secret. Positive thinking alone is only part of the equation. While it provides a solid foundation, positive thinking doesn't guarantee success. As with building a home, a solid foundation only guarantees a good start.

Positive thinking is similar to owning a good website. Today, practically every business needs a website. But just having a website, even a great one, doesn't guarantee success. Of course, that's not what people in the website development business tell you. They run advertisements that say, "without a website, you are up the creek without a paddle." Well, they are correct. Without a website you are practically guaranteed to fail. A great website at least gives you a "fighting chance." But having a great website doesn't guarantee success.

Why? Because having a great website doesn't guarantee anyone will see your site. You can have the greatest website in the world, with no traffic! I personally know many business owners with exceptional, awe-inspiring, state-of-the-art websites...and no customers. They are shocked. They thought having a great-looking website would guarantee success. It doesn't.

The positive thinking philosophy found in *Think and Grow Rich* and *The Power of Positive Thinking* and the positive affirmations found in *The Secret* leave you in the same situation as the person with the beautiful website and no traffic. They provide a fantastic foundation. Positive thinking is certainly crucial to your success. Actually it's almost impossible to succeed without that first step. But all by itself, it will leave you a long way from achieving success.

Why is that? It's because we all live in the "real world." And, the real world is filled with roadblocks, setbacks, rejection, failure, critics, naysayers, and negativity. We all get pounded by negativity every day. The missing ingredient to overcoming these real-world obstacles is the secret contained in *The Power of RELENTLESS*.

Like it or not, the real world is brutal. Bad things happen in the real world...every day. Bad things often happen *every hour* of every day. And, unfortunately, bad things happen to good people like you. And, these bad things can conspire to erode your belief... your faith...the very foundations of your positive thinking.

Plus, when bad things invariably happen, positive thinking not only falls short, it often backfires. People read these books and start to believe that if they simply think positive…and talk positive…and see positive things happening to them…the results will automatically be positive. With all this positive thinking they come to believe they are "bullet-proof." But they are wrong. That's not how life works.

That kind of thinking is dangerous, destructive, and demoralizing when the inevitable happens…and it *always* happens. I see it every day with my coaching clients, with attendees at my speeches and events, and with business associates and friends. They spend months thinking positive, chanting positive affirmations, and visualizing positive images…and then real life intrudes. Life, or fate, or coincidence (or whomever or whatever you want to blame) throws a monkey wrench into their best-laid plans.

Former heavyweight boxing champion Mike Tyson said it best:

"Everyone has a plan, until they get punched in the face."

Bravo, Mike. The real secret of success is how you respond to that punch. The Power of RELENTLESS was written as the answer to what you do *after* you get punched in the face.

Life is like a boxing match. You think your "positive thinking" makes you untouchable, invincible, unbeatable. Then, life comes along and punches you in the face…*hard*. Suddenly you are in shock. You're stunned. Because you realize in that instant that you aren't bulletproof. You are completely unprepared when the "NOs" come raining down on you.

I can hear you thinking inside your head, "This can't be happening to me? I'm invincible." Now you're flustered, dejected, frightened, and depressed. Confidence in your "positive thinking system" is shaken to the core. Your foundation is cracked.

But wait. It gets worse. Life has a way of kicking you when you're down. Now the negativity starts coming in waves (just like punches). What happens when you're at your weakest and you hear "NO" several times in the same day? What happens when people you thought would be impressed by your resume won't even return your call? What happens when people you thought might hire you are instead snickering at you? What happens when people you thought had your best interests at heart instead betray you? *What now?*

Won't your confidence melt away? Won't your positive thoughts turn to panic? That's the weakness of positive thinking alone. It's like a boxer with a good right hook...and nothing else. That boxer will soon find himself lying on the canvas thinking, "What the heck just happened?"

Positive thinking, positive affirmations, and visualizations are a good start. You just need to have a plan in place for when (not "if") you get punched in the face. Trust me, you will get punched in the face. You need to put your positive mindset together with the other half of the equation, The Power of RELENTLESS.

The Power of RELENTLESS is the *real* secret to applying positive thinking in the real world. Relentless is expecting the best, but being 100 percent prepared for the worst (which is what always happens in the real world).

How you react to the worst...how you perform under withering fire...your creativity under fire...your ability to stay positive and enthusiastic under fire...your ability to run over, under, or through massive roadblocks...your ability to turn lemons to lemonade...your relentlessness in the face of a withering flurry of punches in the face...*that is what will determine your level of success.*

At moments of challenge and adversity, most people, especially those who trust that everything will be fine with "positive thinking," pack up their bags, retreat, or quit. They fold like a cheap suit. And after that, they are never the same again.

It's like learning that a person you trust has lied to you. You will never fully trust them again. After the "positive thinking" true-believers fail and quit, they develop a negative attitude. They become more negative and cynical than the people who never believed in positive thinking in the first place. Once they stop believing in their dreams, it's game over.

That's precisely why The Power of RELENTLESS is the real secret of success. It's the missing link in the success equation. It's the second half of a powerful one-two punch. It's the knockout blow.

The Power of RELENTLESS completes the picture. It produces synergy. It's the 2+2=150 math model. Positive thinking is an important ingredient, but you can only succeed with *both* positive thinking *and* The Power of RELENTLESS.

This book will show you how to deal with adversity...with challenge...with rejection...with negativity...with the painful punches coming your way. This book is like a boxing coach that will teach you how to counterpunch like a champion. How to respond to the perfect punch with a *knockout punch!*

This book will show you how to deal with all the negative people trying to smash you in the face and ruin your perfectly laid plans. The Power of RELENTLESS is the perfect solution for what you do when you get punched in the face! You've got to punch back... *hard.*

This book *completes Think and Grow Rich, The Power of Positive Thinking,* and *The Secret.*

This book will change millions of lives by teaching the second step everyone else leaves out—the step that deals with the real world. This is the "secret sauce" of the success formula. *The whole enchilada.*

Without The Power of RELENTLESS, all the positive thinking, dreaming, affirming, visualizing, and chanting in the world won't close the deal. Those three fabulous books are all-time greats. But this book answers the question, "After I develop the perfect positive attitude, then what?" The answer is, you'd better get ready to fight.

This book shows you how to smash back and win.

You're about to learn how to fight like a cornered wolverine...how to take action...how to always play on offense—by always keeping your pedal to the metal...how to become a gunslinger and riverboat gambler...how to relentlessly pursue your dreams...how to live each day with an enthusiasm *unknown to mankind.*

What you are about to read is like the perfect marriage of Mike Tyson, Mother Teresa and Napoleon Hill!

Regardless of where you are in life, The Power of RELENTLESS will provide you with the tools, energy, enthusiasm, confidence and positive mindset to make the right decision and take the *right* action. It is that action that will change your life and turn your wildest dreams into reality.

Relentless people move mountains. Relentless people make the impossible, possible. Relentless people achieve miracles. Relentless people are ready for any challenge. Relentless people don't panic, retreat, or fold when smashed in the face. They expect it and are ready to counteract it with a remarkable plan that smashes right back…except harder! Relentless people are always looking for the knockout shot that makes them the champion.

Yes, it all starts with "The Power of Positive Thinking"…your ability to "Think and Grow Rich"…and, of course, "The Secret." But a happy ending *requires* The Power of RELENTLESS!

In the end, that's the *real* secret.

But as they say in the TV infomercial business …

Wait, there's more!

The Power of Relentless is only made possible by first mastering your inner self. Because before you can master anyone or anything else, you first have to master yourself. That's why I've added a special section to this book—with a proven program called "Positive Addictions."

It is important for you to know up front that this book isn't just "theory" or "philosophy." It's a proven real-world instructional manual. I'm about to empower you with a remarkable, easy-to-follow, step-by-step plan to harness and engage The Power of RELENTLESS.

I hope you ate your Wheaties this morning. Lock your seat belt. You're about to start the ride of your life.

The 1st Principle of RELENTLESS: Relentless HEART

....

*"When you are going through hell, keep on going.
Never, never, never give up."*
—Winston Churchill

I don't have to look far for my perfect model of RELENTLESS. Let me tell you a remarkable, magical, extraordinary story that literally defines relentless—the story of the last hours of Stella Root's story is the perfect illustration of Relentless Principle #1: Relentless HEART.

All success, all progress, all the miracles in this world are based on heart, on spirit, on will, on never giving up or giving in—on being *RELENTLESS* in pursuit of what you love.

My mother and father, Stella and David Root, died of cancer twenty-eight days apart in 1992, the toughest year of my life. I spoke at my father's funeral in New York and flew back to my home in Malibu, California, only to get a call a few days later from my sister telling me that our mom had gone into a tailspin after the funeral. Only days later, she was gone. But it was the remarkable last hours of Stella Root's life that I will remember and cherish forever. They drive me to new levels of RELENTLESS in every aspect of my life.

1

I'll never forget the call I got from my mother's doctor. "Wayne, I'm sorry to tell you this, but your mom is gone. Her brain no longer has activity, so we're disconnecting life support. Please don't rush home. She's gone. You've had enough tragedy in your family for one month. You have a wife and new baby on the way that depends on you. So please listen carefully to me ... be careful, take care of yourself, breathe deep, and don't rush home. She's gone. So there's no reason to rush home. Doctor's orders. Got it?"

That was the phone message I received from my mother's doctor on the last day of her life. Then he handed the phone to my sister (who whispered because she was afraid the doctor would hear what she had to say and she'd sound foolish), "Wayne ... ignore the doctor. Rush home. You and I both know Mom won't die until you get here. *Rush home!*"

I rushed to the airport and caught the red-eye flight that night out of Los Angeles to New York. The flight left late. It taxied on the runway forever. I ordered a car to pick me up at JFK airport to rush me to the hospital in Westchester County. But the car was caught in traffic and arrived late. Everything that could go wrong, did. By the time I walked into my mother's hospital room it had been twelve hours since I got that terrible phone call; twelve hours since life support had been disconnected; twelve hours since that doctor had said, "Don't rush home, your mom is gone."

Yet when I ran through the door to her room, I heard the most beautiful sound:

Beep ... beep ... beep ... beep ...

It was her heart monitor beeping. Despite being disconnected from life support, her heart was still beating. My sister had sat by her bedside all night saying, "Mom, hang on, Wayne is on the way. Don't die, Wayne is on the way." Medical science may have determined that her brain was dead, but that beeping heart monitor told another story. She had lived through the night on sheer willpower.

Some might call it a miracle. I simply call it The Power of RELENTLESS.

I hugged my mom and grabbed her hand. I kissed her cheek. I couldn't stop crying. I said, "Mom, I love you. Thank you for waiting for me. I know how hard that was. But I made it … and you made it. I'll always remember what you did for me. You sure showed those doctors. With all their fancy degrees, they didn't know you like my sister, Lori, and I know you. We knew you'd hang on to say goodbye. I love you … but now it's time to go. You deserve a rest. Heaven is waiting. It's time to go. Your children, both of them, give you permission to *let go.*"

And within seconds, her heart monitor went beep … beeeep … beeeeeeep … beeeeeeeeeeeep … flatline. And she was gone.

Medical science may have considered her brain dead, but somehow, some way, my mother had understood what was being said. She had heard my sister's pleas to hang on all night long. If her brain was dead, how did she know to hang on all night long? How did she will herself to live all the way until the next morning? How did she know that her son Wayne was on the way? If her brain was dead, how did she hear me say that it was time to let go? Why did her heart monitor stop within seconds of my giving her permission to let go?

My mother may not have had any brainpower left, but she had will-power. She had *heart.* And that's the most important thing in the world— no matter what your goal.

My mother defined RELENTLESS. She beat cancer for six long years, coming back a dozen times, unwilling to leave my father alone. She beat the odds because she had a huge heart. She had spirit and relentless will-power. In those last hours of life, she refused to lose faith, to give up, to give in—even though medical science and the best cancer doctors had declared her "brain dead."

Stella Root defined relentless in those last hours of her life. She wasn't going to die without saying goodbye to her only son, her baby boy Wayne.

WILLPOWER TRUMPS BRAINPOWER

Stella Root proved that heart is what matters in life. Heart is more important than the diagnosis of experts, or doctors, or scientists, or science itself. Hard facts don't matter when heart is involved. Heart is what makes miracles happen. Heart makes the impossible, possible. My mom's story proves that if your heart is big enough, it doesn't even matter if your brain is dead. That's The Power of RELENTLESS.

Being smart is a good thing in business. Being educated is a good thing. Connections are a good thing. But they are not the most important things. Willpower trumps brainpower. Heart is the intangible that's impossible to replace. Heart is the game-changer. Heart is that special ingredient that brings it all together to win Super Bowls, and World Series, and political elections ... and the biggest business deals of your life. Heart is what determines champions. Heart is the thing that separates winners from losers on life's battlefield. Heart separates the doer from the follower, the business owner from the employee. Heart, as the younger generation might say, is the *bomb*.

My mother, Stella Root, showed me the real secret is about testing the limits of the human heart. That's how you define "winning." That's how you define "success." That's how you define The Power of RELENTLESS. By testing the limits of your heart, that's how you define *you*.

When I look back on my success against all odds in so many diverse fields, I realize I had one heck of a "model" for success. I inherited amazing levels of spirit, will, and a tenacious, passionate, never-say-die attitude from my mother, Stella Root. I inherited the willingness to test the limits of my heart. With a model like that to follow, it's impossible to lose faith, impossible to give up or give in, impossible to admit defeat, impossible to see any goal as impossible. That's The Power of RELENTLESS.

Think. Think hard. Once you have harnessed that kind of power, spirit, will, tenacity, mindset, HEART, you can make all your dreams come true. You can make the impossible, possible. You can become all you want to be.

Read on. I'm going to show you how. Welcome to my world. Wayne's World!

"If your heart is big enough, it doesn't even matter if your brain is dead."

—Wayne Allyn Root

The 2nd Principle of RELENTLESS: Relentless CHUTZPAH

We are living through the worst economic crisis since 1929. History books will someday call this period "the Great Depression II." The business battlefield is littered with land mines, booby traps, and bodies. For every success story, there are thousands of failures. For every thriving business, there are dozens of vacant spaces that represent lost dreams. For every job opening, there are hundreds of applicants. Unemployment figures are only as low as they are because the government no longer counts those who have given up looking for work, or who are under-employed. The workforce participation rate is the lowest in modern history. And the few jobs being created are almost all crappy, low-wage, part-time jobs. It has never been harder to achieve success and upward mobility.

But in the midst of all this economic carnage, there is hope. It isn't found in your IQ. Lots of bright people are struggling.

It isn't found in your education. College grads are drowning in record levels of student debt, and even Ivy League grads are struggling to find decent jobs.

It isn't found in the energy and creativity of youth. More young people are living in their parents' basements than ever before.

It isn't found in fancy titles. Lots of CEOs are now struggling ex-CEOs. In this economy if you lose a job with a six-figure salary, you may very well find that your next stop is working at Gap.

It isn't found in Dad's connections. Even children of privilege are struggling. Connections are useless if there are no high-quality, high-paying jobs for *anyone.*

In this type of miserable economic environment, one thing, more than ever, separates the winners from the losers, the leaders from the wannabes, the dreamers from the succeeders. One thing allows people the world over to succeed against difficult odds. It is The Power of RELENTLESS!

And, specifically, Relentless Principle #2. Call it grit, staying power, stick-to-it-iveness, aggressive action, intrepidity, perseverance, the ability to bounce back from failures like the Energizer Bunny—in short, Relentless CHUTZPAH!

With that one edge…that mindset…that attitude…that way of thinking and living…you can accomplish any goal. You can turn the agony of defeat into the ecstasy of victory. You can turn lemons into lemonade. You can turn dreams into reality. Anything is possible.

I EAT "NO" FOR BREAKFAST

My life has been dedicated to the principles and actions I'll share with you throughout this book. The tools and attitude you will learn have led me from disaster, defeat, and rejection to the life of my dreams. It can lead you there as well.

Today, I am *thriving* in the worst economy of our lifetime. While so many others are paralyzed by fear, I am excited and enthusiastic about the world of opportunities and possibilities. My life is dominated by rock-solid confidence, while so many others have lost faith. That's The Power of RELENTLESS.

There is nothing else special about me. I'm not any smarter than the next guy or gal. I'd never make it on *Jeopardy.* I'm lost without a calculator. I need my two young sons to help me navigate anything difficult with a computer, or on the internet.

I'm not mechanical; I need to call a handyman whenever a light bulb is out. I have no sense of direction; when I'm lost, instead of using the GPS, I call my sons to talk me through it. I'm no athlete; remember that movie, *White Men Can't Jump?* I'm living proof. Saying that I can't dance or sing would be an understatement.

The list of things I can't do is long. But that list is not the one that matters. What matters is finding what you can do well, then pursuing it with complete disregard for the inevitable obstacles in your path.

Relentless CHUTZPAH is my specialty. It is my "ace in the hole," the one attribute that makes me special, that separates me from the crowd. I never give up. I never give in. I never let rejection or failure stop, or even slow me. For me, "NO" is just the start of a negotiation. In my mind, every "NO" means I'm one step closer to hearing the one "YES" that will make my day or change my life.

I actually crave "NO." C'mon, I dare you—reject me, turn me down, tell me that I can't do something, anything. When you have the power of RELENTLESS on your side, "NO" is powerless. "NO" is meaningless. "NO" just serves as inspiration. "NO" is what gives me that chip on my shoulder. The more I hear "NO," the more I know I'm on the path to victory. I eat "NO" for breakfast.

Challenges, obstacles, and insurmountable odds don't stop me. I just figure out a way around them, over them, under them, or I run right through them ... smashing the stone wall or the glass ceiling to smithereens!

Here's the great news. With Relentless CHUTZPAH, my story can be *your* story.

Life is a series of battles. I've been left lying bloody on the battlefield many times. Yet I never lost faith. I stayed focused, disciplined, motivated, enthusiastic, passionate, committed, confident, and tenacious. I got back up time and again. Then I charged back into battle. I am unbeatable, unstoppable, and incorrigible. That's the power of RELENTLESS.

That is how you beat the odds. That is how you overcome challenges. That is how you prove the cynics, critics, and naysayers wrong about you. That is the only way to put the odds in your favor in the worst economy of our lifetime.

For most people, even in the best of times, nothing comes easy. Forget luck or fate. Like 99 percent of all human beings, nothing I've ever achieved was because of luck. Sure I've had plenty of luck—almost all of it *bad*. I've almost always had to overcome any luck, fate, or coincidence that came my way. But that's easy with the power of RELENTLESS CHUTZPAH on your side.

The adversity I've overcome through the years has been great practice and preparation for dealing with today's miserable economy. While yesterday this power of RELENTLESS made super-achievers special and allowed them to reach the top, today things are so tough that you need this special power just to keep a job. Today you need this power of RELENTLESS every second of every day just to *survive*.

Even before today's "new normal" of mediocrity, extraordinary success never came easy. We often hear the biggest stars in business, entertainment, politics, and sports brag about their amazing success, lives, wealth, and fame. But rarely do you hear about the long journey of hard work, challenge, pain, setbacks, rejection, and failure they experienced to get there. Why? Because to tell the truth would make these super-achievers appear human—just like you or me.

The truth is, celebrities and high profile business leaders pay handlers and publicists to whitewash their faults and failures. Why? To make them appear superhuman, better than you or me, to keep you buying their movies, books, TV shows, their company stock, or their products at your favorite store. They believe that to let you see weakness, to show their struggles and failures, would reveal their humanity. *So they don't.*

What makes this so bad is that it discourages the rest of us. As we experience life's failures, we feel overwhelmed. We feel inferior. We see no hope. The truth is, everyone goes through challenges, adversity, rejection, and failure. The truth is that the winners are just like us—except for the fact they never lose faith, give up, or give in. All that is separating you from these super-achievers is understanding the need to keep the faith, stay the course, and keep fighting with commitment, courage, and the power of RELENTLESS CHUTZPAH. If only our heroes would explain that, it would give millions of ordinary people a desperately needed kick in the butt.

A BLUE COLLAR S.O.B.

I wasn't part of "the lucky sperm club" (born to wealthy, connected parents). I'm a blue collar S.O.B. (son of a butcher) from a dead end street on the Bronx borderline. I had no special talents. I was not born rich or connected. I didn't have a dime to start a business. I've faced massive amounts of rejection. I've failed so many times I've lost count. But I had one thing going for me that set me apart from the crowd—The Power of RELENTLESS CHUTZPAH.

My story isn't unique. In the real world, all of us face challenge and rejection. The odds are rarely in our favor. Most of us are born with no special talents, money, or connections. No one hands you anything. No one sits at the drug store counter and actually gets "discovered" by the CEO of a Hollywood film company. That only happens in a romance novel or fictional Hollywood movie. Fame, fortune, and success don't just drop in your lap. You have to put in your dues for years to achieve "overnight success." You have to fight for it. You have to punch and counterpunch. You have to want it badly. You can't wait for opportunity, because it will never come. You have to seize it. To do that, you'll need to harness The Power of RELENTLESS CHUTZPAH.

That one trait separates the winners from the losers. That's the one common ingredient in virtually every success story.

THE NEXT JIMMY THE GREEK

My story started with a dream. I wanted to be Jimmy "The Greek" Snyder. He was the most famous sports gambler and oddsmaker in Las Vegas. When I was a kid growing up on the tough streets of New York, every kid I knew wanted to be "The Greek." The difference was, I made it happen.

At age sixteen, I hustled my way into a feature story in the local newspapers. They called me "The Next Jimmy The Greek" and "The Betting Whizkid." Nice start. I stayed focused on my goal. When I met Doug Miller years later and he asked me what my dream was, I was quick to respond, "I want to be Jimmy 'The Greek.'" The point is, it took twelve more years (from 1977 to 1989) of promotion, hustle, tenacity, creativity, and mind-numbing RELENTLESS CHUTZPAH to achieve my goal. That newspaper story may have started it. But, it took another *twelve long years.*

Along the way I was rejected by literally thousands of TV, radio, and media experts; thousands more executives, producers, news directors, agents, and consultants rejected me too. *For twelve long years.*

Along the way, the media called "The Greek" himself and asked him about this young kid Wayne Root. Jimmy said, and I quote:

"You tell Wayne Root that in every city, town, and village in America there are a thousand guys who want to be Jimmy The Greek. Get in line."

I never stopped moving. I never stopped fighting. I never stopped dreaming. I never lost faith. Thousands of rejections didn't slow me. Unlike those "thousand guys" with the same dream, in every city, town, and village in America, I was RELENTLESS.

Yes, some really awful and depressing things happened along the way. One ABC television producer, thinking he was talking to my agent, said, "Wayne Root has absolutely no talent. Hell will freeze over before he lands a TV job." *Except I had no agent.* He was actually talking to *me.* Now when you have to hear those words about yourself—said directly to you—that's a tough day.

One Fox television executive actually saw promise in me. He invited me to Los Angeles for an interview "in the future." He didn't know I would take his offer literally. I had less than $500 in the bank, so I spent my last penny to buy a plane ticket to L.A. to meet him. I showed up unexpectedly on his doorstep one month later. The only problem? He no longer had a TV show to cast. The show had been cancelled. I had spent my last dollars on a three-thousand-mile wild goose chase.

I finally landed a big break. I was hired by NBC Radio to talk sports on over one hundred stations. Three months later, NBC spent $15 million to hire Casey Kasem for *America's Top 40.* In order to afford Kasem's big salary and make room for him on the air, they fired me. Only three months into my first starring role, it went up in smoke.

I can laugh about it now. But back then it was painful. However, when you are relentless, nothing can stop you. When you have The Power of RELENTLESS CHUTZPAH on your side, incidents like that motivate you, light the fire inside you, make you that much *more* committed to achieving your goal. The Power of RELENTLESS pushes you beyond your comfort zone, beyond what you thought possible.

After another year of relentless pursuit of my dream, another year of rejections, another year of disappointment, I finally hit pay dirt. I was hired by CNBC (known then as Financial News Network) as anchorman, host, and network oddsmaker. The interview that got me the job of a lifetime came after I made fifteen calls to the General Manager of the network, Arnie Rosenthal. Fifteen calls over two years, without a callback. I hit pay dirt on call number sixteen. That's RELENTLESS CHUTZPAH!

Within a few weeks of settling into my new job and life in Los Angeles, my boss asked me to come up to his office. I knocked on his door and opened it to see the most amazing sight of my life. Sitting in front of the desk was Jimmy "The Greek" Snyder himself. After all those years of fighting and struggling to replace "The Greek," this was the first time I'd ever met him.

My boss said, "Wayne, meet your new co-host. I'm teaming you guys up for your own television show." There may have been thousands of young guys in every city, town, and village in America waiting in line to be the next Jimmy "The Greek." But I had just moved to the front of the line! It took twelve years, but I had turned my wild, crazy, seemingly impossible dream into reality. That's The Power of RELENTLESS.

The way I had done it was even more miraculous. My competition was hundreds of experienced television hosts and anchormen from across the country and thousands more hungry young graduates of broadcast journalism schools.

Yet the guy who landed the job was me! I had never spent one hour on TV, not even on a local cable access channel. I had never taken a single broadcast journalism class. I had never been an intern or assistant at a TV network. I didn't have one connection in the TV business. Yet I had just become one of the youngest national television hosts and anchormen in America. And, as far as becoming the network oddsmaker went, I'd never spent one day in my life as an oddsmaker either! I'd never even *been* to Las Vegas.

I was so raw, I didn't know what a teleprompter was. Remember, these were the days before Obama. This was 1989. No one mentioned that word in those "old days." The GM had been so impressed by my in-person interview and a videotape of me sitting at an anchor desk that he hired me on the spot without asking my background. He had no idea I'd never been to broadcast journalism school or on TV. My first segment at the anchor desk, on national TV, was one for the ages. Since I'd never seen a teleprompter, instead of reading the words on the screen, I just kept talking. The result? I was so good no one cared. But when I got off the TV set, I was greeted by the executive producer of the network. He congratulated me on a great first thirty minutes, then asked, "Why didn't you just read what we wrote for you? Why did you ad lib the entire thirty minutes?" I answered, "Oh, those words on the screen? You wanted me to read those?"

The producer flipped. He paged my boss. They held an emergency meeting. They gave me a one-month warning. I was on "probation." I had four weeks to accomplish two things: a) get rid of my New York accent and b) learn to read the teleprompter. Or I would be fired and my dream would be dead before it started.

Well, what does a kid with RELENTLESS CHUTZPAH do under that kind of stress and ultimatum? He makes it happen. I hired a speech coach, Dr. Lillian Glass, to get rid of my accent … and I practiced teleprompter reading day and night in my off time. By the time the deadline arrived, I had no accent. I sounded like a Midwesterner. And I was the best damn teleprompter reader at Financial News Network. That's The Power of RELENTLESS.

I never looked back. I went from almost being fired to hosting five shows! No one ever threatened my job again. I settled in as the star of the network. I had beaten impossible odds. I had beaten out much more qualified competitors. I had made myself into a professional television broadcaster by learning "on the fly" in record time. I had turned a wild dream into reality. That's The Power of RELENTLESS.

But as they say in TV infomercials, *"Wait, there's more!"*

For me, RELENTLESS CHUTZPAH isn't just a story or career highlight. Being relentless is a way of life, a way of thinking, a way of acting, a way of living. My never-give-up attitude, grit, and determination have smashed down doors for the past thirty years. The goals were always ridiculously large; the odds against me ridiculously long; the rejections unending. Yet my RELENTLESS CHUTZPAH always won out.

SOMETHING MORE THAN TV

I was just getting warmed up. After two years of hosting five shows for CNBC, I realized I wanted something more than being a TV anchorman. That "more," I decided, was to turn my skills for picking the winners of sporting events into a business. I set a goal to become the leading sports prognosticator and oddsmaker in the country. I thought I had found what I wanted when I was hired by a Las Vegas handicapping company. I was soon making several hundred thousand dollars a year selling my prognosticating advice. It bought me a mansion in Malibu and a job working from home that would be the envy of 99 percent of all American men. But not me. To me, it was just that, a job with someone else in control of my life. I came to realize that I was a born entrepreneur and would not be happy until I ran my own business and had total control over my life.

Recognizing I would need help in accomplishing that goal, I approached my long-time friend and mentor Doug Miller. He had the business experience that I needed to complement my sales, marketing, and promotional know-how. Behind almost every famous entrepreneur you will discover a behind-the-scenes business partner who "minds the store" day to day. For me, that was Doug.

Now that I had that piece of the puzzle in place, it was time to face the seemingly impossible odds again. They were long indeed. The first thing I needed to do was raise about $10 million. Then I would need to find a national TV network to air my television show, hire and train a sales staff of one hundred employees, build a business infrastructure to handle over ten thousand phone calls per week, and build a website, which in those days was no easy task.

The challenges and obstacles were monstrous. The biggest was the stock market crashing and the internet bubble imploding right at the start of my money-raising campaign. In response, investors simply closed their checkbooks.

But that was only the beginning of the challenges. Numerous "experts" said no TV network would ever pick up my television show because sports gambling was *persona non grata* on television. At the start they were right—every network I pitched said "NO" to my show.

Wall Street was even colder. They didn't understand my business plan. I was rejected by dozens of investment bankers and private equity gurus.

So-called financial experts said I could never raise one dollar, let alone $10 million.

Both the so-called media and financial "experts" advised me to walk away before I wasted any more time or money. But those experts didn't understand my RELENTLESS CHUTZPAH.

I knew that in the end if I remained relentless I would accomplish my goals. After about two dozen rejections, I finally found a TV network to air my show. Over the next decade the show aired on high-profile national cable TV networks Fox Sports Net, Comcast Sports Net, Discovery Channel, Superstation WGN, and Spike TV. Luckily I didn't listen to the "experts." With The Power of RELENTLESS, you won't have to either.

In the end I didn't raise $10 million. I raised almost $20 million! And since the hot shots on Wall Street weren't interested, I did it the old fashioned way with small investors (one $50,000 check at a time). For every check given to me, I was rejected at least twenty times. That's a lot of rejection. But I persevered and surpassed my goal. The investment bankers didn't understand my business model, so I did it without them. The lesson is, "Don't listen to the naysayers, even if they are so-called 'experts.'" With RELENTLESS CHUTZPAH, you can accomplish anything.

I won't tell you it was easy. Raising money one investor at a time is so slow and tedious; the business almost failed because of a lack of money early in the game. Within six months we were at death's doorstep. We were so close to running out of money that one worried investor asked a high profile "turnaround specialist" buddy of his (with vast experience at saving failing companies) to meet with us. He spent two days with Doug Miller and me. Then he called his buddy (the investor) and said, "Forget about this business. Let it die. Wayne Root can't succeed. He doesn't even have enough money left in the bank to make payroll next week. This piece of junk is dead, dead, dead. It's going down like the Hindenburg."

He was wrong. A week later, I wrote the payroll check with a personal check. In all my years in business, I have never failed to meet a payroll—although there were more paydays than I would care to remember when

I wasn't one of those who got paid. I have always believed you can't call yourself a true entrepreneur until the end of the week—when on Monday morning you know payroll is coming up Friday, you don't have the money to pay it, but you have the confidence you will find a way. If you do, *you are an entrepreneur!*

The business stayed afloat because I bought us some time with that personal check. I worked hard, caught a break, and closed a financing deal the next week. We turned the business around. It lasted almost a decade, until we sold it to a publicly traded UK company.

As with most small businesses, during that decade we faced crisis after crisis. In pioneering an industry in its infancy we didn't encounter just those everyday minor crises that are the nature of every business. We faced the kind of crises that put most normal businessmen out of business. We were left for dead at least a dozen times. But I'm creative, resilient, and resourceful. I am a walking advertisement for RELENTLESS CHUTZPAH. I changed our entire business model several times to bring the business back from the dead. I'm like Freddy Krueger of *Nightmare on Elm Street.* I just keep relentlessly popping back up from the grave.

What's so crazy is that this story is *not* unusual. Every business or career I've been involved in has required this same level of energy, enthusiasm, focus, intensity, tenacity, creativity, commitment, faith … along with an axe, jackhammer, and blowtorch for good measure.

This is what all entrepreneurs face on a daily basis. It's a nonstop battle for survival against bad luck, bad decisions, bad employees, bad government, lawyers, competitors, thieves, taxes, regulations—you name it, the list is endless. As a business owner, every day is a new challenge. If you don't have RELENTLESS CHUTZPAH, you have as good a chance of being struck by lightning as you have of long-term success.

I am immensely proud of all the good this one small business did during that decade. Granted, it was good for me. But it was also good for the employees, good for the economy, and good for America. We pumped about $60 million into the U.S. economy during that decade. We paid about five hundred payrolls. We paid salaries and health insurance for one hundred employees for almost decade. This is the American spirit at its best. This is capitalism. This is entrepreneurship. This IS RELENTLESS CHUTZPAH.

Are you starting to get "it"? RELENTLESS CHUTZPAH is hard to define in just a few words, but it's willpower, it's mindset, it's your refusal to give up or give in. You will never, never, never, ever give up. You won't hesitate to burn your bridges and remove your path of retreat, because there is no turning back. It's succeed or perish. You know those are your only options.

THE KING OF VEGAS

When I became an anchorman in 1989 at CNBC, I was inspired to create a TV series that I could sell to Hollywood. I spent the next sixteen years pitching a show called *The King of Vegas*. SIXTEEN YEARS! That's a long time to stay committed. That's a long time to stay positive. But when you have The Power of RELENTLESS on your side, it's a walk in the park!

I was rejected by virtually every TV network in America, some multiple times. I made countless trips to Los Angeles and New York over those sixteen long years—all ending in rejection and crushing disappointment. But in 2005 I finally heard one "YES." I sold the TV series *King of Vegas* to Spike TV. With my TV business partner Michael Yudin, I became the creator, co–executive producer, and co-host of the show. It was one of the highest-rated shows in Spike TV history. RELENTLESS CHUTZPAH had just paid off again.

Was it worth it? Like most success achieved through RELENTLESS CHUTZPAH, that first success was merely a stepping stone—a door opener. Today, again with Michael Yudin, I am a co-producer of *Ghost Adventures*— the highest-rated show on Travel Channel for eight straight seasons. We recently celebrated our one hundredth episode. It drew over one million viewers to an episode and was Travel Channel's single highest-rated show ever.[1] Without sixteen years of pitching *King of Vegas* it would never have happened. One little bit of success led to a bigger success.

I'm currently busy creating and pitching two new reality TV shows. One is called *Vegas D. A.* about the justice system in Las Vegas, the high-profile tourist capital of America. I have great hopes for this show. Everything is bigger in Vegas, even the crime! But again, the show would never have been possible without my relentless pursuit. It took me numerous meetings, phone calls, and e-mails over four years to finally convince Clark County district attorney (and now friend) Steven Wolfson to agree to the show. Without RELENTLESS CHUTZPAH it never would have happened.

RUNNING FOR PRESIDENT

It took that same RELENTLESS CHUTZPAH for me to become a national political figure. How unlikely was it for me, with no prior national political experience, to have a chance at the 2008 Libertarian Party presidential nomination?

I was told "NO" (and much worse) by every politician, political leader, consultant, and "expert" that I met. I constantly heard, "A Vegas odds-maker running for President? Absurd." That's why no one should listen to experts. They only know what has worked in the past. They can't think out of the box. They don't see possibilities. And they don't know you or your passion. They don't understand the difference made by RELENTLESS CHUTZPAH.

Libertarian Party insiders called me "Don Quixote," meaning I was tilting at windmills with zero chance of success. The media called my goal "impossible." There's that word again. That word stops most normal people, but it *inspires* me.

My main opponents, former Republican Congressman Bob Barr and former Democrat U.S. Senator Mike Gravel, never took me seriously. The *Washington Post* left me out of their article on the Libertarian Party debate.

I was on that stage as one of three leading contenders for the Libertarian presidential nomination. But the photo in the *Washington Post* only showed two candidates. I had mysteriously vanished through the magic of camera angles. My name wasn't mentioned in the article about the debate either.

I was ignored, denigrated, and laughed at by the critics and naysayers. But I just kept fighting relentlessly and ignoring the experts and critics.

Eventually, I lost the presidential nomination in one of the closest convention races in political history. The six ballots to determine the winner took all day. The last time that had happened at a major presidential convention was when Franklin Delano Roosevelt won the Democratic nomination in 1932.

But this unknown small businessman and Vegas oddsmaker beat out the former United States senator, ending his political career. I also beat out several lifelong Libertarian activists who had far bigger followings within the party. Congressman Bob Barr ultimately won the nomination and was so impressed by my relentless personality that he asked me to join his presidential ticket. He stepped on stage and asked the delegates to vote for "Mr. Relentless." The convention delegates then elected me as the Libertarian vice presidential nominee. I spent the rest of the night giving an acceptance speech and thanking the delegates who had just put me on a national presidential ticket.

My critics were flabbergasted. The media was befuddled. Longtime Libertarian leaders were shocked. They kept saying "How the hell did Root do that? What are his qualifications?" Well, my main credential was RELENTLESS CHUTZPAH. That's really all you need.

I was also bold, brash, confident, full of ideas, and conveyed them with tremendous energy and enthusiasm. I never lost faith, never gave up, and never stopped fighting. I was always willing to roll the dice and gamble everything on my dreams. And I didn't just talk or dream, I took action. That's how a "nobody" puts himself or herself on the map and becomes a "somebody."

Now keep in mind that I was only a third party vice presidential nominee. No, we were never a serious threat to win the presidency. But in the history of the greatest nation in world history (since George Washington in 1789) there have been only forty-four Presidents and fifty-six presidential elections. If you count various major third party candidacies, that means there have been perhaps one to two hundred serious candidates for vice president on the ballot in the history of America. I made it into that super-exclusive club, and I'm in for life. No one can take it away from me. That's pretty amazing! That's the Power of RELENTLESS CHUTZPAH.

Generally vice presidential nominees are never heard from again. They are as in-demand as a Maytag repairman. Remember that old TV commercial? Maytag washing machines were supposedly so dependable that Maytag repairmen were lonely because no one ever called. That also sums up the life of a former vice presidential candidate. But a third party vice presidential nominee? Only one word describes them—*anonymous*. That is, until I came along. I turned my fifteen minutes of fame into a career as a political commentator, author, and national media personality. That's RELENTLESS CHUTZPAH.

By the way, it's never easy. It's like the famous quote attributed to Gandhi. "First they ignore you, then they laugh at you, then they fight you, then you win." Great quote. Gandhi was obviously familiar with my brand of relentless. At first, I was ignored by the media. But I kept hounding and hammering them. I kept pushing and pitching. I kept submitting my articles and press releases. I kept relentlessly promoting myself. I kept suggesting story ideas. I started to get a trickle of interviews. Then dozens. Then hundreds. Finally it turned into thousands of media appearances. About eight thousand of them since 2008. *EIGHT THOUSAND.*

Today I'm a frequent guest on conservative media, from Fox News to thousands of talk radio stations across the country. I'm a syndicated columnist for a dozen conservative web powerhouses including Fox News and TheBlaze. My opinion pieces appear regularly in places like the *Washington Times*. All this happened because I never gave up faith in my dream. And it all happened because, unlike any sane person, I refused to accept the word "NO." That's the power of RELENTLESS CHUTZPAH.

How did I apply RELENTLESS CHUTZPAH to achieve my goals? By never giving up, never losing my enthusiasm, and never letting my critics or detractors think for a second they'd beaten me. I just kept coming. That's RELENTLESS CHUTZPAH.

The formula is fairly simple. First, I just wear people out. I keep coming back at them so many times, they eventually give up. Often they agree to the deal just because they are so exhausted from trying to say "NO" to me. When someone like me refuses to accept "NO," people don't know how to react, or what to do. So they eventually say "YES." But, there has to be talent and proven success to back it up. They say "YES" knowing I will bring incredible levels of energy, enthusiasm, action, creativity, and tenacity to the table. They know my energy always inspires superior results. That's The Power of RELENTLESS.

If I had been at Custer's Last Stand, outnumbered by Indian warriors, I would have charged the Indians! My guess is they would have been so confused, they would have turned tail and run. RELENTLESS CHUTZPAH isn't just a mindset, it's a way of life!

THE RELENTLESS TRIBE

"Chutzpah" is the Yiddish word for audacity (or in my macho mindset terminology: balls). As a proud Jewish American—and a New Yorker, to boot—I come by my RELENTLESS CHUTZPAH naturally.

I am very proud of my Jewish heritage. I am also bursting with pride for the people of Israel. But the question for you is: Can *anyone* learn RELENTLESS CHUTZPAH?

The answer is a resounding YES. The Chinese are obsessed with learning how to succeed and obtain wealth. Over one third of the books sold in China are about financial success. And a large portion of those books are about *Jewish success*.

Some of the bestselling business book titles in China in the past decade:

- *The Eight Most Valuable Business Secrets of Jewish Wealth*
- *The Legend of Jewish Wealth*
- *Jewish People and Business: The Bible of How to Live Their Lives*[2]

The Chinese people aren't interested in being Jewish. They are interested in what they can learn from the Jews: Learn how to think like they think. Learn their mindset. Learn the traits that have made Jews so remarkably successful. Learn to harness the power of RELENTLESS CHUTZPAH.

It seems to be working well. China is the fastest growing economy in the world. They passed America in the past year to become the #1 economy in the world based on consumer spending. And they are poised to overtake America as the overall #1 economy in a decade or two.[3]

As Steve Jobs of Apple once said, quoting Pablo Picasso, "Good artists copy, but great artists steal." The success secret the Chinese are so desperate to steal is RELENTLESS CHUTZPAH.

Now it's your turn to learn from the most relentless people in the history of the world. This tribe literally invented relentless. This tribe has survived and thrived against incredible odds for over six thousand years with The Power of RELENTLESS. You could say they are the model for this book. They are the Jewish people, and even more specifically the Jews of Israel.

Israel is a nation of some six million Jews. It is one of the smallest nations in the world. Its size is about eight thousand square miles—just about three times the size of Delaware and only slightly larger than Fiji. It is only two hundred sixty miles at its longest, seventy miles at its widest, and nine miles at its narrowest.

Would you be surprised to learn the three countries that lead the world in venture capital dollars are America, China and … *Israel?* Yes, Israel. This tiny country attracts venture capital investment at a rate that's thirty times higher, per capita, than the entire continent of Europe.

Let's look at a few remarkable facts about the amazing people of Israel:

- Israel ranks third in the world for entrepreneurship and has the number one spot among seniors and women.
- Israel has more high-tech startups, per capita, than any nation in the world.
- Israel has more biotech startups, per capita, than any nation in the world.
- Israel has more business startups, per capita, than any nation in the world.
- In raw numbers, Israel has the second most business start-ups of any country in the world, behind only the United States.
- Israel has more companies listed on the NASDAQ stock exchange than any other country in the world, other than the United States and Canada. More than Europe, India, China, and Japan combined.
- Relative to its population, Israel is the largest immigrant-absorbing nation on earth.
- Israel leads the world, per capita, in patents for medical equipment.
- Israel's has the highest computer-to-citizen ratio in the world.
- Israel's citizens have the highest university-degree-to-population ratio in the world.
- Israel leads the world in the number of scientists and technicians in the workforce, with 145 per 10,000, as opposed to 85 in the U.S., over 70 in Japan, and fewer than 60 in Germany. With over 25 percent of its work force in technical professions, Israel places first in this category as well.

- Israel has the highest number of Nobel Prizes, per capita, in the world.
- Wikipedia reports the Israeli economy is ranked as the world's most durable economy in the face of crisis. The Bank of Israel is ranked first among central banks for its efficient functioning. Israel is also ranked first in the world in its supply of skilled manpower.
- With only seven million citizens, Israel's economy is bigger than those of her twenty-two Muslim Arab neighbors combined, with a population of over three hundred million.
- Israel is the Hong Kong of the Middle East, with a booming economy even in the middle of a global economic collapse. Israel's GDP growth was 4.7 percent last year.[4]

So the question becomes WHY? What accounts for all this outrageous economic success by such a small tribe as the Jewish people?

The answer is simple: the Jewish people lead the world in RELENTLESS CHUTZPAH. Throw anything at them: hate them, persecute them, steal their property, enslave them, torture them, murder them, yet they survive. More than survive, they move on and thrive. That's the power of RELENTLESS CHUTZPAH.

My recommendation to Israel's enemies: you are far better off studying the Jewish people and emulating them, than fighting with them, because you'll never win. No one in history has ever defeated the Jewish people ... and no one ever will. That's the power of RELENTLESS! If you can't beat them, why not learn from them? Wouldn't it be ironic if Israel's enemies greatly improved their citizen's lives by becoming more like the Jews?

My many Jewish friends and relatives often lament that God did not bless the Jewish people. They say history shows a pattern of unmatched pain, prejudice, adversity, and tragedy suffered by this tribe. Yet I would argue that all the pain has been a blessing. It has created the most unstoppable, unbeatable, and relentless people in world history. One could argue that was God's plan all along. Perhaps God was playing the role of Marine drill sergeant. Those hard-asses embarrass, humiliate, exhaust, starve, and often torture their soldiers. But there's a reason. It toughens them and keeps them alive in the future when they are under withering enemy fire.

Soldiers survive, then go on to thrive because of their hard-ass Marine drill sergeant. Later in life, long after they've left the Marines, gotten married, had kids, and lived their lives, soldiers think back fondly on the lessons they learned from the torture dished out by that drill sergeant. The RELENTLESS CHUTZPAH of the Jews was forged by God's tough love. I guess God was the original Marine drill sergeant!

The Jews, and in particular the Jews of Israel, are Exhibit A for the famous saying, "Anything that doesn't kill you, makes you stronger." Fire turns iron into steel. The Jewish people were mentally forged as steel.

Once you've been discriminated against, persecuted, robbed, hunted, enslaved, and tortured, something as simple as asking an investor to write a check or refusing to accept NO in a business transaction doesn't seem like such a big deal.

THE NINE RULES OF RELENTLESS CHUTZPAH

What did generations—actually centuries—of pain, persecution and tragedy teach the Jews? *The nine rules of RELENTLESS CHUTZPAH.* If you want to be as successful, as entrepreneurial, as disaster-proof as the Jews, these are the rules you have to embrace and make your own:

THE FIRST RULE OF RELENTLESS CHUTZPAH: Accept that you must be relentless to survive.

If you set your mind to be relentless, to never give up or give in, no matter what, no one can defeat you. That mindset has been the foundation of my life.

THE SECOND RULE: It's good to have a chip on your shoulder. Jews are always the underdog. They are always either ignored or treated with disdain. That's a big advantage. It drives you, it makes you perform at your best, and it makes you over-perform.

I've lived my life with a chip on my shoulder. I've gone into every business deal with a chip on my shoulder. I'm always motivated to shove that smirk off my opponent's face and make him eat crow. That's my "winning edge" in business and life. Invite the world to disrespect you and underestimate you. Then spend your life proving them wrong.

THE THIRD RULE: Stop complaining. Complaining gets you nowhere. Take action. Do something about your lot in life. Take the time you might have wasted complaining and use that time to take action. You'll find what a waste of time it was to even consider complaining in the first place.

I don't waste my time complaining. I always take action (although at times that action is complaining). But I only complain if I believe the complaint will result in action and resolution. Taking action is your best revenge!

THE FOURTH RULE: Life is short, so take action N-O-W. Don't wait for tomorrow, or next week, or next month. You never know what tomorrow will bring, so do it now. Today is as good a day as any to get started turning your dream into reality. If you put it off until tomorrow, it may never happen.

I always take action—aggressive action—at the earliest possible opportunity.

THE FIFTH RULE: Turn lemons into lemonade. God never promised to make life easy. Ask the Jews. But you can turn each challenge and setback in life into a learning experience.

When something bad happens, don't give up. Learn from your mistake, get back up, use that failure as motivation and newfound wisdom to succeed the next time.

THE SIXTH RULE: Take control of your life. Jews have experienced what it's like to be under a tyrant's control, to be enslaved, to feel helpless. It's horrible. So Jews learned to control their own destiny by taking personal responsibility and being self-reliant. The only people you can depend on are you and your own family. Never, ever, ever think you can depend on government. The first concern of government—and that includes every elected official as well as every government employee—is not you. It is their own job and well-being.

How do you take control of your own life? You educate yourself to take control of your mind; find a job you love and, if possible, always create your own business; own your own home; invest wisely so you are in control of your own retirement. Let me reiterate: if you can't find a job you love, stop complaining and create your own. NEVER depend on government or the kindness of a stranger to save you. Remember, as Robert Schuller said, "If it's going to be, it's up to me."

I've only had a job with a boss a couple of times early in my life. I learned what I needed to learn, then quickly left to start my own business. I love working for the most generous boss in the world—*me!*

THE SEVENTH RULE: Be willing to do what no one else wants or is willing to do. Do what others consider "low class" and beneath them. Whatever you do—*SELL!* Sell homes, stocks, cars, clothing, mortgages, insurance, gold, books, entire companies, or money (banking). Sell yourself. The product doesn't matter. You get rich by selling *something.* People who work at Ford Motor Company may think they work for a company that manufactures cars. WRONG! They work for a company that *sells* cars. You only have the right to make it after you sell it. Otherwise you become that worst of all possible companies—a company with a lot of expensive, worthless inventory.

In the California Gold Rush, more people got rich selling picks, shovels, food, and clothing to the miners than got rich working the mines. Who are the wealthiest people in every society? The business owners and salesmen. Guess who gets the last laugh? The tribe doing that "low class" thing—selling anything and everything!

I've been selling products and services my entire adult life. But in each case the number one commodity that I'm selling is me! Selling isn't "low class." It's the best way to make enough money to live a life that is "First Class."

THE EIGHTH RULE: Be FEARLESS. What's the worst thing that could happen? It's hard to get any worse than the infamous Holocaust. Over six million Jews were wiped from the earth after first having their property, homes, businesses, jewelry, and even their gold teeth stolen.

After having something like that in your history, it's tough to scare you. After torture and the death of the people you love, everything else seems like a walk in the park. Little things no longer bother you. You become fearless. And that's the key to success in almost every field, but especially in business: NO FEAR. Few people have that trait. Those that are fearless can achieve anything. Those that are fearless can make the impossible, *POSSIBLE.*

I've been fearful about physical challenges my entire life. I don't like heights. I'm not big on swimming in deep water. I don't climb mountains. I don't ride motorcycles. But I'm fearless when it comes to financial challenges. I risk my money on a moment's notice … which brings us to the last Rule of RELENTLESS CHUTZPAH.

THE NINTH RULE: Take risks! The final lesson learned by the Jews from centuries of pain is a tolerance for risk. To be successful in life and earn the serious money you need to be a gunslinger and riverboat gambler. You don't get rich from a safe weekly paycheck. You don't get rich by settling. You don't get rich off a "job."

To be successful you need to risk your own money. I consider riding motorcycles and jumping out of airplanes stupid risks. That's risking your life and your health for what, a momentary thrill? A smart risk is putting your money into a business. A smart risk is investing in yourself.

The business world may be brutal, but not compared to the lifetime experiences of the Jewish people. The business world may sometimes seem like war, may sometimes seem bloody, but not when compared to what Jews have lived through.

That is why the Jewish people, particularly the Jews of Israel, have more RELENTLESS CHUTZPAH than any other people in the world. They never stop fighting for their goals; never let a challenge or setback slow them down; never give up or give in. They never stop starting businesses, no matter how many times they have already failed. They never stop asking strangers for money, no matter how many have already said "No." Like me, the people of Israel see the word "NO" as merely the start of a negotiation. That is how they have managed to produce their stunning record of economic success.

The 3rd Principle
of RELENTLESS:
Relentless AMBITION
and GOAL-SETTING

....

"It took me twelve years to turn my dream of becoming Jimmy The Greek into a reality. It took sixteen years to sell my first television show to Hollywood. It took eighteen years of relentless plotting and planning to realize my dream of seeing my daughter Dakota accepted into Harvard and Stanford. Dreams take time. You'd better be relentless!"
—Wayne Allyn Root

What are you aiming for?

I'm a firm believer in aiming for the stars. There's no point aiming for something "normal" or average. Why aim to have just enough money to "get by"? Why not aim insanely high? Why not aim for the stars? If you miss, you still might land in Beverly Hills. If you aim for the curb and miss, you might wind up in ... Detroit.

Take my career. I didn't aim for town council. I aimed for President of the United States, and wound up on a presidential ticket. I didn't aim for a local radio show. I aimed for national TV, and wound up a host of five shows on CNBC. I didn't aim for being like Jimmy The Greek on some local cable access show. I aimed to replace Jimmy The Greek on national TV ... and I did. I didn't aim to self-publish an e-book. I aimed to write a national bestseller ... and I did. I didn't teach my daughter to aim for a local community college. I taught her to aim for Harvard and Stanford ...

as a homeschooler. How ridiculous. How absurd. What audacity! Yet she was accepted at both.

If you're going to aim at something, be optimistic about something, fight relentlessly for something—be sure it's worth fighting for! Be sure you're aiming for the top, the highest rung in your industry, the pinnacle.

I've never aspired to be in the mafia. But if I did, I'd have aimed to replace John Gotti. I've never belonged to a union. But if I did, I'd aim to become a modern-day Jimmy Hoffa. I've never aimed to become a police officer, but if I did I'd aim to become police chief of New York City. That's ambition, drive, cajones, balls, chutzpah.

As Charlie Sheen might say ... the point is "WINNING!"

The key to where you end up is where you aim. No, not everyone will become #1 in their field. Lord knows I'm not. I didn't become president. But I did win the Libertarian vice presidential nomination. I'm not a billionaire business mogul, at least not yet. But, I did become a self-made millionaire by age twenty-nine, with a home on the beach in Malibu. I don't host my own show on Fox News. But I am a regular guest on hundreds of political TV and talk radio shows, as well as a bestselling political author. Without the audacity to aim for the stars, I might be stuck in an apartment in Detroit, rather than a mansion in Las Vegas.

How did I make it this far? Relentless AMBITION and GOAL-SETTING.

HOMESCHOOL TO HARVARD

I call this story "Homeschool to Harvard." It's the story of my remarkable superstar daughter Dakota Root. This story may be more impossible than even becoming an anchorman at CNBC without any prior experience.

There is nothing that requires The Power of RELENTLESS more than raising a child from birth through college ... *and doing it right!* But this story is over the top. My daughter Dakota was homeschooled her entire life. She sat in the first classroom of her life in the hallowed halls of Harvard.

Dakota scored perfect SAT scores in reading and writing. She was a National Merit Scholar and Presidential Scholar nominee. She was accepted by many of this nation's finest universities including Harvard, Stanford, Duke, Columbia, Penn, Brown, Chicago, Virginia, and Cal-Berkeley. She actually had the confidence to turn down an early admissions offer from Yale—the offer came from the Yale fencing coach—before she had gotten any of her other acceptances. *My kid turned down Yale cold!* I must tell you, Mr. Relentless himself thought she might be out of her mind.

What was her reason for turning down one of the five best colleges in the world before she knew if any other college would take her? Her heart was set on Harvard. It was her #1 choice, and she reminded me that her dad taught her to be relentless in pursuit of #1, never settle for #2. You could have knocked me over with a feather. The kid out-relentlessed her old man!

Dakota went on not just to graduate from Harvard, but to conquer Harvard! She graduated right at the top of her class, magna cum laude, as well as earning "first class" honors at Oxford University in England, signifying she was in the top 5 percent of her class during her time there. Her senior thesis at Harvard was on the legality of NSA surveillance on the American people. After Harvard she was accepted at Cambridge for her master's degree, but turned them down, at least temporarily. Dakota decided to take a year off to teach yoga around Europe. As I write this, she is teaching yoga at a spa in the south of France. The Power of RELENTLESS leads to quite a life.

There is just one more thing a proud father wants to share about his oldest daughter. Dakota is both a scholar and an athlete. As a high school senior she won the Pacific Coast Fencing Championship and fenced in the Junior Olympics and Nationals. She represented the U.S.A. at World Cup events all over the world. Fencing for the elite Harvard team, she earned Second Team All-Ivy honors. I take credit for raising her to be relentless, but she made it happen.

She is the complete package! I am proud to say Dakota is among the best and brightest ever produced by the great state of Nevada. She represents what all of us hope and pray for our children.

But it didn't just happen. The story is one of Relentless AMBITION and GOAL-SETTING from the very beginning. From the day she was born, I told Dakota she was destined for Harvard or Stanford. I prayed with her at her bedside every night, including a prayer that she'd attend Harvard or Stanford as both a scholar and athlete, making Mom and Dad proud. We took her on campus tours of Harvard and Stanford. I bought her Harvard and Stanford pens, pencils, and sweatshirts. In each of my books I wrote that my brilliant young daughter was going to attend Harvard or Stanford one day on an athletic scholarship (which would, of course, save me money). From the age of five I knew she had the talent to do it and relentlessly reinforced that image in her mind.

Some might call it relentless brainwashing. I call it relentless faith. When Dakota went out and delivered, it was not by luck or coincidence. She was put into a position to deliver excellence. She is a success story that might be titled, "Think and Grow Harvard."

Of course the last laugh was on me. Only after she was accepted at Harvard did I learn that Ivy League colleges don't give athletic scholarships. My dream was getting her in … without Dad having to pay. Instead I got stuck with the full bill, about sixty-five thousand per year. Oh well, I better get even more relentless pursuing new business deals. I have three more kids headed to college, and they too are aiming for #1.

What makes Dakota's story so remarkable is that she was educated in Las Vegas, the same city that produces some of the worst public education results in America. Las Vegas students' test scores, drop out rates, and graduation rates are among the worst in the country. So how did Dakota's success happen? What was in the water at the Root household? Can others learn from Dakota's story? Can others replicate her remarkable "Homeschool to Harvard" story? YES, they can! But you better be committed to being relentless for twenty-two years from your child's first breath until his or her college graduation ceremony.

It doesn't take a village, or a government, or a teachers' union to raise a child—it takes Relentless AMBITION and GOAL-SETTING.

It takes a mother and father who can paint the vision, show the child how to dream big, instill them with unshakable faith and contagious enthusiasm, and then teach them work ethic, discipline, sacrifice, and personal responsibility. It takes a mother and father who can teach a child to never, ever, ever, ever give up on a dream. In other words, like anything else you want, first you have to clearly see it, then believe it, then take action, and finally harness The Power of RELENTLESS to achieve it. That's how you turn dreams into reality.

If you know what your goals are, and you have 100 percent faith in your vision, you will unleash the power of RELENTLESS discipline and sacrifice. I'm up early each day. I start work early. I put in long days. I take calls, texts, and e-mails 24/7. I'm never "off" except for Christmas Eve and part of Christmas Day. Other than the news, I don't waste my time watching much television. I don't waste time or money at nightclubs or bars. I don't drink, smoke, or do drugs. I work out religiously and pray every day. I taught Dakota the exact same relentless discipline and sacrifice. The fact is, 99.9 percent of all kids will never get into Harvard, Stanford, Duke, Columbia, Penn, or Brown—let alone all of them. Even fewer will graduate at the top of their class at Harvard and Oxford. That's how you become part of that infamous and hated "1 percent."

But there are no mistakes or coincidences in life. My favorite saying is "Luck is the residue of design." Most people in the "1 percent" earned it. My daughter was studying when other kids were partying, hanging out at the mall, gossiping, drinking, doing drugs, or getting pregnant. Few of those kids will lead a special life. Making the wrong decisions and taking the wrong actions will damage your prospects, potential, and opportunities in life. I taught Dakota to sacrifice what some see as "fun" as a teenager, in order to live a life few will ever experience or even imagine as an adult. Dakota listened and learned. She is living an amazing life because we SET GOALS for her and instilled Relentless AMBITION in her from the beginning.

CONCRETE STEPS FOR SETTING YOUR GOALS—AND ACHIEVING THEM!

One of the key lessons of Napoleon Hill's famous book *Think and Grow Rich* is that you must have detailed, specific goals. You can't "ready, shoot, aim." We all need to know the target we're aiming at in order to hit it. *Think and Grow Rich* actually used the word *obsession* to describe the attitude about your goals that is necessary to achieve success.

Even Relentless HEART and CHUTZPAH will not take you far, unless you first identify your goals. Goals are nothing less than the magical way you turn your dreams into reality.

Unfortunately, right here is where so many other books leave the subject. This is where I start! I'm going to take you step by step through the detailed process of how to create your goals and how to then turn them into reality. It's a twelve-step process.

1. FIND YOUR PASSION AND PURPOSE.

It is not possible to set goals until you first identify your passion and purpose—your Relentless AMBITION. Identifying the things you are passionate about will lead to enthusiasm, commitment, tenacity, energy, relentlessness, and eventually success.

As you know from my own story, my personal passions and purpose have changed several times over the years. It will probably be the same for you. If so, more power to you. As we age and change (and accomplish success), our goals change too.

2. MAP OUT YOUR GOALS.

Once step one is out of the way, it is time to map out your goals. This doesn't need to be long. You can do it on the back of a napkin. Lay out your goals for the short term (six months and one year), and then long term (two years, five years, and ten years). Know that it is natural that these will evolve and change along the way. Just update them as they change.

3. CREATE A DREAM BOOK OR VISION BOARD.

This is a powerful tool used to help clarify, concentrate, and maintain focus on specific life goals. Fill it with images that represent whatever you want to be, do, or have. I prefer both an old fashioned "photo album" where I place photos of my goals and a vision of my future—and also a "vision board" that I mount on the wall of my office where I see it throughout the day.

Today's youth would no doubt prefer an online vision board kept on your computer. The reason I prefer an old-fashioned photo album is that I place that album on my nightstand. I can't go to sleep without seeing it. That is my reminder to look at it each night before bedtime.

What is the point of a dream book or vision board? Humans are busy and constantly bombarded by distractions. A vision board helps you:

- Identify your vision and give it clarity.
- Reinforce your Relentless AMBITION daily.
- Keep your focus on your intentions.

Don't forget to update it as goals are reached and new goals are set.

I've made at least four specific dreams or visions happen as a direct result of my dream book and vision board. For many years I put my dream Las Vegas mansion in my dream book. That vision inspired me to finally take the bold step of moving my family and business from Los Angeles to

Las Vegas. And the home I bought in Las Vegas looked eerily like the one I had stared at in my dream book for five years.

Once I moved to Las Vegas, I added a new dream. For years I hung on my wall a photo of a beautiful home on a ski slope in Park City, Utah. Eventually I bought my own dream home on a ski slope in Park City. It took about three years of seeing it to make it happen. But the key was that I put it in front of my eyes 24/7. I saw it every day. I couldn't miss it. I wanted it so badly, I could taste it, hear it, feel it. There it was, on my wall, staring right at me every day. And then ... *it was mine.*

I also put photos of my dream sports car in my dream book—a black Aston Martin DB9 Volante convertible. It was right out of the James Bond movie. I stared at it every night before I went to bed. Then in 2006 I bought it. In black—exactly as I saw it in my dream book.

Once you turn your dream into reality, it's time for a new dream. So I soon set my sights on a white-on-white Maserati Quattroporte. It's basically an exotic racecar disguised as a four-door ultra-luxury car. On the outside it is beautiful. On the inside it is luxurious. But under the hood it's an Indy racecar—with a twin turbo-charged Ferrari engine capable of going from zero to sixty in about four seconds and a top speed of 190 miles per hour. Last October I brought my white-on-white Maserati Quattroporte home.

Who says dreams don't come true? They most certainly *do* when you have a dream book or vision board!

4. CREATE A CONTRACT WITH "ME, MYSELF, AND I."

This means exactly what it says. Write a contract with yourself identifying the goals you will attain (not want to, or wish to, but "will" attain). Most importantly, in the written contract include the specific steps you are committing yourself to take and agree to follow through on to accomplish those goals. Contracts are important. Most normal people don't break contracts. You are legally obligated to keep your word. Your subconscious mind sees written words and your signature on a contract and believes you are obligated—just like in every other legal contract you've ever signed.

This is just one more piece of the puzzle to create a positive, confidant, relentless mindset.

5. WRITE YOUR OWN OBITUARY.

Yes, you heard me. How do you want to be remembered after you're gone? What are truly the most important things you want to have accomplished? Think about it, then write your obituary as it will appear in the newspaper or online after your death. Now ... start working in reverse. Live your life that way, to make it happen. Talk about Relentless GOAL-SETTING. This is the "end goal" of all end goals!

6. KEEP A "BLACK BOX."

A black box is the recording device on planes that investigators use to piece together and solve a mystery as to why a plane crashed. The "black box" saves lives by making sure we learn from tragedies, thereby never repeating the same mistake. Well, that's the exact same purpose for your personal "black box."

Basically it's a weekly journal, where you write about your mistakes, frustrations, rejections, failures, defeats, and of course your victories too. I fill it in once per week at bedtime. Then I review it once per week as well. Like a "black box" does for the airlines, your journal will save you from making the same mistakes again and again. Write your results down for just five minutes once per week. And review it once per week for five to ten minutes. You'll see patterns developing. You'll start to see why the same bad things keep happening to you. And you'll *correct* it.

This journal's sole purpose is to be just like a football coach making notes on his clipboard, which he studies so he can make halftime adjustments. Its purpose is to record and review what happened during the week and make the adjustments and changes necessary to get the intended results.

Life gets busy and so many people, once headed in a direction (whether good or bad) simply run on "automatic." They are too distracted to change direction. Don't be one of those. Instead be a person of Relentless AMBI-TION and GOAL-SETTING. Then you can make the necessary "halftime" adjustments. A daily journal gives you the information and tools to do exactly that. Isn't it sad that life-improving tools like this aren't ever taught in school?

7. MAKE A DAILY "HIT LIST."

Just like a mob "hit list"—only yours is a straightforward list of what you want to do each day to make your dreams come true. Make it as specific as possible, so you can check off each line item as you achieve it. Then on to the next and the next. Until you've crossed each "hit" off your list. Those you don't complete, add to tomorrow's list. That is how you are forced to follow up.

8. CHOOSE AN "ACCOUNTABILITY PARTNER."

This is a peer, a friend or co-worker, who understands your goals and preferably is headed in the same direction. They should be a cheerleader—always ready to offer positive reinforcement. This is someone you can always call to go over goals, motivate you, uplift you, stop you from doing negative things, hold you to your Relentless AMBITION. This is the person to whom you are accountable, forcing you to make the phone calls, go to meetings, or job interviews, or take whatever actions are necessary for you to succeed. It is especially powerful if this is a spouse or business partner (so you see them daily). The key is you have to do the same for them.

I've never been to an AA meeting—I thank God that I've never had a problem with drugs or alcohol. But AA does wonderful things for people with addiction issues. The key is they are each assigned a "sponsor." That sponsor is just like an "accountability partner." Your sponsor looks out for you. They are always willing to take a call and give you strength or counsel. Well, we all need a "sponsor" in our lives. Not just addicts. Here's your chance. They will help you and you will help them, by holding each other accountable.

You may think I have overdone the importance of accountability and follow-up. But the fact is, they can't be overdone. All the Relentless GOAL-SETTING in the world will not work without discipline, accountability, personal responsibility, follow-up, and the commitment to do the work.

9. FIND A MENTOR.

Unlike an accountability partner, this is not a peer. This is someone older, wiser, and preferably much more successful than you. Someone who has already achieved great success and/or celebrity. This is not someone that has time to talk to you every day, or at all hours of the day and night. This kind of person is too successful to be bothered by nonstop calls from you.

This is a once per month or once per quarter call for general advice and motivation. Find someone you believe you can learn from. Don't hesitate to ask someone older, higher up in your own organization, or even someone who might be considered famous, or who you might think has no time for someone like you. You'll be amazed how many people love to be needed and are ready to help. Most smart and successful people want to "do good" and give back. You are giving them a chance. If you handle the relationship properly, a good mentor will also be aware of your goals and where you are in your career and may make introductions or present you with opportunities they come across.

My relationship with my mentor, Doug Miller, has been crucial to my success. Every step of the way Doug gave me good advice and counsel and kept me focused. It wasn't just that he was there to guide me through the hard times. He was also someone to high-five and celebrate my successes.

My relationship with Doug started over thirty years ago and continues to this day. As he recently told me, "Over the years this has become very much a two-way relationship that has undoubtedly helped me as much as it has you." *Everyone needs a Doug.*

10. FIND A BUSINESS COACH.

A business coach is similar to a mentor, but this is a professional coach giving you much more of their time and input—*for a fee*. You can ask them anything, you can bother them whenever you want—because you're paying for it. And you can be sure they're good at keeping you motivated and on track, because this is what they do for a living. A good business coach is there to keep you on track and be brutally honest with you when you're creating both a long-term and daily game plan.

As most of you know, one of my passions in life is sports. It is no secret that the most important "player" on any team is the coach. Quite frankly, coaching is everything—not only in sports, but in business, relationships, and life itself. A good coach can make all the difference in the world. A good coach can take a losing team and almost overnight turn them into a winner. When that coach leaves after a decade of nonstop winning, the next coach rarely ever succeeds at the same level. Why? Because coaching is an art. Few have that "it" factor. Find one and hire them to guide you.

A sports writer once said of legendary Alabama football coach Paul "Bear" Bryant, "He can whip you with his players … or he'll give you his players … take yours … and he'll whip you with your players!"

Business coaching has become a big business. Just remember, as in all professions, there are only a few good ones, a lot of mediocre ones, and way too many bad ones. Once you find a good one, keep him or her for life!

11. KEEP A PROGRESS AND REWARDS CHART.

A common method of training children is to keep a "progress chart" with rewards if they clean their room, mind their manners, do their homework, etc. It works like a charm for kids, but it will work even better for you!

As you check off your daily list of tasks, assign yourself points for each positive achievement. On days you fail, take points away. Decide beforehand how the point system will work and what the rewards will be when you reach predetermined levels. Rewards can range from: an afternoon off, a day off, a three-day weekend, day spa, a massage, dinner at a five-star restaurant, going shooting at a gun range, a new suit, dress, or shoes … all the way up to a vacation or new car.

And remember—DON'T CHEAT!

The point of this is motivation. As long as you're honest with yourself, this progress and rewards chart will super-charge your motivation. We all want gifts. It started at a young age on Christmas and birthdays. It never went away. It never will. That's why everyone loves Christmas. We all feel like kids on Christmas morning. Getting gifts is a wonderful feeling. So write down all the things you want, crave, make you happy, float your boat, etc. Then assign points for good days, good actions, good results. And as soon as you reach a target, go buy a gift for yourself. Soon you'll train your mind to fight for those gifts, to never give up … to never accept "NO." Because that gift you want is waiting. All the naïve people who claim "greed is bad" don't understand life or human nature. "Greed is good" (as Michael Douglas said in *Wall Street*), *if* it's used in a positive way as motivation for achievement.

And if you are one of the rare people in this world who thinks material things are bad, then by all means set up your rewards as the chance to give donations to charity, or trips to the hospital to volunteer with sick kids, or days dressed as Santa to ring that bell for the Salvation Army at Christmas, or a day volunteering at an animal shelter.

Maybe your reward is that each time you close a big deal, you rent a big truck, fill it with groceries, and head to a poor neighborhood to hand out turkeys or free groceries. *Great!* I like this idea so much, I think from now on my reward system should include both material rewards and a charitable component each time I hit my target. I just made this decision while writing my own book!

The fact is, rewards work. Use them as motivation to do great things … achieve great things … hit targets … beat the odds … and make the impossible, *possible*. Use rewards to supercharge your Relentless AMBITION and help you sprint through your goals.

12. FOLLOW UP ON YOUR GOALS.

Rarely does anyone ever teach you this in school, at the workplace, or in life. But the reality is that "the follow-up" is more important than creating your goals in the first place. Follow-up is more important than taking action on your goals. Success is all in "the follow-up." Without follow-up, it's all wasted. You did all that work for nothing. Because rarely does anything ever work the first or even second time. It takes persistent, dedicated, committed *relentless* follow-up to achieve any kind of success.

Relentless AMBITION and GOAL-SETTING is a mighty force for good in all aspects of your life. To unleash The Power of Relentless, set Relentless GOALS, and use my twelve-step plan to follow through on them. Aim high. Set your ambition on something you will be willing to work and sacrifice and exercise RELENTLESS discipline in pursuit of, even if it takes eighteen years of RELENTLESS plotting and planning, like my "Home-school to Harvard" story.

Speaking of planning, next up is Relentless Principle #4 ...

The 4th Principle of RELENTLESS: Relentless PREPARATION

....

"Luck is the residue of design."
—Branch Rickey

You've got Relentless HEART. You've set Relentless GOALS, and you're committed to pursuing your Relentless AMBITIONS with Relentless CHUTZPAH.

What will it take to make those ambitions a reality? Relentless PREPARATION.

KEEPING YOUR PIPELINE FILLED

You must keep your pipeline filled. If you're wondering, "What's my pipeline?" it's your potential deals, jobs, careers, investors, and opportunities. Like a talented circus juggler who keeps a lot of balls in the air, you need a pipeline full of opportunities that you are always juggling and pursuing. But how does your pipeline get filled? Relentless PREPARATION.

I have multiple careers. I'm a speaker, author, CEO of multiple companies, spokesman for multiple companies, TV pitchman for multiple products, Vegas oddsmaker, and political commentator, as well as a TV producer. I never rely on just one career. I keep my pipeline filled. I'm always juggling twenty-five to fifty balls in the air.

The average person juggles just one or two balls at the most. They depend on one job, or one career, or one paycheck, or one working spouse, or one sugar daddy, or perhaps government to "save" them. That is a tragic mistake. And if that describes you, it is time to fill your pipeline. You need to start creating options and backup options—and backups for your backups. Not just with one, two, or three balls, but a bare minimum of twenty-five to fifty balls. Fill your pipeline using Relentless PREPARATION.

As an example, I might be raising money for a new business idea. Let's say I need to raise $500,000. I would never rely on one investor to write that check. If he says "No," I am left with nothing. Instead, I'll most likely be speaking to twenty-five to fifty investors who are each capable of writing the check I need. And I'll have twenty-five more in the pipeline as backups in case the first fifty fall through.

If you're a cop or fireman or teacher, why not use your free time to build a small business, or open a retail store, or build a multi-level marketing home-based business, or become a salesman, or raise money on the phone for a charity. Better yet, do all of them! *Always* keep your pipeline filled.

If you're an actor, don't read one screenplay or script. Read twenty-five scripts. And while you're working on your acting career, start writing and directing too. *Always* keep your pipeline filled.

If you're a stockbroker and have two hundred clients, congratulations! But never rest on your laurels. Be sure you set aside a couple of hours per day to find another hundred. *Always* keep your pipeline filled.

If you're a realtor and you have fifty listings, congratulations! But you still need to set aside a couple of hours per day to hunt for new listings. Go get fifty more. *Always* keep your pipeline filled.

Here is the point. Never leave your life in the hands of others. Always have backups…and make sure your backups have backups…and those backups are backed up by more backups. *Always* keep your pipeline filled.

But how can you find time to plan and prepare for new opportunities? Where does Relentless PREPARATION actually fit into your life?

Most people are constantly REACTING. They are always running behind, barely keeping up with the demands of their current job, their current deal, their current opportunities. They're just trying to catch up with what life throws at them. They're not calling the plays, planning two moves ahead, making things happen in their future. They will never fully utilize The Power of Relentless.

If you want to be PROACTIVE instead of REACTIVE, you need a PLAN.

THE AMAZING TRIAD

That's why I'm going to share with you my secret for making Relentless PREPARATION a daily part of your life. This secret will transform your career and set you up for undreamed-of success. It's my RELENTLESS DAILY SCHEDULED ACTION PLAN for taking your life from "normal," "average," and "just getting by" to EXPONENTIAL.

THE RELENTLESS TRIAD: THE REMARKABLE, INCREDIBLE, MAGICAL, SCHEDULED DAILY ACTION PLAN THAT WILL CHANGE YOUR LIFE BY 9:00 A.M.

If, like me, you believe "Luck is the residue of design" and "God helps those who help themselves," then you need a detailed system to put you in a position to succeed.

Why is this plan called the Relentless TRIAD? First, because it divides the start of your day into three meaningful periods of improvement and empowerment. The Relentless TRIAD gives you three remarkable things:

1. A mental head start to the day.
2. A physical head start to the day.
3. A financial head start to the day.

The second reason it is called the Relentless TRIAD is because it harnesses The Power of Relentless to allow you to accomplish three remarkable things.

Who wouldn't like to change your mindset and attitude for the better every morning by 9:00 a.m., before you even settle in at work?

Who wouldn't like to get a head start on your competition before the official workday even starts?

Who wouldn't like a head start that puts you thousands of "actions" ahead of your colleagues and competition over the next decade?

That's the power of the TRIAD. That's The Power of Relentless PREPARATION.

The timing is optional. You choose how long you have for the Relentless TRIAD. Some will choose the shorter version, some the longer version. It's up to your schedule.

I wake up every day at 6:00 a.m., start my day at around 6:15 a.m., and do three hours of the Relentless TRIAD. So by 9:15 a.m. or so, I'm in the greatest mindset of my life! I'm ready to take on anyone and anything. My energy is through the roof. My confidence is at "def con BRIGHT RED." That means I'm a serious threat to everyone I do business with! I'm off to a head start that no one I'm competing with can match. And it's only 9:15 a.m. My day has not even really started yet!

But for most people with kids to take to school (I'm a homeschool dad) and a job to get to (I work out of my home office), three hours is asking too much. So for practical purposes treat TRIAD as a ninety-minute scheduled action plan.

Try it for ninety minutes per day, experience it, and once you've felt the amazing benefits and seen the remarkable results, you will be inspired to expand it.

This is your opportunity to super-charge your career, business, and entire life in only ninety minutes per day. This is your opportunity to unleash your inner genius and give yourself a head start over your competition for the rest of your life, in only ninety minutes per day. This is your opportunity to give yourself a huge advantage over every competitor for the same job, career, sale, or raise, in only ninety minutes per day.

The Relentless TRIAD is about building your life around motion and action—PLANNED and SCHEDULED motion and action. It is all about you being in control of your life—not circumstances, or fate, or a boss without your best interests in mind. This is what Relentless PREPARATION is all about.

As you first read about the Relentless TRIAD, you'll think "this is so simple and just common sense." That may be true, but sometimes the answer to a huge problem is sitting right in front of your face. Sometimes the simplest answer is the one everyone ignores. The Relentless TRIAD is a powerful, life-changing action plan to supercharge your life ... assuming, of course, you are one of the few who will have the hunger to change your life, the drive and intensity to succeed, and the discipline to follow the plan every day.

Here is how it works. Adjust your personal schedule so you have ninety minutes before you need to leave your home. For example, if you get up at 6:00 a.m. each day and you start the Relentless TRIAD by 6:15 a.m., you'll be done by 7:45 a.m. If you get up at 7:00 a.m. and start by 7:15 a.m., you'll be done by 8:45 a.m. If you are a commuter and need to leave your home by 7:30 AM, you will need to start at 5:30 to leave time for shower, dress and breakfast. (If you aren't already in the habit of waking up that early, see my "Positive Addictions" at the end of this book.)

But it will be more than worth it! The time you spend on the Relentless TRIAD will be the most amazing ninety minutes of your day. These ninety minutes will leave you in the best mood of your life—filled with optimism, confidence, energy, enthusiasm, and focus. Those are the qualities that empower you to harness The Power of RELENTLESS. These ninety minutes will put you in position, each and every day, for the best day of your life.

It's called the Relentless TRIAD because that magical ninety minutes to start your day is divided into three distinct parts.

- **PART I: MENTAL IMPROVEMENT.** The first thirty minutes of your Relentless TRIAD is dedicated to putting your mind in motion and achieving mental improvement: prayer, meditation, visualization, affirmation. Read more about resources for meditation and mental improvement in "Positive Addictions" at the end of this book. As time permits, you can read inspirational books such as the Bible, or a biography. (Or your favorite book, *The Power of RELENTLESS*. Wink-wink.)

- **PART II: PHYSICAL IMPROVEMENT.** The second thirty minutes of the Relentless TRIAD is dedicated to putting your body in motion and achieving physical improvement with your daily walk, aerobic exercise, weight training, yoga, swimming, etc. Read more about how to use this time in "Positive Addictions" at the end of this book.

- **PART III: FINANCIAL IMPROVEMENT.** This final thirty-minute period is dedicated to financial motion and taking action for financial improvement (increasing your income, or building your career). You'll have two choices of direction here. You might sometimes want to use this thirty minutes to build (and reinforce) your current career or job. This is the time for setting and reviewing your goals (planning out your day), developing and maintaining your hit list (who you need to contact today). But if you really want to harness The Power of RELENTLESS, you will choose to devote many of these thirty-minute blocks of time to truly Relentless Preparation—to change, improve

or expand, to create new opportunities, businesses, clients
or careers.

This is your time to plot, plan, and dream. This is the time you use to
create new ways to explode your income. This is the time to build a second
or third career. This is the time to write your book. This is the time to
create videos that can be used to solicit business. This is also the time to
update your "Hit List"—identify who you need to contact, who you need
to send videos to, who you need to follow up with *today* to turn your goals
into reality.

Your goal for this thirty-minute session is to choose and write down
four actions each day that will advance your goal(s). Then of course you
need to take those actions during the rest of your day—just thinking or
talking about them is not good enough. And finally you need to follow up
those four actions. Let me give you a couple of personal examples. In my
case, I never work on my current deals in this period. I use this time just
for creating new ideas, opportunities, clients, or careers:

a. Suppose I have a current book deal and several regular
speaking deals. I'll work on those during my regular hours.
The Relentless TRIAD is the special time I use to dream up
new book ideas and new speaking opportunities. I use this
time to create a pitch and make a list of *new* clients, agents,
publishers, and organizations I want to contact. This thirty-
minute period is where I make *new* contacts each day.

b. I have a business I'll work at during the rest of day. During this time I'll dream up a *new* business and draw up a game
plan to get it launched.

c. I am the creator and producer of a hit TV series. But I'll
deal with producing that show later in the day. I'll use this
thirty minutes for dreaming up ideas and contacts for a *new*
TV show.

d. I am a real estate broker. I'm working on ten different listings. But I don't use the Relentless TRIAD time for those ten potential sales—that's what I'll be doing that for the rest of the day. I use this thirty minutes every day to find *new* listings and *new* clients.

e. I am a manager of a company from 9 to 5. But I use this daily thirty-minute period to create a *new* career that I've always dreamed of—writing my first movie screenplay, or my first novel.

f. I am a teacher or police officer 9 to 5. But I use this time to build a *new* second career in MLM (multi-level marketing) or sales.

g. Or perhaps you don't want a second source of income, or another career. Perhaps you are an insurance agent, you love your job, and you're darn good at it. Your only goal is to become the #1 performing agent at the firm. So you can use this thirty-minute period to plan out your day, schedule your calls, and make four new contacts each day—*before* your actual workday begins.

This is what's lacking for 99 percent of your competition in the business world. They are always thinking about their current job, career, or business. They are thinking about their current customers or clients. But my "winning edge" in life is that I always keep the pipeline filled. I'm never relying on one career or business. I never want to rely on my pipeline of old clients, or old deals. I want to fill my pipeline with new clients and new deals. This is the thirty-minute period to <u>fill your pipeline.</u>

Most of your competitors don't understand this concept. Relentless PREPARATION is a concept unknown to them. They get too busy or distracted to expand or dramatically improve their income and their life. They have one business, or one job, or one career.

The Relentless TRIAD is your winning edge. The TRIAD puts you in good stead to "attack the day with an enthusiasm unknown to mankind." The Relentless TRIAD helps you get a jump on your competition. It jump-starts your day, jump-starts your career, jump-starts your income, and gives your Relentless AMBITION an outlet to explore, take action, and make things happen.

This is your thirty minutes to dream and be bold. Nothing is better for defeating depression and doubt and creating a positive outlook than to know you are taking action to bring your dreams to fruition. *Go for it.*

If you're having trouble getting started, use a journal, a dream book, or a vision board to brainstorm about where you want Relentless PREPA-RATION to take you. Remind yourself of your Relentless AMBITION and the GOALS you have set for yourself, and consider what are the concrete steps you could take to bring them closer to fruition.

You can and should work ten plus hours per day on your present career, job or business. That's just the "minimum requirement" to succeed nowadays. But if you want to become a super-achiever and taste wealth and financial freedom, you must set aside special time to improve yourself and expand your options and opportunities.

TRIAD is your time to nourish your body, mind, spirit and soul. And it's also your time to think only of new deals, new jobs, new clients, new employees, new partners, new buyers, new distributors. This is how you stay three steps ahead of the competition. While you have your current job or deal ... always be thinking about the next one. This is what separates you from the crowd. This is what allows you to juggle fifty balls in the air at once.

If in this thirty-minute period, you average **4** actions per day (6 days a week) that equals **24** *new* actions (or contacts) per week ...

That adds up to **96** *new* actions (or contacts) per month ...

That's **1,152** *new* actions (or contacts) per year ...

That's **11,520** *new* actions (or contacts) per decade!

That's **11,520** MORE actions (or contacts) than 99 percent of your friends, co-workers, and, most importantly, competitors will ever take over the next decade.

Now let's expand those numbers to include your entire career. From age twenty-two when you graduate college to age seventy when you might retire (if you're the retiring type), that's 55,296 more actions than any of your competitors.

That's how you improve your life. All before 9:00 a.m.! That's 55,296 actions or contacts over your career, before any of your days ever started.

Most important, it's not just any old motion and action. It's scheduled, *structured* motion and action. It's making Relentless PREPARATION a part of your daily routine. It's on your daily calendar—like a doctor's appointment, or client appointment, or a meeting with your boss, or a parent-teacher conference. Those are all scheduled. You never miss them. That's the point of putting these appointments in your schedule. If they are "scheduled" you know you'll make it there, and usually on time.

So I'm asking you to schedule your mind improvement, your body improvement, and your financial improvement. They are just as important as any meeting with a client, doctor, or your boss. This is how you ensure you nourish your body, mind, spirit and soul, and take the actions you need for success.

I'm sure author Napoleon Hill would agree; this is how you create the time to "Think and Grow Rich." And author Reverend Norman Vincent Peale would agree that this is the time necessary to practice "The Power of Positive Thinking." And author Rhonda Byrne would agree it's the time to practice "The Secret." I know for certain that author Wayne Allyn Root agrees this is how you harness The Power of Relentless.

Now, if you can arrange your life to work from home (like I do), then I have a new and improved game plan for you. I personally do three *HOURS* of the Relentless TRIAD each day. I give each of these steps an entire hour each and every day. And I practice the TRIAD six to seven days per week. That's my personal version of the perfect head start to each day (even weekends). That's how I create the *perfect* relentless mindset. You are only as strong as your weakest link. So I want my mind to be strong seven days per week, 365 days per year.

To perfect the Relentless TRIAD even further, add fifteen minutes of scheduled time every night for review. That way, every day, you'll have the chance to look back and judge how the plans and dreams of your Relentless PREPARATION in the morning actually panned out under the pressures of the daily grind. Use this review time to keep a daily journal, review your dream book or vision board, and read a chapter from an inspiring book, or a passage from the Bible.

That's it. The Relentless TRIAD is the foundation of my life. I leave nothing to chance. NOTHING.

Luck is the residue of design. The TRIAD is your personal design.

And God *does* help those who help themselves. The Relentless TRIAD is how you help yourself emotionally, physically, spiritually, and financially.

The Relentless TRIAD is how you fill your pipeline.

Practice the TRIAD religiously, and you will see all your dreams come true.

And keep reading for more RELENTLESS principles that will give you a boatload of ideas for how to use your TRIAD time to bring you closer every day to the life of your dreams.

The 5th Principle
of RELENTLESS:
Relentless BRANDING

....

*"The secret of success in life is for a man to be ready
for his opportunity when it comes."*
—Benjamin Disraeli

When I married my wife back in 1991, I gained more than a wife. I gained a grandpa—Norm Johnson, known to one and all as "Grandpa Norm." It was love at first sight. Grandpa Norm and I got along like we'd been grandpa and grandson our entire lives. We shared a love of God, family, sports, sports cars, and most importantly fitness. We were both workout fanatics. Our relationship was meant to be.

With all we had in common, there was one big difference. I was already a well-known personality in the media and sports world and Grandpa Norm—well, Grandpa Norm was a retired blue collar print shop worker. He was loved by all his family and his many friends. But the truth was, he had been an anonymous working-class guy his entire life. I never considered that might bother him. But I soon found out it did, *a lot.*

One day, out of the blue, Grandpa Norm said, "Grandson, I love you and am going to ask you for a huge favor. I'll be ninety-two on my next birthday. As a special gift, can you make me famous? I've been a 'nobody' my entire life, but before I die, I want to be famous. I want to live your life, even if only for a few days. I want my fifteen minutes of fame. Can you do that for me?"

THROW GRANDPA FROM THE PLANE

Wow! How do you pull off something like that? But Grandpa Norm had faith in me and knew I was relentless. Once I got an idea in my head, I never stop until it becomes reality. He counted on that. He was right. I dreamed up one heck of an idea. I would use Relentless BRANDING to give Grandpa Norm his birthday wish and make him a celebrity. I would create a celebrity brand for him with a concept I called "Throw Grandpa from the Plane." A week later I came back to Grandpa Norm and told him, "I have the idea that will turn your dream into reality, Grandpa. Are you ready to be famous? You'll need to take a leap of faith with me. Literally. We're going to celebrate your ninety-second birthday with a grandfather-grandson skydive! You do that with me, and I'll make you famous. Are you willing to jump out of a perfectly good airplane from thirty thousand feet up, then dive down to earth at over 120 miles per hour?"

Grandpa never hesitated, "Grandson, I'm in. Let's take that leap of faith!"

Now came the hard part. I had about five months before Grandpa Norm's ninety-second birthday to make this happen. If I failed, Grandpa would be crushed. The disappointment might kill him—*literally.* The weight of the world was on my shoulders. So, as usual, I turned to The Power of RELENTLESS. I went on the offense. I attacked the media with abandon for the next five months. I bombarded them with press releases, calls, FedExes with my invitation to the event. I peppered them with reminders about Grandpa Norm, the ninety-two-year-old who was going to jump from an airplane. I didn't wait for their reply. I hounded them with follow-up calls. I wouldn't take NO for an answer. I wouldn't rest until I made Grandpa Norm famous. I was, in short, RELENTLESS!

Then came the big day. My Relentless BRANDING of Grandpa Norm had paid off. When Grandpa and I landed safely, we had over thirty news organizations waiting for us. Most every news station in L.A. was waiting for an interview. Local NBC News opened the 5:00 p.m. newscast in the second largest city in America with our landing and an interview with Grandpa Norm! All of Los Angeles watched. Grandpa was a star for the first time in his ninety-two-year life. Grandpa made the most of the opportunity, trying to pick up the beautiful anchorwoman, Colleen Williams, on live TV with the whole "Southland" watching. He said, "Colleen, I know you're married, but that's okay. We can still be friends."

But making Grandpa Norm into a local hero was only the start. I delivered an even bigger prize with my relentless media attacks—taking the Relentless BRANDING of Grandpa Norm to a new level. I convinced Rosie O'Donnell to interview Grandpa. There, behind the thirty TV news crews in a feeding frenzy interviewing Grandpa, was a limo to race us to the airport for a flight to New York to star on *The Rosie O'Donnell Show*. It was the first limo ride of Grandpa Norm's life and his first ever flight in first class. When we got to New York, Grandpa informed me that it was his first ever trip to Manhattan, too. It was certainly his first time on national TV! Rosie had him *OPEN THE SHOW* by introducing her. Next she interviewed him about his life. Then she showed her thirty-five million television viewers the video of the sky dive. She asked Grandpa, "Why did you do it?" Grandpa Norm pointed to me and said, "There's the guy who MADE me do it. My grandson, Wayne, pushed me out of the plane!" The audience roared with laughter. Grandpa was a hit! To end the interview, Rosie's producers rolled out a cake with ninety-two candles and the entire studio audience sang "Happy Birthday" to Norm. With thirty-five million people watching, Rosie and Grandpa blew out the ninety-two candles and hugged each other—to wild applause.

But wait. We're not done. Grandpa's dream day was just heating up. His favorite actress was Drew Barrymore. Guess who was sitting backstage waiting to come on the show as the next guest? Drew Barrymore. She hugged and kissed

Grandpa and said he was her star. SHE asked for Grandpa Norm's autograph. But Grandpa's day still wasn't over. Grandpa's favorite TV show was *Golden Girls*, about a group of elderly ladies enjoying life as single chicks. As we walked outside to catch our limo, one of the stars of *Golden Girls*, Estelle Getty, was arriving for her guest appearance on *Rosie*. She asked Grandpa why he was there. Grandpa, the old ham, told her his entire story. She jumped up and down with glee and gave Grandpa a big kiss and told him, "You are my hero."

When we got on the plane, the pilot for American Airlines asked Grandpa if he'd enjoyed his trip to New York. Grandpa told him every detail of his story. Once we took off, the pilot announced over the intercom what an honor it was to be flying "the most famous ninety-two year old in America." Then he asked the entire crew and all the passengers to join him in singing "Happy Birthday" to Norm. For the rest of the flight, Norm was asked for autographs by dozens of passengers. Finally the flight attendants had to ask people to stop coming up to first class because they were creating a mob scene.

Grandpa came home to receive the key to the city of Pasadena, his home. Blue Cross Blue Shield awarded him their "Ageless Wonder" award and featured a story on Grandpa Norm in their nationwide newsletter. Stories appeared in newspapers and on TV news shows across the country. Other elderly people were soon in the news, inspired by Norm's stunt to jump out of airplanes themselves, including one eighty-nine-year-old woman. And then there were the marriage proposals. Dozens of women sent letters to Grandpa Norm proposing marriage, some of them twenty years younger. Norm got a real kick out of that.

The power of Relentless BRANDING was able to turn an ordinary ninety-two-year-old print shop worker into a national celebrity. Norm died a happy man, but only after going racecar driving with yours truly at 150 miles per hour at the California Speedway in Fontana, California, in front of a crowd of reporters—to celebrate his ninety-third birthday! I loved Norm, but I swear a part of me was relieved when he died before his ninety-fourth birthday. I had no idea how to top those stunts!

But you know I would have ... because I'm *RELENTLESS!*

FLOYD "MONEY" MAYWEATHER

Are you already using branding to grow your business, attract clients, and ratchet up your success? Why not?

Look at Floyd "Money" Mayweather. Boxing is a dying sport. TV ratings are in the toilet. Seats at the events are empty. MMA (Mixed Martial Arts) and the UFC (Ultimate Fighting Championship) have killed boxing. Yet a great brand can overcome *anything*.

The biggest brand in boxing is Floyd "Money" Mayweather. As I write this chapter the Mayweather/Pacquiao championship fight is days away in Las Vegas. It is the most talked about event in Las Vegas history. It's bigger than the Super Bowl. CNN reports it's the biggest payday for any athlete in world history.[1]

Mayweather will earn about $180 million for this one night's work. Manny Pacquiao will earn $120 million for this one night.[2]

Even in the middle of a terrible economy, every seat at the MGM Events Center is sold out at prices that defy reality. The nosebleed seats are being sold by ticket brokers for $8,000 to $10,000 per SEAT! To get a ringside seat you'll need a $250,000 credit line![3]

Hotel rooms are the most expensive in Las Vegas history. Rooms that normally cost $130 per night are going for up to $2000 per night.[4]

And the Pay-Per-View price to watch at home will be $95, the highest in history. The economy is gasping for air. It doesn't matter. Boxing is a dying sport. It doesn't matter. People are hungry for success … celebrity … winning. When people find a brand name "valuable," they will pay anything to feel like a winner. *That's branding!*

"BROADWAY" JOE NAMATH

"Broadway" Joe Namath is a brand. If you just look at Joe Namath's stats he was average. His career win-loss record is 62 wins vs. 63 losses.[5] Joe Namath's career completion percentage was a mediocre 50.1 percent. His career touchdowns-to-interception ratio was terrible—Namath actually threw far more interceptions than touchdowns (173 TDs vs. 220 INT).[6]

Yet he'll go down in history as one of the great NFL gunslingers and greatest brands ever! Why? Relentless BRANDING. Namath had a knack for promotion and a bigger-than-life personality. Putting your personality out there in the public spotlight is what defines and sells a brand—and that's exactly what "Broadway" Joe Namath did.

He was bold enough to predict his team would win the 1969 Super Bowl as 19-point underdogs. That prediction branded him for life. He wore fur coats on the sidelines of games.[7]

He did a TV commercial wearing women's pantyhose.[8]

His bigger-than-life personality made Joe Namath one of the biggest brands in sports history. His net worth is $18 million.[9] Not bad for a guy with more interceptions than touchdowns. Not bad for a guy who won 62 games and lost 63.

That's Relentless BRANDING.

And it's the same reason people are paying to see the Mayweather fight—because Floyd has put his bigger-than-life personality out there and made himself a BRAND. Personality makes people feel alive. It can be positive or negative. You may love it or hate it. But it makes you *feel.* It's memorable. It gives you energy, electricity, and excitement. People pay big money for "memorable!"

RALPH LAUREN

I'll bet many budding young fashion designers think they are "too good" to worry about sales or promotion. They believe their products will "sell themselves." But one of the "best" fashion designers ever certainly understood the importance of Relentless BRANDING. His real name was Ralph Lifshitz. But he understood rich women would never buy his clothes, no matter how fashionable and classy, if he didn't project the right image.

He changed his name to Ralph Lauren and created a dream image of a wealthy, tan, WASP playboy riding horses at his estate in Greenwich, Connecticut ... as opposed to the truth: a short (5′6″) Jewish kid from the Bronx named Lifshitz, who used to be a broke tie salesman. Can you imagine women bragging, "This is my latest dress from Lifshitz"? *It's all about BRANDING.*

I'll bet there are many young lawyers who think they are "too good" to worry about their brand. They think it's all about their legal skills. One of my lawyer friends proves them dead wrong. He is one of the most famous and powerful lawyers in America. I walked into his office one day and was completely intimidated by the walls lined with media headlines celebrating his many winning cases. I said to my friend, "That's really impressive—you must have a 100 percent winning record." He laughed and said, "Actually I'm 50-50, but I only put the winning cases on the wall to impress and intimidate anyone walking into my office." *It's all about the WINNING BRAND.*

THE U.S. MILITARY

Do you think young men and women join the Army or Navy only because of patriotism? Not true. The Army and Navy spend tens of millions of dollars on ads each year. They hire Madison Avenue executives to design those advertising campaigns. Those ads don't show a sobbing mom and dad at a funeral. They don't show a soldier in a psych ward with Post Traumatic Stress Disorder. They never interview a kid who has no legs or arms, or whose best friend died in his arms. That would be too frightening and negative.

Instead, Madison Avenue shows images of fun, independence, and a proud young person in a perfect shiny uniform dripping with medals. They show scenes of friendship, camaraderie, and bravery. They have slogans like "An Army of One." It's enough to make a patriotic kid run to the Army recruiting office and enlist! *It's all about Relentless BRANDING.*

LAS VEGAS

A great example of the importance of branding has to be my hometown of Las Vegas. Five words—"I'm going to Las Vegas"—produce an instant smile on faces all over the world. But what separates Las Vegas, Nevada, from Las Vegas, New Mexico? In this Vegas we understand the power of the brand! We don't just understand it, *we live it*. Everything is image. Everything is branded. Everything is memorable. Everything is bigger than life. Everything is based on slogans.

Vegas is "Sin City" ... the gambling capital of America ... the tourist capital of America ... the convention capital of America ... the fun capital of America ... the sex capital of America ... the low tax capital of America ... and of course, "What Happens in Vegas, Stays in Vegas."

All of that that memorable branding makes you forget that Las Vegas is in the middle of a sweltering hot, godforsaken, ugly, tumbleweed-infested desert. Until Vegas embraced gambling, booze, sex, and quickie divorces, it was an empty town where you stopped for gas on your way to Los Angeles. Relentless BRANDING changed that just a bit.

Because of the success of that sales job and image makeover, well over 40 million tourists visited Vegas last year (an all-time record). Over 22,000 conventions were held in Las Vegas last year.[10] Nevada gaming revenues were over $11 billion last year.[11] Nevada was the fastest growing state in America for nineteen consecutive years.[12] Las Vegas is home to at least half the reality TV shows in America.[13]

And then there's the amazing statistic about Las Vegas nightclubs. Seven of the ten top-grossing nightclubs in America are found in one city: Las Vegas. Vegas's top clubs and bars grossed $612 million in 2014. Second place went to Miami with $192 million, with New York in third place at $181 million. Just one Las Vegas nightclub—X/S at Wynn Resort—grossed more than every nightclub and bar in Los Angeles combined ($105 million vs. $97 million).[14] This ugly desert town has used Relentless BRANDING to become the most famous town in the world!

THE SAD STORY OF PHIL TOBIN

But now let me tell you the story of the polar opposite, a story of a humble man who never understood the power of the BRAND. His name was Phil Tobin, and what makes this an amazing dichotomy is this man was the "Father of Las Vegas."[15]

I'll bet you've never heard of him. Neither has anyone else. He died anonymous and invisible—the opposite of everything about Las Vegas.

But without Phil Tobin, Las Vegas, Nevada, would be no more famous than Las Vegas, New Mexico. Tobin was a "cowboy legislator" in the Nevada State Assembly in the 1930s. At the time, Las Vegas was a town of five thousand people. It was a stop on the highway on the way to Los Angeles until Phil Tobin dreamed up legal casino gambling and fought for it for years in the Nevada legislature. He said, "If gambling is made legal, Las Vegas will become the playground of the United States." What a visionary. That's exactly what happened. After three tries, Tobin finally got his bill passed.

Satisfied and sick of politics, he went back to ranching. But his timing was awful. It was in the middle of the Great Depression. Tobin lost his ranch. He wound up as a ranch hand working for others. He lived in a tiny, dirty bunkhouse and slept on a dirty, stained mattress. He died penniless at age seventy-five in 1976.

When he died, stories appeared in Nevada newspapers honoring Tobin as "the father of legalized casino gambling" and "the father of Las Vegas." His friends and fellow ranch employees were shocked. They told the newspapers that Tobin was polite, humble, nice, and never bragged about himself and never said a word about his role in legalizing gambling. "We had no idea" was the phrase heard most often by reporters at his funeral.

I'm sure Phil Tobin was a nice man. Yet Tobin never made a penny off his vision, or his heroic efforts to turn his dream into reality. I'm sad to report that "nice" isn't enough in this competitive, dog-eat-dog world. I don't think God wants anyone to be so humble that they die penniless and anonymous. "God helps those who help themselves." If you want success, you need to relentlessly promote your brand.

THE "WALL STREET PORN STAR"

My final example of branding is an X-rated one. While I'm not endorsing this career choice, sometimes even a negative choice can prove the value of branding. Paige Jennings was an anonymous part-time intern at a Wall Street stock brokerage firm in early 2015. She decided she wanted a career in porn and needed an angle. The angle? She became the "Wall Street Porn Star." She submitted "selfies" taken in the bathroom of her Wall Street firm to an adult film company searching for a star for a new film.[16]

Thousands of women submitted their photos. Guess who got a call back in three hours? The "Wall Street Porn Star."[17]

Branding works. Thousands of women applied, but only one had her own brand, "Wall Street Porn Star." Next Ms. Jennings set up a Twitter account. Within hours she was being inundated with media interview requests from across the country. The "Wall Street Porn Star" made headlines in the *New York Post* and *Business Insider*. Soon she was fielding offers from media all over the world. The "Wall Street Porn Star" was offered a six-figure sponsorship deal—something that had never happened in the history of the adult film industry. Keep in mind she was just a lowly intern—she really had nothing to do with Wall Street. Yet she got a major six-figure sponsorship deal and was soon paid an unheard of sum to star in her first movie, even though she had never done an adult movie scene in her life. *That's branding!*

THE NECESSITY OF HOOKING

No, not *that* kind of hooking. I'm talking about the kind of "hooks" that create hit songs. Success in the business world is no different from success in the music business. You need the right hook or angle to create a hit. Why? In the music business there is so much competition that singers are a dime a dozen. To catch listeners' attention, to stand apart from the crowd, every singer needs a "hook." One such hook is a memorable song verse that resonates with people. You know, like Lionel Ritchie's "Easy like Sunday morning." I personally love Sundays. I always have, always will. It was the only day of the week my hardworking blue-collar dad was home with the family. The verse "Easy like Sunday morning" from Lionel Ritchie's hit "Easy" was released almost forty years ago, but I still remember that verse like it was yesterday. That's the power of a "hook." By the way, that song hit #1 on the Soul charts. Today Lionel Richie is worth over $200 million.[18] A good hook is worth its weight in gold!

I went from nowhere to one of the top online syndicated political columnists in America because of my "hooks" (i.e. headlines). You can write a great story, yet no one will read it without a compelling, memorable headline to catch reader's attention. That's my specialty. Hooks and headlines are BRANDING.

I always use the *New York Post* as Exhibit A for the value of outrageous headlines.

The classic headline in newspaper history, used to describe a murder victim found in a strip club:

"Headless Body Found in Topless Bar"[19]

Another great headline used to describe a monumental mistake on the golf course by Tiger Woods, who dropped his golf ball in the wrong place:

"Tiger Woods Puts Balls in Wrong Place Again"[20]

A classic *NY Post* headline to describe the murder of a gay mob boss:

"Mobster Sleeps with The Swishes"[21]

A classic headline to describe the NY Yankees beating the Boston Red Sox on the one hundredth anniversary of Fenway Park:

"100 Years of Ass-Kicking"[22]

I credit my success as an entrepreneur to having grown up reading and learning from the *New York Post*. To this day it's my favorite newspaper.

My favorite website is the DrudgeReport. Matt Drudge has an amazing "touch" for picking the most colorful, fun, outrageous and controversial headline. It is an art form. That talent has made the DrudgeReport one of the most-read websites in the world—with over 27 million page views per day.[23] Drudge drives more traffic than Twitter and Facebook combined![24]

Drudge has three employees, Matt Drudge plus two others. The site is worth close to $1 billion.[25]

A great "hook" is what empowers Drudge to stand out in a web world with millions of sites.

I have applied that talent to my entrepreneurial and political careers. I always try to think of a headline in my political commentaries that will attract attention and stand out in a crowd. Every advertising headline I write is designed for "shock value." If it doesn't shock, it's a loser.

Everything you do and say as an entrepreneur should be measured by how much attention you attract and how many leads you attract (phone calls or sign-ups on your website). "Hooks" are how you stand out in a crowded field. The reality is you're either a "talented hooker" or you're just screwing yourself!

Branding means something simple. It means something memorable. It sets you apart from the crowd. Your name, "hook," or brand is what people remember and pay for. Relentless BRANDING is a crucial part of success in any field. What is your brand? What sets you apart from the crowd?

Use your morning TRIAD time to brainstorm about what's unusual and compelling about you and your business … what's memorable about your personality or product. What do you have that's unique, that no other person or company can offer? It may be a new product or business idea. It may be something in your personality or style that makes doing business with you an experience unrepeatable anywhere else. It may be a marketing concept or a fundraising scheme. Whatever it is, it's something that sets you apart from the competition and makes you unique. That's your BRAND. Once you know what it is, you just have to sell the world on it with Relentless BRANDING—just like "Broadway" Joe Namath, or Las Vegas, or the "Wall Street Porn Star," or my personal favorite, Grandpa Norm. I gave Norm's skydive story a name, "Throw Grandpa from the Plane." The media ate it up! Keep reading to learn more secrets of how to sell your BRAND—with Relentless STORYTELLING!

The 6th Principle of RELENTLESS: Relentless STORYTELLING

....

"Newspapers are dying because no one likes to read anymore. People want to watch. One video can change your entire life, career, or business. One video can say more than a hundred thousand words on a piece of paper. People learn and absorb through visual images. People forget the words on a page within minutes. But they remember iconic video images for the rest of their lives. Video can change everything in an instant. Ask Ray Rice how one powerful video can change public opinion."
—Wayne Allyn Root

I've sold hundreds of million of dollars of products, as spokesman and pitchman in over twenty diverse product categories. How? By Relentless STORYTELLING. The key is I always have a personal story for every product. My speaking career is a hit because I always have a personal story. I'm a hit with the media because I always have a colorful and entertaining personal story. My books are always filled with entertaining personal stories. The truth is people get bored by facts. "Facts tell and stories sell." If you want success at anything, you must learn to tell stories.

Have you ever watched the Olympics? They aren't popular because of sports. They are popular because of the compelling personal stories of each individual athlete. Those stories are packaged with emotional music by TV networks to great effect.

Why is the Bible the bestselling book of all time? Because the Bible is filled with the greatest set of compelling human-interest stories ever told. How many Bibles have been sold? *5 BILLION* and counting.[1]

Politics is nothing but storytelling. The winning candidates are always the ones with the most compelling personal stories. The losing candidates are usually the ones with loads of facts on their side. No one remembers and, unfortunately, no one cares. But a great story—voters remember those forever!

Stories are memorable, facts are not. After I've given any of my speeches (business or political), not one person in the room ever quotes a single fact I've told. But they're all quick to tell me how much they enjoyed certain stories I told: my journey to become Jimmy The Greek, my presidential campaign, my homeschooled daughter graduating from Harvard, Grandpa Norm jumping out of a plane, my nonstop relentless business success stories. They remember those stories with ease!

"Facts tell and stories sell." Remember that, and you'll be a star at whatever you choose to do in life. With Relentless STORYTELLING, your BRAND will take the world by storm.

THE POWER OF VIDEO

Today there's a tool that makes it easier and more effective to tell stories—and get those stories in front of the eyes of hundreds, thousands, even millions of potential customers, clients, and investors—than ever before in world history. As you'll see, this tool has been a key secret of my success at every stage of my career: VIDEO.

If there was ever a perfect tool for The Power of Relentless, this is it! And, in today's high-tech, smartphone, social media world, it is more important and prevalent than ever. Today almost everyone is using video. But few use it as a tool to create wealth and success.

First, let me tell you that video changed my life. Video is at the root (excuse the pun) of almost every miracle and great achievement in my life.

Nowadays the competition is fierce. Nothing is more important than finding a way to separate yourself from the crowd. Video gives me that separation, that *winning edge,* and it can give it to you as well.

What exactly does video do? Video tells a story. Video allows you to tell *your* story in your own way. Success is about great personality, great communication skills, great energy and enthusiasm. Video allows all those great traits to be combined to tell great stories. Facts are boring. Unless you're a contestant on *Jeopardy,* no one succeeds by being an encyclopedia of facts. Never forget: "Facts tell, stories sell." So to achieve great success in business, in relationships, in life . . . you need to learn how to tell great emotional stories.

Video is the way to tell a great story—a *memorable* story, an *emotional* story, a story that moves people, preferably the people you need to impress in order to get a job, or get a promotion, or build a career, or build a business, or sell your business, or sell your products.

Remember my mother Stella Root's amazing story? She proved that if your heart is big enough, you don't even need a brain. Well, a video is all *heart.* A video gets people's attention. The people you want to do business with will forget your words on a resume, letter, or e-mail in five minutes. But they will remember the right video images for years to come! That's why RELENTLESS VIDEO is the *heart* of The Power of Relentless.

Virtually everything that is sold is sold by telling a story, usually on video. Hollywood sells their stories on video (TV, movies, the internet). The media tells their story on video (ABC News, NBC News, CBS News, CNN, Fox News—whether on TV or the internet, it's all on video). Madison Avenue tells and sells their stories on video (think TV commercials). Whether it's cars, homes, stocks, mortgages, insurance, pharmaceutical drugs, or music, they are all sold on video. Your ability to use video to tell your story, to sell your product, to sell yourself, is a powerful tool to separate you from the crowd.

There is a reason that newspapers are dying. People would rather watch than read. They watch TV and surf the internet watching videos. The web has turned your computer into a television set. So today people primarily do two things: they watch television on their TV screen, and they watch videos on their computer screen. In other words, they communicate, entertain, and educate themselves almost exclusively through video.

Why? Because words on a piece of paper convey very little emotion. But video makes you feel something. Video is *heart*.

Let me ask you a few questions. Would the Beatles have been as important a cultural phenomenon if you had read about them in a newspaper? No. It's the video images of them landing in America to hysterical mob scenes and the young girls fainting during their first appearance on *The Ed Sullivan Show* that we all remember.

What made the JFK assassination the memory of a lifetime? Not a newspaper article. It was the video of JFK being shot in his limo on that fateful day in Dallas ... and then days later the video image of his three-year-old son John Jr. saluting as his father's casket drove by.

Will you ever forget the O.J. Simpson car chase in the white Ford Bronco? Of course not. Why? Because we all watched it live on television. Those video images are seared in our brains for life.

How about 9/11? None of us can ever forget the iconic video image of the Twin Towers collapsing and the toxic clouds of smoke that followed. Those images will be seared in our brains forever. No newspaper could have told that story the way video images did.

Then there's *The Secret*. It is the not only the bestselling self-help book of modern times, it became a *cultural phenomenon*. There are now over 21 million copies in print. *TWENTY-ONE MILLION. The Secret* has been translated into 46 languages. It was on the bestseller list for 146 consecutive weeks. Revenues now top $300 million.[2]

Amazing, right? "The law of attraction" sure worked for the author of *The Secret*. But was it "the law of attraction" or "the law of video" that turned *The Secret* into a phenomenon?

Because before there was ever one book sold there was a video called *The Secret*. It was released on March 23, 2006, as a documentary film.[3]

It was screened and shared by millions of people online. Then it was turned into a DVD bought by millions of people. And only then, in 2007, was *The Secret* released as a book.

It was the video images of *The Secret* that created a worldwide phenomenon. To this day, *The Secret* is the only self-help book I know of that was first promoted and sold as a film. Brilliant marketing, because the author of *The Secret* obviously understood the power of RELENTLESS VIDEO.

Here's more evidence of the power of video: video even saved the entire billion-dollar music industry. The music industry was dying in 1982. Record sales were in a nosedive. *Billboard* reported record shipments down by 50 million between 1980 and 1982. August 13, 1982, was known in the music business as "Black Friday." Half of the marketing department of CBS/Epic Records was laid off on that day. Nothing like that had ever happened before in the music business.

Then a video came to the rescue. Music played on the radio may have been dying a painful death, but music played on video was just what the doctor ordered. Michael Jackson's *Thriller* album debuted on November 30, 1982.[4]

The earth moved. At *Thriller*'s peak over one million albums per month were being sold. Today it is still the bestselling album in history. In the range of fifty to sixty million copies have been sold internationally, although the Michael Jackson estate claims over 100 million have sold worldwide.[5]

Thriller has gone Platinum twenty-nine times. After the release of *Thriller*, the music business exploded. Billions of dollars were made because of *Thriller*. History was changed. Why?

Why else? Because of a video. CBS/Epic Records decided to take a gigantic gamble. The typical music video in those days cost $30,000 to $40,000 to produce. Epic spent over $1 million on a fourteen-minute video for the title track "Thriller." The video was released on December 3, 1982. That video for "Thriller" became a pop culture phenomenon. It told an emotional story. It touched hearts. The National Film Preservation Board has included "Thriller" on its list of significant films of all-time.[6]

MTV was a fledgling new TV network. "Thriller" turned MTV into one of the most popular TV networks in history. MTV had never paid one cent to play a video. Record companies were glad to give them free copies of videos so MTV would play them. "Thriller" changed all that. MTV paid $1 million for the exclusive rights to play the "Thriller" video. It became the sensation of all-time. MTV played it all day long. It was such a phenomenon that a one-hour film documentary was made called "Making Michael Jackson's Thriller."

Yes, it's true that I'm "Mr. Relentless." Yes, it's true that I'm more relentless than my competition. Yet my success isn't due to just being relentless. It's due to my #1 relentless tool—*the video.*

From an early age I had a unique understanding that videos could take any product to another level. Video is how I tell my personal stories. Video is how I sell my products. Video is how I sell my number one product—*me!* Video supercharges The Power of RELENTLESS.

When you apply your relentless mindset to "the video," you are taking advantage of life's great multiplier—*synergy!*

TEN MIRACLES BROUGHT TO YOU BY RELENTLESS VIDEO

Let's look at ten distinct miracles in my life, and I'll show you how in each case I relentlessly used video to tell a unique and memorable story, thereby making the impossible, *POSSIBLE.* These examples should help you decide how to use video in your own journey to success.

MIRACLE #1: A blue-collar son of a butcher managed to escape his working class roots, escape death at his dangerous, high crime urban high school, and get accepted at Columbia University. How? *With The Power of Relentless and ...*

THE RELENTLESS STORYTELLING POWER OF VIDEO: Even as a teenager, I realized the power of a video. At the age of seventeen, I produced a powerful video answering the question of why I deserved to be accepted at Columbia University. I told my story of being a blue-collar son of a butcher almost killed in my urban high school. I explained that fate intervened and I had been given a second chance, when my parents begged my grandfather to save my life by sending me to an exclusive private school (Thornton Donovan School in New Rochelle, New York)—where I graduated valedictorian of my class. My life had a purpose, and that purpose was Columbia University. I explained on that video that while Columbia would admit hundreds of rich spoiled kids whose parents went to Columbia, they'd have only one chance to admit a S.O.B. (son of a butcher). I promised them they wouldn't be sorry. I was the one who would change the world. I left that video with the Columbia admissions officer. I guarantee you that back in "the Stone Age" of 1977, I was the only applicant with the chutzpah to create a video about my life and leave it with the admissions officer. I was accepted at Columbia. Yes, I was relentless, but the video was my tool. Video had changed my life for the first time. It wouldn't be the last.

MIRACLE #2: Then that same kid with no money, connections, prior education, or experience in the TV industry talked his way into becoming the #1 anchorman and host of five shows on Financial News Network (now CNBC). He did that after twelve years of massive failure and rejection. He said he'd become the "Jimmy The Greek" of his generation. He wound up becoming Jimmy's co-host on national TV. How? *With the power of RELENTLESS and…*

THE RELENTLESS STORYTELLING POWER OF VIDEO: Remember I had no resume to offer; I'd never been a TV anchorman or host. I had no degree to offer (I'd studied political science at Columbia). I never took a course in broadcast journalism. But I had THE VIDEO. My success at gaining admission to Columbia led me to try The Video again. I rented a TV studio, sat at the anchor desk and acted like what I thought a TV sportscaster should look and sound like. Then I created a second segment with me sitting at the anchor desk portraying my version of a young

"Jimmy the Greek" on an NFL pregame show, portraying a Vegas odds-maker, and picking point spread winners. Then I added some scenes of me appearing as a guest on TV talk shows. I then relentlessly sent that video to every decision-maker in the TV sports business. It was roundly rejected hundreds of times. But all I needed was that one "YES" that changes your life. The Video did it—*again*.

MIRACLE #3: That kid, now a man, without any prior experience in creating, producing, or financing a TV show, sold a TV show to a major cable network, then two shows, now three. He did that after sixteen years of rejection. How? *With The Power of RELENTLESS and ...*

THE RELENTLESS STORYTELLING POWER OF VIDEO: The TV business obviously understands video more than any other. Yes, it took sixteen years, but eventually I got that first YES that changed my life by showing them a short video, known in the TV business as a "sizzle reel." The key was that I stayed relentless for all those years. I relentlessly kept pitching my idea. I relentlessly kept sending out my video. And I was eventually rewarded. My life changed because of The Video—*again*.

MIRACLE #4: That same man built a multi-million dollar business that was an industry leader, with over three million clients, and was awarded a star on the Las Vegas Walk of Stars. He did all that despite never-ending criticism, naysayers, cynics, and rejection. How? *With The Power of RELENTLESS and ...*

THE RELENTLESS STORYTELLING POWER OF VIDEO: This time it was "all video, all the time." I raised almost twenty million dollars by showing investors a video of my vision for the company that I planned to build. I also showed TV networks a video of the vision of the NFL pre-game show I intended to create. Once the business was launched, the TV show itself was one big video. It was the all-important marketing vehicle for my business. We received over ten thousand calls most every Saturday morning because of that thirty-minute television show. Next we'd send each potential customer a fifteen-minute video, "A Day in the Life of The

King of Vegas—Wayne Allyn Root." That video showcased my career as America's leading Vegas oddsmaker and sports handicapper. It followed me behind the scenes. It introduced viewers to my family. It showed them how I think, how I pick more point spread winners than anyone else in the world. That video cost about three thousand dollars to produce and attracted several million dollars in sales. My life changed because of Video—*again*.

MIRACLE #5: That same man, now a well-known sports gambler and Vegas oddsmaker, decided to run for president. He beat out a U.S. senator, almost beat out the congressman who led the impeachment of President Bill Clinton, won the vice presidential nomination of the Libertarian Party, and became one of maybe one to two hundred people in the history of America to run for the office of vice president on a serious presidential ticket. How? *With The Power of RELENTLESS and ...*

THE RELENTLESS STORYTELLING POWER OF VIDEO: By now I understood the power of video. I had used video to achieve almost every goal in my life. So while my competitors for the Libertarian presidential nomination handed out campaign literature, I handed out DVDs and also pointed potential voters to my website, which featured dozens of videos of me being interviewed by the media.

I put all those political talk show appearances on a video, along with a professionally produced TV interview about why I wanted the Libertarian presidential nomination. Then I sent that video to every delegate to our national convention. That video turned me from a nobody, with zero chance to win the presidential nomination, to one of the three favorites to win the nomination. Then at the convention I introduced myself to the crowd with another video of national TV and radio talk show host Mancow Muller (of *Mancow in the Morning* fame) endorsing Wayne Root for president. I won the vice presidential nomination and forever changed my life because of a whole bunch of videos—*again*.

MIRACLE #6: That same man turned a third party vice presidential nomination, normally a dead end, into a career as a national TV political commentator, pundit, and syndicated columnist. How? *With The Power of RELENTLESS and…*

THE RELENTLESS STORYTELLING POWER OF VIDEO: By now you should be getting the picture. I had used media interviews to make a name for myself, establish credibility, and win a place on a presidential ticket. Now I took all the TV media interviews during the presidential campaign, put them on video, and sent that video to every TV and radio network in America. That video was my calling card. Who needs a boring resume that looks like everyone else's, or a business card that says nothing special? I created a unique calling card, a video featuring me as a star on Fox News, CNBC, CNN, and MSNBC. Next thing you know, I'm a media personality and political commentator. My life changed because of a whole bunch of videos—*again.*

MIRACLE #7: That same man became a national bestselling author. Despite my having no background or credentials to write books, you're now reading my tenth book! How? *With The Power of RELENTLESS and…*

THE RELENTLESS STORYTELLING POWER OF VIDEO: Each of my book deals was sold with a video sent to publishers showcasing my media credentials and star power on TV. Did you think publishers buy "words on a piece of paper"? Not today! Today, before they even look at what you want to write, they want to know how you—not they—are going to sell your book. They want to see you live and up close on video. They want to see you "in action" in media interviews. Without powerful videos sent to publishers, I never would have gotten the chance to write ten books.

But my success as an author goes much deeper than the videos that closed my book deals. I also used web videos to attract attention and sell my books. I created multiple videos for each book to convince potential book buyers to buy my book. Those videos featured colorful topics and often OUTRAGEOUS headlines! I created one or two distinct new videos each week. I then put each video up at my website, at my publisher's website, on Facebook, and on Twitter, and I e-mailed it to my database of thousands of followers. My life changed because of a whole bunch of videos—*again.*

MIRACLE #8: That same man became a spokesman and TV pitchman for many national and international companies, selling hundreds of millions of dollars of products in over twenty different genres and industries. He did this despite NOT being Brad Pitt, George Clooney, or Donald Trump. How? *With The Power of RELENTLESS and …*

THE RELENTLESS STORYTELLING POWER OF VIDEO: I landed each of my spokesman deals by sending a video called "Meet Wayne Allyn Root" to the CEO of the company. In many cases these were total strangers that I "cold called." Yet, because of a powerful, relentless sales tool—The Video—I was able to close big deal after big deal. They would have never read a letter or a plain vanilla e-mail. But they all watched my video.

But getting the job to star as a spokesman in TV and radio ad campaigns is just the start. Achieving success selling tens of millions of dollars of the products is quite another thing. Once again "The Video" did the trick. I've never sold a product with words on a piece of paper, or words written on a boring, static website. In each of the twenty-two different cases, I sold the products with TV ads, TV infomercials, webinars, and, of course, a website with powerful videos. My life changed because of a whole bunch of videos—*again.*

MIRACLE #9: That same man fulfilled the last wishes of his ninety-two year old adopted Grandpa to turn an anonymous working-class man into a celebrity for his ninety-second birthday. How? *With The Power of RELENTLESS and…*

THE RELENTLESS STORYTELLING POWER OF VIDEO: This one was easy. To attract media attention, you just need cute kids, adorable pets, an emotional story, or a ninety-two year old jumping out of a plane. *I had one of those!*

So I interviewed Grandpa Norm about his upcoming skydive. He gave funny and colorful answers to my questions. I asked him "What happens if this goes wrong and you die?" Norm said, *"Who cares? I'm ninety-two years old, and I'll be jumping out of a plane in midair. If something goes wrong, I'll be halfway to heaven!"*

I knew the media would eat the story up. I sent the video to news stations and TV networks. Everyone I sent it to wanted to cover the story. *Everyone.* The rest of it is history. Grandpa Norm's life changed because of a video. *It works every time.*

MIRACLE #10: That same man took a young girl and molded her into a relentless super-achiever, producing one of the most remarkable stories in the annals of education called "Homeschool to Harvard." How? *With The Power of RELENTLESS and…*

THE RELENTLESS STORYTELLING POWER OF VIDEO: I knew Dakota was competing with over thirty-five thousand of the smartest, most remarkable teenagers in the world for a few slots at Harvard and Stanford. The year Dakota was accepted at both elite colleges, they were the two most competitive in the history of education. But Dakota knew how to separate herself and stand out from the crowd. After all, she had learned from the best!

I knew Dakota had to use Relentless BRANDING to make herself memorable to Harvard and Stanford admissions officers. Her brand was "the brilliant homeschool girl." That made her special and unique to Ivy League colleges. She was also branded as a fencing champion, another unique brand that set her apart. Then she added The Video to her package. The Video featured Dakota giving her dad's nomination speech for President of the United States on national TV. Not many teenagers could compete with that! Just like her dad, Dakota's life changed because of a video. *It works every time.*

BONUS MIRACLE DUE TO THE RELENTLESS STORYTELLING POWER OF VIDEO: I have a "bonus" story to tell about The Power of Relentless Video. The point of this entire chapter is "you have to see it to believe it." People are cynical and skeptical. You need "Show and Tell" to get their attention. A video does that. It shows and tells a story that you could never convey on a piece of paper, brochure, business card, resume, or business plan. Sometimes even I need to be reminded of that lesson!

In the past two years my income has improved dramatically—because I built a powerhouse niche business by mistake. It was never my intent. It just happened…because of The Power of Relentless Video.

For a decade I've been a business and motivational speaker at business conferences and conventions worldwide. But I never utilized The Power of Video in my speeches. I spoke for 90 minutes, got a big ovation, signed books, then flew home. I did that for over ten years. To me the speaking business was only about ... *speaking.*

Then one of my mentors, a brilliant success coach and legendary business speaker named JT Foxx, challenged me to expand my presentation and come up with a product to empower the people in my audiences. He wanted me to be more interactive and create something the audience could take home with them to improve their lives and increase their income. Because of my respect for JT, I agreed. I gave it thought. I prayed about it. I meditated on it. I took a walk each morning thinking about it, as I walked through my favorite park. Then the idea struck.

I decided to offer audiences my talents as a spokesman for THEM. I would create a business as an endorser and spokesman for small business owners, professionals, and independent contractors. Big business of course already does it every day. They hire celebrity spokesmen. But small business and individuals can't afford to hire Brad Pitt, George Clooney, Sly Stallone, William Devane, Denis Leary, or Jennifer Lopez. Who is the spokesman for small businesses? Until I came up with this idea ... ***no one.***

I asked myself, *"Why can't I create a professionally produced video that will market, promote, and brand any small business or professional? Why can't I use my national media exposure, brand name, and credibility to give credibility to any small business?"* The answer, of course, was "I can."

So I tried it out. I gave a speech and offered this new product, a video hosted and produced by me, to promote the business or product of small business owners in the audience. Great idea, right? No one bought it. *I bombed.*

Some might have decided the product was just that, a bomb, and folded their tent. But I'm relentless. My motto is: "If it doesn't work, try and try again until you make it work, preferably with a video that tells a great story." That's exactly what I did.

I went back to the drawing board and created a new presentation, complete with a half dozen videos to be played throughout the presentation. These videos were all examples of how I used The Video in my life: to supercharge my career, to make miracles happen, to make the impossible, *possible*. I used The Power of Video to paint a picture, to help my audience understand how a video could help promote their business and sell their product. I used the power of "Show and Tell."

It worked like magic. Suddenly half the audience was racing to the back of the room to stand in line to buy a Wayne Root spokesman video. The results were over the top. The videos had done the trick. I had to paint the picture of the importance and power of a video ... by showing the audience *a bunch of videos!*

By my second presentation I had added even more videos to my presentation. And the results were even *more* spectacular.

Now I *really* started thinking. Why not open the entire event with a video introducing me to the audience? Wouldn't that be even more powerful? Wouldn't that paint a powerful picture before I even walked on stage? So I created a six-minute video, "Meet Wayne Allyn Root." That video was shown as an introduction before my next presentation. The results were *spectacular*.

That inspired me to add more videos. Today I sprinkle up to a dozen videos into my presentation. The purpose is to "Show and Tell"—to show the power of The Video, then tell my emotional story. The result? I hit *the mother lode!*

Today creating videos for small business owners, professionals, and independent contractors to promote their business, career, or product is my number one income stream. I have a whole new career! Even in the midst of a struggling economy, this business is exploding, and it is all because of The Power of Videos to paint a picture. Without The Video, no one wanted this product. I couldn't give it away. With the videos painting the picture, I can't keep up with the demand. *That's The Relentless Storytelling Power of Video!*

BARACK OBAMA

Many of my political followers and friends are about to be shocked. Because I'm going to praise President Obama!

I am undoubtedly one of our current president's harshest critics. For more than six long years I've warned of catastrophic results if Obama was allowed to get his way with taxes, regulations, entitlements, spending, and debt.

Well, he has gotten his way, and the results are even worse than anyone could have imagined. Because of Obama, the workforce participation rate is the lowest in modern history. America has dropped on the economic freedom index for six years in a row. For the first time in history our middle class is no longer number one in the world. More people now collect welfare and entitlements than work in the private sector. For the first time in history more businesses close each day than open. Entrepreneurship rates for young adults (under age thirty) have plummeted from 10.6 percent in the 1980s to 3.6 percent today.[7]

And our national debt has skyrocketed by over $8 trillion dollars.

Obama's policies are damaging this once great country, entrepreneurship, the economy, capitalism, and the American Dream. His policies are damaging not just our current lives, but our children's future—for generations to come.

But while I believe Obama has been the absolute worst and most destructive president in modern history, there is one thing I *respect* about Obama. He clearly understands and shares my mindset—The Power of RELENTLESS. And he is one of the top practitioners in world history of THE RELENTLESS POWER OF VIDEO.

Obama and I are polar opposites in every possible way. But when it comes to being relentless, we are twins. We co-own the patent on The Power of RELENTLESS.

Say what you want about Obama, he has gotten pretty much everything he ever wanted: massive increases in spending … massive increases in the power of government … a massive stimulus program … massive debt …

massive tax increases ... the most government regulations in history...
massive entitlement spending ... a government takeover of healthcare
(Obamacare) and student loans ... the virtual halt of deportations of illegal
aliens and eventually a complete amnesty for 5 million or more illegals ...
a complete overhaul and even more government control of the financial
industry (Dodd Frank) ... and a takeover of the internet—just to name a
few actions that Obama has taken to give big government far more control
over our lives.

Obama certainly understands The Power of RELENTLESS.

A great example of the relentless mindset I am teaching you in this
book is how Obama handled the biggest landslide defeat in modern political history. In case you didn't notice, that occurred in November of 2014.
The election was a complete repudiation of Obama and his policies. He
publicly dared voters to make him the centerpiece of the election.[8]

The result? An overwhelming, historic landslide by the GOP at every
level of politics and government: Senate, House, governors, state legisla-
tures, even local offices. The American public spoke loud and clear—
repudiating Obama and everything he stands for, with Republicans
winning everything, *everywhere*.[9]

Any normal person would have been humiliated when his own Democrat candidates treated him like the plague. Democratic Senate candidates
across this country not only refused to be seen on the same stage as Obama,
they acted as if he didn't exist and they had never voted for anything he
ever proposed. In short, his own party disowned him for the election. They
refused to campaign with him. They ran ads disassociating themselves
from him. They turned down offers to have him speak on their behalf.
Virtually no Democrat anywhere in the country wanted to be in a picture
with Obama. He was, in a word, *toxic*.

Then came the results: landslide, tsunami, a final nail in the coffin,
the end of Obama ... a total repudiation.

Anyone else would have hidden from public view for the last two years
of his presidency with his tail between his legs, licking his wounds. Anyone

else would have hidden in the Oval Office among his few remaining loyal friends and confidants. Anyone else would be in severe depression. Anyone else would have realized that his presidency was over and the chance to pass any meaningful legislation was dead. Just hide in the White House, go to fancy state dinners, then quietly slide into retirement. See George Bush for a perfect example of that philosophy. That is the exact description of Bush's last years in office after the humiliation of Hurricane Katrina.

But how would a truly relentless president respond? He'd completely ignore his party's stunning defeat at the polls. He'd act like it never happened. It would be "business as usual." He'd make believe it didn't bother him. He wouldn't let it slow him down. He'd just go ahead and ignore the will of the people, make believe he was in the right, and snub his nose at the Constitution and the American people by implementing every single thing he wanted via executive order, without Congress's approval. And he'd do it with a smile on his face.

That's exactly what Barack Obama has done. As much as I hate what he's doing, I appreciate the way he does it. Obama is the perfect example of the success that comes from harnessing The Power of RELENTLESS.

Obama and I are Yin and Yang. He will fight with every breath to impose socialism upon America, weaken and try to kill capitalism, redistribute income, regulate business to death, and put government in charge of *everything*. He believes "The State" always knows best. He will use The Power of RELENTLESS to grow government ever bigger. He will not let anyone stop him … *unless they are equally relentless.*

I will fight with every breath to make government smaller, reduce its power, lower taxes, cut spending, cut regulations, drastically cut entitlements, support capitalism, and champion small business. Hopefully you will all join me in using The Power of RELENTLESS to give power back to the people—just as our Founding Fathers intended.

The point is that this amazing RELENTLESS philosophy and mindset work for either side, for any goal, to turn any dream into reality. God help the people on the other side who don't understand The Power of Relentless.

Obama has easily run roughshod over the GOP and imposed his agenda. The GOP establishment is not relentless. The opposition has no understanding of this mindset. The opposition has no idea how to deal with a relentless president. The opposition naively believed that "elections have consequences." The opposition naively thought that if you defeat your opponent, it's over. He loses.

Not true if your opponent understands The Power of RELENTLESS. Obama has proven that a historic landslide defeat and repudiation won't even slow down a relentless president. He didn't even pause to reflect on what had happened. He just revved up his relentless engine and moved ever forward.

This is one heck of a battle. I may not like anything Obama stands for, but I respect his mindset and style. I respect him as a worthy adversary. He is quite simply ... *relentless.*

And what's the top tool Obama uses in his relentless fight for his political agenda? The president recognizes THE RELENTLESS STORY-TELLING POWER OF VIDEO. His political opposition, the GOP, are like "the old me," giving speeches with no video to paint a picture. Obama is like "the new me," always using video to tell an emotional story.

Obama constantly uses "The Video." No matter the issue, Obama barnstorms the nation, relentlessly giving speeches and interviewing people affected by whatever he's implementing. These speeches and emotional stories are always videotaped to ensure they are shown on the evening news and in campaign ads. Obama is "all video, all the time."

He uses the magic of the video on a TV or computer screen to paint a picture, to tell an emotional story that tugs on your heart. Obama was able to pass Obamacare, a bill that damages the lives of tens of millions of Americans, because Obama knows how to twist public opinion by pulling at people's heartstrings with a video or speech showcasing one person's emotional story.

Meanwhile, Obama's Republican opposition stands helpless with a shocked look on their face, never knowing what hit them. They argue back with words. It's no surprise that their words are ignored. A video image beats words every time. Obama knows that.

The GOP may not know what hit them … or why they seem to lose to Obama at every turn. But I certainly know what happened. It was THE RELENTLESS STORYTELLING POWER OF VIDEO.

With that tool in your toolbox, no one can ever stop you … But even if they did … *who cares?* You'd just get back up … dust yourself off … get back in the saddle … create another video … relentlessly promote it … and start the process all over again—until you succeed!

There is no stopping someone who has the power of RELENTLESS … a powerful video in his or her tool box … and a willingness and courage to show it to everyone and anyone!

Remember, "If it is to be, it's up to me." TOMORROW MORNING, use your TRIAD to ask yourself how video can help you sell your product, your brand, your business, your career, your latest great idea.

And don't let a lack of technical know-how discourage you! The foundation of my business success was … a nine-year-old. My son, Hudson, now fifteen, is a high-tech whiz kid who has been the director, videographer, and editor for all of my videos since the age of nine. Can you imagine? The truly RELENTLESS always find a way!

RELENTLESS PITCHMAN

By now you are well aware of just how relentless I am.

So I'm going to include one shameless plug right here.

I was born with a gift. Like my college classmate, President Obama, I'm a great reader of the teleprompter. That gift served me well as an anchorman at CNBC. It served me well as the star of my sports handicapping TV show, *Wayne Root's WinningEDGE*. More recently, it has served me well as a pitchman and spokesman for many national companies. I can do a near-perfect TV commercial on the first take 99 percent of the time. Yet I typically do six to eight takes on every commercial. Why? If the first one looks great, why do five more takes? Because I don't accept "near perfect." I want perfection. In each case, the first commercial would have been fine. No one watching would know the difference. But I'd have known. I can tell if one word ... one smile ... one glance is not perfect. I demand perfection at all times.

For me "close" isn't good enough, and you can't let it be good enough for you either. I expect everything I do to be the best. I want every client to say, "WOW, you are the best I've ever seen." If I didn't love striving for perfection, I couldn't work those extra two to four hours per day to make sure my work is the absolute "best there is."

I worked relentlessly on this book. I aimed for perfection. My desire is for the ideas in this book to change your life ... to make your life better ... to make your bank account bigger ... to put a smile on your face. While most authors would have finished this book a month earlier and pressed "send" to the publisher, I kept writing for another thirty grueling days. If that helps one reader live a better life, then it was worth it. I hope as you're reading this book, you can feel the time, effort, and relentless energy I put into it. That's "Relentless Perfection."

I wrote this book to empower millions of people looking to take control over their financial lives. People just like you. My spokesman videos change lives, save businesses, and dramatically increase sales, revenues and profits. Putting my energy, enthusiasm, and relentless mindset to work as the promoter of your business, product, or career is a smart move. At the end of this book you'll see a page with contact information. That is how you can contact me and engage me to produce a Wayne Root spokesman video, where I endorse and promote your unique business or career. Grab the opportunity and allow me to change your life!

The 7th Principle of RELENTLESS: Relentless AGGRESSIVE ACTION—Hunting, Hammering, Hounding, Pitching, Promoting, Marketing, Selling, and Follow-up

....

"Many of life's failures are people who did not realize how close they were to success when they gave up."
—Thomas Edison

You've got enough HEART and CHUTZPAH to take on the world. You've identified your Relentless AMBITION and set Relentless GOALS. You're using The TRIAD to start every day with Relentless PREPARATION and an enthusiasm unknown to mankind. You've got your BRAND and you're ready to sell it with the Relentless Power of Storytelling of Video. Now it's time to take AGGRESSIVE ACTION.

The greatest lie ever told is "Opportunity only knocks once." The truth is, opportunity doesn't knock at all. You have to search for it like a heat-seeking missile, attack it, knock it over the head with a club, seize it, and drag it home like a caveman!

The real world is brutal. Opportunity is not sitting around waiting for you. It's not knocking. You have to create and seize opportunity by taking aggressive action. Nothing good comes from sitting still, waiting, or procrastinating. Good things only come from action and motion.

GOD HELPS THOSE WHO HELP THEMSELVES

Let me tell you a great story about seizing opportunity. Back in the mid-1990s my wife's best friend's mother came to me with a request, just like Grandpa Norm did. To protect her privacy, I'll call her Harriet. This is the classic story that proves "God helps those who help themselves." Harriett was divorced and living alone for many years. What little money she had, she used to play golf on public courses in the Los Angeles area. Golf was the love of her life. But she desperately wanted a man to share it with.

She often said to me, and it is undoubtedly true, "The odds of getting struck by lightning are better than the odds of a single woman over the age of fifty-five finding a husband in Los Angeles."

What she asked me to do was "find her a husband." My advice was: "Take action. Don't sit around waiting for the man of your dreams to find you … take the bull by the horns … take aggressive action … and go find him!"

I recommended Harriet take a personal ad in the newspaper. Harriet said, "Are you crazy? You'll get me killed by an axe murderer!" I said, "No, I won't, because we're going to take the advertisement in the Beverly Hills newspaper." But I went a step further. "Let's promote your two best attributes: You're a beautiful woman who plays golf. Every guy wants a beautiful wife to be his companion on the golf course."

So Harriet's journey began. Instead of sitting home complaining about the impossible odds of finding a good man, she took action. Action always attracts good things. Her advertisement was a hit! Several *hundred* men responded. Because it was in the Beverly Hills newspaper, they were doctors, dentists, lawyers, and millionaire businessmen. Harriet struck gold. She found one she liked and married him. He was a doctor <u>AND</u> a lawyer. That's called a jackpot! Taking action changed Harriet's life. It will change yours too.

Today, of course, no one needs a newspaper ad to find a relationship. Anyone can join Match.com, or any of the hundreds of online dating sites. That makes it easy to take aggressive action. Now you can go shopping for a date every night on the privacy of your computer! You can go hunting for opportunity with the click of a mouse. No one ever has to be lonely again. Anyone can find a relationship. Just don't sit around on the couch complaining.

Action works just as effectively for whatever your goal might be. It's a numbers game. Action doesn't guarantee success, but it guarantees a fighting chance. It gets you "in the game"! You attract good things to your life with motion. Motion is energy. Take action, and good things are attracted to you like a magnet.

"God helps those who help themselves." Get off the couch, stop complaining, and take Relentless Aggressive Action.

RELENTLESS SALES AND PROMOTION

Life revolves around sales and promotion. That's why we all need to ABS, and ABP—"Always Be Selling" and "Always Be Promoting."

The problem is that most people were never taught this law of success. Or worse, they know it, but they refuse to do it. They won't "lower themselves." They think selling or promoting is beneath them. They are wrong. If you want to succeed, if you want to do good things for others as well as yourself, if you want to provide quality products to others, if you want to educate and empower others, then sales and promotion are positive principles that allow you to spread your quality service or products to more people.

We are all in sales, whether we know it or not. Teachers often think they aren't in sales. Really? The best teachers are constantly selling, marketing, and promoting education to their students. Your level of enthusiasm and salesmanship is what will motivate your students to crave learning, to look forward to coming to class.

Plumbers may think they aren't in sales. Really? If you are the best plumber in the world, but no one ever calls because no one knows about your talents, is that a good thing? How can you help people in need if no one has ever heard of you?

DAVION NAVAR HENRY ONLY

Aggressive action isn't always about money. Fifteen-year-old Davion Navar Henry Only stood in front of a church in St. Petersburg, Florida, in 2013 to sell himself and promote his cause. Davion was an orphan, born in prison. His cause was to plead for a parent to love him. He said, "I know God hasn't given up on me, so I'm not giving up either … I'll take anyone to love me. Old or young, white or black, dad or mom, I don't care. And I'll be really appreciative. The best I could be." Cameras were rolling (remember, a video always helps tell your story). The church also understood the value of aggressive promotion. They sent the video and publicity about the story to the media. The media certainly understood what a great story they had on their hands. The story made headlines across the globe.[1]

How powerful is aggressive action to promote yourself? For fifteen long years before Davion made that sales pitch, he was alone in the world. But with a little sales and promotion everything changed in an instant. Within hours the church had received ten thousand requests to adopt him (five thousand by e-mail, five thousand by phone). Parents offered to adopt Davion from America, Canada, Mexico, Australia, the UK, India, and even Iran! With the right story and relentless promotion, word really gets around!

Realize that without sales and promotion that little boy would almost certainly have stayed an orphan for the rest of his life. Sales and promotion create *miracles* for any business or personal goal. That's the power of

AGGRESSIVE ACTION. If you don't toot your own horn, why should anyone else? Sales and promotion aren't "low class" or "beneath you." They are the keys to living the life of your dreams. Relentless Sales and Promotion are as essential to success as breathing is to living.

HITTING AND PITCHING VS. BITCHING

Now the question becomes "What kind of action do I take?" The answer is simple: pitch, pitch, and pitch some more. In other words, take action to aggressively search for clients, customers, investors, deals, jobs, and opportunities like a heat-seeking missile.

I start the process with a "Hit List." I make a list of my targets of opportunity. Then I go after them like a Canadian Mountie—I *always* get my man! I go down the list each day and start attacking. I e-mail them … I call them … I text them. If I don't reach them, I move them to tomorrow's list. I only cross them off the list once I get a resolution. Once I cross them off the list, it's time to find new targets of opportunity, or, as I call it, "refill the pipeline."

What do I do to people on my infamous "Hit List"? I hunt them, hound them, hammer them, and pitch them on either doing a deal, or hiring me as spokesman, or investing in my latest project, or buying my latest book idea, or hiring me to give the keynote address at their business conference. I do so much pitching, I should win the Cy Young award!

I send hundreds of e-mails per day. I make at least a hundred calls per day. I attack business opportunity the same way Harriet attacked searching for a husband. The difference is, she only had to do it once. I take the same kind of whirlwind action every day, six to seven days per week. In business the action never stops … *as long as you never stop!*

How do I know my relentless hunting, hounding, and hammering really work? Because I receive about 200 e-mails per day, every day. Do you have an iPhone? Look down at the e-mail icon at the bottom of your screen. It gives a number for how many e-mails are in your account. As I write this chapter of my book, I have **63,199** e-mails in my account! I'm a busy boy. I also get 100 phone calls per day. That's 3,000 calls per month.

But it doesn't happen by accident. If I wasn't aggressively hunting, hounding, and hammering, it would all stop. I'm the straw that stirs the drink. All those people are contacting me because I'm contacting *them!* I create the energy and it boomerangs back to me.

How do I know this to be true? When I'm stuck in a TV studio all day shooting a spokesman video, or hosting a TV infomercial or webinar ... when I'm out of contact all day giving a speech or seminar at a business conference ... if I'm flying all day on a business trip ... my e-mail volume and phone call volume drops off by 50 to 70 percent (or more).

Or take the three months it takes to write a book like this. Because I'm writing five hours a day, my time to "go hunting" is limited. And because I'm not initiating contact and making things happen, it gets quiet. If I'm not relentlessly stirring the pot, nothing happens (and that's not good). That's what most people's life is like ... all the time. They spend their lives waiting for the phone to ring ... and it never does.

For me, silence is the worst sound in the world. It means no one wants to do business with me. It means I'm not wanted. It means my income and opportunities are drying up. It means my pipeline is empty. It means I'm skating on thin ice. I get petrified. My definition of "heaven" is when I have deals, investors, and opportunities lined up "ten-deep" like jets on an airport runway. Silence isn't golden, it's *depressing.*

That's why I'm always in motion. Most people spend their lives bitching. I spend my life *pitching!* From the moment I wake up until the moment my head hits the pillow at night, I'm pitching "me, myself and I," my brand, my companies, my products, my talents. If people spent less time bitching and more time pitching, they'd have nothing to bitch about!

Bitching vs. pitching: the difference in outcomes is startling. It's a crime that no one teaches you this stuff in school. There should be mandatory courses in relentless hunting, hounding, hammering, hitting, and pitching.

RACHEL MARTIN

Rachel Martin is a Manhattan real estate broker, as well as an officer in the U.S. Naval Reserve. If there's one thing you learn in the jungle of Manhattan real estate it's to be relentless.

In 2012 this thirty-three-year-old realtor was called up by the U.S. Navy for a 330-day tour of duty in Kandahar, Afghanistan. She was now 6,800 miles from home in a dusty, barren, unforgiving country, at war with the Taliban. End of her real estate career, right? *Wrong.* Relentless Rachel took AGGRESSIVE ACTION.

Rachel found herself in a war zone living in a converted container storage unit covered by barbed wire. When you're at war, you grab any shelter you can find. Yet this relentless warrior decided to continue her Manhattan real estate career ... *from the war zone.* I guarantee you Rachel Martin was the only soldier in Afghanistan or Iraq (on either side) selling real estate.

Keep in mind she was dealing with even bigger impediments than being in a container storage crate in the middle of a war zone. Her only phone was a bulky, heavy-as-a-brick satellite phone. But when you are committed to taking AGGRESSIVE ACTION, nothing else matters. No obstacle (or phone) is too big.

Using that awkward old-fashioned satellite phone ... with poor reception ... from her barbed-wire-encased storage container ... in a war zone ... Rachel stayed in contact with her real estate clients and fellow real estate brokers assisting in her quest to sell upscale condos.

Rachel hit pay dirt. She sold a $1.9 million luxury condo at Trump Place. Yes, "The Donald's" building. Her commission was $114,000, almost double her $65,000 annual Navy salary. Her amazing feat earned her a full page story in the *New York Post* with the headline "Condo Warrior." Overnight, U.S. Navy Lieutenant Commander Rachel Martin became the most famous realtor in Manhattan.[2]

Rachel proves you can sell anything ... even from the middle of a war zone 6,800 miles away ... even in the middle of a devastating recession.

Rachel proves you can sell part-time while you have another full-time career. Rachel proves it's possible to stay in contact with your clients, no matter how busy you are ... *even with the Taliban shooting at you*. Rachel proves you can succeed while under intense stress—even while living in a converted container crate. Rachel proves you can call people, even while bombs are bursting in the background.

Now tell me again ... what's your excuse? Why can't you set sales records? Why can't you build relationships? Why can't you stay in contact with your clients? Why can't you start your sales career part-time, while keeping your full-time "day job"? After hearing Rachel Martin's story, no entrepreneur or salesperson has a valid excuse. There is no reason not to start taking AGGRESSIVE ACTION *TODAY*.

By the way ... Rachel is a relentless marketer and brander as well. She uses her military background and famous *NY Post* headline as her "brand" to separate her from thousands of other realtors in a crowded, competitive Manhattan real estate market. If I was buying a condo in Manhattan, I know I'd hire Rachel as my broker.[3]

MEZA HARRIS

Meza Harris is a Southern woman with another amazing *relentless* real estate story. Known as a "party girl" who spent her free time playing tennis and bridge, she was divorced in the early 1990s. With her back against the wall, Meza had to find a way to earn a living, pay the bills, and support her children.

She decided to get a real estate license in her hometown, Bentonville, Arkansas, also the home of Walmart. She was fifty years old, had never sold anything, and was starting from ground zero without a single listing or client.

The odds of Meza succeeding were slim to none. Soon after graduating from real estate school she was assigned "floor duty," manning the phone and answering questions and requests from callers. Denise West, an executive from Walmart, called asking if someone could show homes to a prospective Walmart recruit.

All the established agents knew that Walmart had a deal with another agency and that a call like this only came when the agents at the other office were too busy or passing on the client—and it never resulted in a sale. Not wanting to waste their time, they all said, "No, I'm busy too." But Meza said YES and took the client to see homes. The date was May 16, 1994. That decision changed her life.

The recruit never relocated, but the Walmart executive, Denise West, was impressed and thankful that someone had taken the initiative and made the potential recruit feel welcome. Denise told her boss, Coleman Peterson, Walmart's Director of Human Resources, about Meza.

Peterson decided to reward Meza by sending her another client. Meza did a great job once again. So he sent another one, then two, then three, then a dozen. Soon she was also getting the listings of Walmart executives who were themselves relocating away from Bentonville. Meza treated the Walmart clients like family, so the calls from Walmart kept coming. As Walmart grew to become the biggest employer in America, guess who kept getting the calls? M-E-Z-A.

Meza went the extra mile. She took calls at midnight and at 6:00 a.m., she picked up clients at the airport, she became a full-service broker with answers to every question. She found financing for her clients. She knew the right neighborhoods with the best schools for families with young kids. Then, when the executives eventually relocated again, she re-sold their homes.

She became the model for how a realtor should aggressively take action. She out-worked and out-hustled the competition. She cold-called strangers and followed-up leads. Meza was *relentless*.

The result? In 2006 she sold $56 million dollars of real estate. That made her #1 in the state and started a run of her being ranked #1 in the state by the Arkansas Business Journal for nine *consecutive* years and eleven times since 1998.[4]

In the odd years when she wasn't ranked #1 in the state, Meza was #2.

She was also voted #1 Realtor in Northwest Arkansas by *Celebrate* magazine year after year.[5]

Then the Great Recession hit in 2008. The bottom fell out of the real estate market in Northwest Arkansas. Fifty percent of all real estate brokers left the business. Meza just became even more relentless. Here is a sampling of her results:

2007—$33.7 MM in sales[6]

2010—$24.7 MM in sales[7]

2011—$24 MM in sales.

2013—$29.19 MM in sales.[8]

In Meza's career she has sold about $500,000,000 of real estate. **Yes, that's a *half billion dollars.*** This was achieved in *Arkansas* where homes are relatively inexpensive.

Remember, her career started at age fifty, with no prior experience in sales of any kind. Meza has won so many awards that she is no longer known by her first name. Everywhere Meza goes, the words "Number One Realtor" are the first words you hear when she is introduced.

Meza Harris proves that Relentless AGGRESSIVE ACTION can move mountains ... and a half billion dollars of real estate.

AGGRESSIVE ACTION BUILDS RELATIONSHIPS

Success doesn't happen by mistake or coincidence. Yes, Meza works long hours. And she also understands the value of relationships. Meza knows everyone in Northwest Arkansas and everyone in Northwest Arkansas knows her. She's at their weddings, she coordinates their fundraisers, she knows their anniversaries, she's at lunch and dinner with her clients, her weekends are spent showing homes during the day and meeting new contacts at night. She sells homes to the children of people that bought a home from her twenty years ago. Relationships matter.

Do you know why Meza does all these things? Because she loves what she does! You will only be able to be Relentless if you truly love what you do. I don't have a magic wand to tell you how to accomplish this. All I can tell you is that it is vitally important to truly pursue the life of your dreams. It is my hope that this book will give you the tools to successfully pursue your personal dreams.

If you want to be successful in life and business, then there are three AGGRESSIVE ACTIONS you need to take to build relationships:

a. **Build a list of contacts every hour, of every day.** Never stop networking and connecting. Never stop contacting new people. Make everyone you meet your friend and then add them to your list of contacts. That list is priceless. Use it to find clients, customers, deals, jobs, business partners, and opportunities. Use it to announce your achievements and success. Use it to introduce people you know to other people you know. It will be repaid in spades.

b. **Build a list of testimonials from this list of contacts.** Utilize the saying, "If you don't ask, you don't get." Ask everyone on your list to write an endorsement of you, your career, your company, or your product. Testimonials are the most effective way to sell anything. It's great that you sing your own praises, but when others sing your praise, it's the most effective advertisement of all.

c. **Build a "Wall of Fame" on your office wall.** Everyone should have a Wall of Fame. It's a testimonial to your success. It's also a neon billboard that screams out to all future clients or business associates. When people walk into your office and see the impressive and influential people you know, they will want to do business with you too. My wall is a "Who's Who" of American politics, business, entertainment, and sports. The centerpiece of my wall features photos of me with presidents of the United States, past presidential candidates, and future presidential candidates: George W. Bush, Ronald Reagan, Mitt Romney, Ron Paul, Rand Paul, Jeb Bush, Dr. Ben Carson, and Newt Gingrich. It features me with billionaires like Steve Forbes, Jim Rogers, and Steve Wozniak, co-founder of Apple. It features me with entertainment icons like Al Pacino, Arnold Schwarzenegger, and Gene Simmons of KISS fame. Those are all brand names. Associating with brand names makes your brand more valuable.

Relationships matter. Take AGGRESSIVE ACTION to pursue new relationships every hour of every day. Then stay relentless in maintaining "constant contact" with your list.

THE ULTIMATE TEST

AGGRESSIVE ACTION is the ultimate test of RELENTLESS. I have built a successful career as a business and motivational speaker. It all started with a "NO." I bothered well-known national seminar organizer JT Foxx to include me in his events around the country. He is a superstar in the industry—one of the highest-paid success speakers and coaches in the world. He rejected me for two years. I bothered him so much that finally, just to get rid of me, he said he'd "allow me" to give a speech for FREE at one of his events, just to see how his audiences reacted. He offered me ninety minutes at an event in Chicago, taking up two days of my time for no pay. I accepted with gusto.

The result? I was the hit of the event—including twenty speakers over four days. The audience filled out forms and rated me the best speaker of the event. JT Foxx was so impressed that he hired me, for the fee I asked, to do one seminar. Then two. Then three, and four, and five. Since then I've spoken at JT Foxx events all over the globe, from South Africa to Singapore to Amsterdam.

Now I speak worldwide at many different business conferences. But I owe my start in the business to JT Foxx ... and of course, to Relentless AGGRESSIVE ACTION. If you ask JT, or Damien Elston, the dynamic president of his company, they'll tell you that I simply wore them down. But JT and Damien are glad that I wore them down. Audiences are passionate about my presentations. So it's good I was relentless, because it turned into a win-win for everyone!

Or take the TV spokesman business: because I'm relentless, I wear a lot of hats! I have numerous careers, and hopefully more still to come. Today my main career is as a spokesman, the public face or voice in TV and radio advertising and marketing campaigns for many different companies and products. Certainly you need to be relentless to be a TV pitchman. Think of the greatest ones in history: Billy Mays, Ron Popeil, Tony Little, Jack LaLanne, Susan Powter, George Foreman, and Richard Simmons, to name just a few.[9]

Each could be described as a relentless, high-energy ball of fire. Yet they were all known for one product, or one genre—exercise, or diet, or cooking, or home gadgets. The Power of RELENTLESS was certainly the key to their success. Each of them had "an engine that never stopped," and they were famous for repeating their key sales message over and over and over again. That's The Power of RELENTLESS.

But I have a claim to fame none of those superstar TV pitchmen can match. I'd guesstimate I've sold hundreds of millions of dollars of products in over twenty completely different fields, most of which I had zero expertise or knowledge about before I became the product spokesman. Here are the genres, fields and products I've successfully sold on TV, radio, billboards, and the internet:

- Precious metals—gold and silver
- Rare collectible coins
- Vitamins and nutritional products
- Energy (oil and gas)

- Diamonds
- Student loans
- Financial education products
- MLM (multi-level marketing) products
- Sports-handicapping advice
- Horserace wagering
- Fantasy sports
- Legal services for law firms in multiple cities
- Survival products
- Sports memorabilia
- Golf clubs
- Las Vegas resort casinos
- Currency-trading products
- Political PAC fundraising for Libertarian causes
- Political PAC fundraising for Republican and conservative causes
- My own books
- My own seminars
- Gluten-free cereal

That's one heck of a list. Even I was flabbergasted when I compiled it! How does someone not named Brad Pitt, George Clooney, or Donald Trump wind up as the public face and voice of so many diverse products? By taking AGGRESSIVE ACTION!

For example, you saw on the list above that I've been a spokesman for law firms. Here's the back story on that one! To be blunt, I'm not a fan of lawyers. They are often the enemy of business owners and wealth creators. The legal fees from abusive lawsuits kill jobs and cost legitimate wealth-creators time, trouble, and money.

I may not be a fan of the legal profession, but I also know that when you need a lawyer, you'd better find a great one! One day a decade or so ago, I found myself sitting at the table of one of the most prominent lawyers in Las Vegas at a charity event. I told him bluntly, "Lawyers know nothing about business, they only know how to damage a perfectly run business. Even worse, lawyers are terrible salesmen. Even though I can't stand lawyers, I'll bet I can sell your legal services better than *you* can sell yourself!"

We spent the night good-naturedly debating and arguing. We swapped business cards and said goodbye. Guess who followed up? It sure wasn't the lawyer! I followed up relentlessly for two years. To prove I could sell his law firm better than any lawyer, I offered to be his TV spokesman for FREE for three months. That was a decade ago.

I served as the only non-lawyer spokesman for legal services in the state of Nevada for many years on billboards all over the city of Las Vegas, on television commercials during the evening news, and even on the cover of the Las Vegas phone book. Today I serve in the same role for a Los Angeles law firm.

I'm sure my mom and dad are looking down from heaven with pride. They always wanted me to become a lawyer. Now ... *I PLAY ONE ON TV!*

AGGRESSIVE ACTION is the secret to my success in publishing, as well. I decided to write my first book in 1989. It was rejected by dozens of publishers. But one said "YES!" That's all you need.

In the years since, I've written nine more books. Every one of them was roundly rejected by numerous publishers. I kept right on writing, and finally *The Ultimate Obama Survival Guide* became a national bestseller, one of the top ten bestselling political hardcovers of 2013, and #1 in three categories at Amazon. The key to success was that I never gave up aggressively writing, pitching, and selling my books. Not for a New York minute. I knew I just had to stay committed and tenacious long enough to find the one "YES" that would change the narrative from failure to success. As usual, I did ... *ten times!* That's The Power of RELENTLESS.

The Ultimate Obama Survival Guide was published by Regnery, the largest conservative publisher in America, with over fifty *New York Times* bestsellers. My deal came after two years of hounding them relentlessly. Regnery rejected at least a dozen of my book ideas.

Then they finally said, "YES." Without my constant Relentless AGGRESSIVE ACTION, it would never have happened. I hounded the publisher, Marji Ross, until she could not get me off her mind. Finally, the day after President Obama's re-election in November of 2012 she called me to offer a book deal. If I had not "gently" reminded her continually for two years, it would never have happened. My guess is she gave me the book deal just to make me leave her alone!

Keeping your name, product, or idea on people's minds and lips is key. That eventually leads to pay dirt. If you simply wait for people to think of you, or remember you, or do you a favor, well, good luck. It never happens, except in fictional Hollywood movies and fairy tales. The reality is that people often hire or do business with whoever is on their mind at the moment they make their decision. <u>I make sure I'm always that guy.</u>

A PERSONAL STORY

I met my wife, Debra, at a Grammy party at a nightclub in L.A. She was a former Miss Oklahoma and the lead singer for the famous rock group Emerson, Lake & Palmer. She was also a very religious evangelical Christian who never went to nightclubs. *Never.* And she certainly had no interest in meeting a man at a nightclub. She'd recently had a bad bicycle accident and had been recuperating for weeks. She had almost died. One side of her face was badly injured, and she almost lost her lip and ear. This was her first week "back in circulation." Her friends begged her to go with them to this Grammy party. They dragged her out of the house.

Neither of us smoked or drank alcohol. So we both wound up downstairs at the pool table. We played on the same team for an hour. Then we talked for another two hours. I had to get home because I had to host a TV show at 6:00 a.m. the next morning. As I turned to leave, I gave Debra my business card. She pushed it away and said she would NEVER call a guy she met at a nightclub. I spent the next thirty minutes trying relentlessly to convince her to take my card. She rejected every argument I made. She kept giving back my card ... I kept putting it back into her hand.

Finally I left, but on the way out I stuck my card in her hand again for at least the twentieth time and said "If you don't call, it will be the biggest mistake of your life. You'll miss out on marriage, kids, and the whole rest of the wonderful life we can have together."

She laughed and said, 'I'm NOT calling."

Two weeks later she saw my card in her purse and called her best friend three thousand miles away in New York. During the conversation she told her about this crazy, RELENTLESS guy she had met at a nightclub in L.A. Debra asked if she should break her vow to never call a guy she met in a nightclub. The friend said, "Tell me this guy's name?"

Debra read my business card and when she said my name, "Wayne Allyn Root" to her best friend, sitting in her apartment in New York, her friend repeated it out loud to her husband. The husband said, "Wayne Allyn Root? That's my *cousin!*"

Debra immediately called to relate this one in a billion story. She said, "Now you're no longer a stranger that I met at a nightclub ... you're like family. You're my best friend's cousin-in-law. Now we can go on a date."

Sixty days after that I asked her to marry me. Ten months later we were married in a ceremony on the beach in Malibu, beneath my beach-front home.

Relentless AGGRESSIVE ACTION isn't just effective for business deals. It's effective for relationships, finding love, and building a family. You can never give up because you just never know where the road may lead you!

It's like Jimmy Stewart in the famous movie *It's a Wonderful Life*. Without the repeated actions I took to pitch, promote, and sell myself to this woman I met over a game of pool in a nightclub, my four beautiful children wouldn't exist. My entire life would be dramatically different.

RELENTLESS REMINDER AND REPETITION

You might ask "Why do I have to always be on the attack?" and "Why can't I wait for others to notice me?" and "Why do I have to keep reminding people of my talents?"

The answer is simple: "Out of sight, out of mind." It's a proven law of human nature. You may think you're on the mind of your business associates, or your potential customers, or clients, or bosses, but you never are. It's your responsibility to remind them about you or your products. You must hunt, hound, hammer, hook, hit, and pitch them … and then remind them again. There is no such thing as reminding people too often of your value to them or their company. If you don't remind them relentlessly, you are usually forgotten—no matter how talented, famous, or successful you are.

And remember: you are *never* too big or too important to take AGGRESSIVE ACTION to remind potential clients, customers or partners that you're valuable to them. You need to constantly remind people, or they forget you, take you for granted, or hire someone else because that person was on their mind at the moment they made an important decision (and you weren't). Timing is everything in life. That's why I want to be on your mind at all times. My timing is … *always and forever!*

By the way, reminding others that you exist is not just for your benefit. You do it for *their* benefit. You are valuable to them. You will make their life better. So you're doing them a favor by reminding them of your value!

Why do they need reminding? Remember, "Out of sight, out of mind." Life is busy and distracting, and they are getting inundated every day with thousands of other ideas, things, people, clients, events, deals. It is also true that many if not most people are somewhat lazy and will do what is easy. If your phone number is in front of them, it is the one they will call.

Think of how repetition works in advertising. A radio advertising campaign must be bought for the long term. Be prepared to buy hundreds or even thousands of ads over a long period. Why? Because few customers ever respond the first few times they hear an advertisement. The calls only start coming in after listeners have heard the advertisement twenty or fifty or even a hundred times. It finally hits home because of the magic of repetition.

You'd think people remember you, but they don't. You'd think they'd respond to you after hearing your story, but they don't. So, swallow your pride and keep reminding them. No one is too big, no one is too important to stop reminding and repeating.

Think of politicians. They campaign with relentless repetition. Their TV and radio ads run thousands of times in each market. Their fundraising phone calls and e-mails never stop. As I was writing this book, I received dozens of e-mail fundraising requests for each declared GOP Presidential candidate. Dozens of e-mails from *each* in a matter of days. They never stopped hounding and hammering me. Because politicians know *repetition works.*

Think of Viagra. Doesn't every man in America already know the name? Yet they keep advertising relentlessly. They never want a day to go by without Viagra on your mind. Why would a company keep spending hundreds of millions of dollars to advertise a household name? They're not wasting money! Advertisers have tested this strategy for a hundred years and they know … *repetition works.*

Think of GM, Chrysler, Mercedes, and BMW. We all know the names. So why do they keep spending hundreds of millions on advertising? Why do these car companies sponsor every sporting event they can get their hands on? Because they've tested it thousands of times. They know *repetition works.*

They also know that if today is the day you are going out shopping for a car, you'll go to the dealer whose TV advertisement you saw today. Even if you've known the name Audi for thirty years, Audi knows they need to put their brand name in front of you today, on the day you are going car shopping, because if you see a BMW commercial, the odds are good you'll go to their dealer instead. They know *repetition works.*

Think of national pharmacy chains. Why do these pharmacies put signs in front of their door saying "Flu shots available today"? Why do they have the same sign in the aisle? Why do they have the checkout gal verbally remind you as you're leaving, "Have you had your flu shot yet?" They know *repetition works.*

"Relentless Reminder and Repetition" works like magic. If it's good enough for big business, why should you be embarrassed to use the same technique?

I've been represented by the same international speaking company for many years. Yet I'm seldom booked for a speech unless I call them, e-mail them, or follow up on my previous calls and e-mails. And they always say, "Wow. Great timing. I'm glad you called. We're just now planning an event for next month. Would you like to speak at our event?" Hunting, hounding, hammering, repeating, and reminding even my own biggest clients works like magic. If I didn't remind them, I would lose half of my income. That's despite being an outstanding performer for these same companies repeatedly for many years. "Out of sight, out of mind."

I'm a guest on hundreds of radio talk shows. Some of them have me on as a guest monthly. Some weekly. But the primary reason they book me is because I send them my latest press release or commentary three times per week. I'm always booked immediately after I contact them. Coincidence? They just needed reminding of what a great guest I am. Why would they need reminding if I'm such a great guest? "Out of sight, out of mind." That's why I'm always in sight!

You have to keep banging on their door with a hammer and a chainsaw. You need to keep chopping away at that cherry tree with your axe. Eventually it will fall. That's the power of Relentless AGGRESSIVE ACTION

RELENTLESS INTERNET

AGGRESSIVE ACTION means hunting, hammering, hounding, pitching, promoting, marketing, and selling by every means you can find. But the internet is a great place to start. The internet is where you hunt for new deals, new clients, new customers, new partners, and new business associates. The internet is the vehicle you use to go hunting!

Remember the Relentless Power of Storytelling on Video? Well, the internet and e-mail are the perfect vehicles for showing your video to others. Just film a video on your Smartphone, iPad, computer webcam, or video camera and add a link to your e-mail. You instantly have a unique, colorful, animated message for your target!

The internet and e-mail are the perfect platform to expand your day. In the old days, even if you wanted to work sixteen-hour days, you couldn't contact anyone beyond normal business hours. I never call anyone before 8:00 a.m. nor after 8:00 p.m. But today the internet and e-mail allow me to make contact, cold call, respond to calls, follow up on deals, and make detailed proposals at all hours of the day and night, plus weekends.

My potential customers will open and read the e-mail at their convenience. I'm not limited by so-called "normal work hours." That's how I get so much work done from 6:00 a.m. to 9:00 a.m…. and from 8:00 p.m. to 11:00 p.m.

I can work while others are playing, relaxing, watching a movie, dining out, hanging with the kids, or sleeping. I probably send out fifty e-mails each morning before 9:00 a.m. And I send at least twenty-five more after 10:00, after my kids go to sleep (and I've got quiet time to think).

That means a ton of my "hunting, hounding, and hammering" gets done before the day starts … and after the day ends (for normal people). That's time set aside just for hunting new deals, new jobs, new clients, new opportunities. That frees up the normal nine-to-five work hours for making calls and following up responses for all of my present deals.

Here's what the internet and e-mail has done for me and can do for you:

a. The internet allows me to find and contact the people I want to do business with. I can find anyone on Google. I mean *anyone*. All the info you need is there, including their e-mail address. If Google doesn't have it either Facebook, Twitter, or LinkedIn does. In the old days, if you found their phone number their "gatekeeper" would block access. But now you just send an e-mail. If they answer, you've scored! If they don't, move onto the next "target of opportunity." It's all a numbers game.

b. It saves time ... and time is money. I accomplish so much more by expanding my workday to earlier and later hours. I'll bet 50 to 60 percent of my income comes from deals I initiated before 8:00 a.m. or after 8:00 p.m. If you don't expand your day, you've lost the battle before it's begun. I've kicked your butt before you even sit down at your desk with your morning coffee.

c. It saves money. I used to send out ten to twenty packages per week to potential clients, customers, partners, etc. They were filled with my resume, bio, multiple videos, and two or three of my books. I was spending thousands of dollars per month on Express Mail and FedEx. Now I send my entire presentation, including resume, bio, videos, audios, and Power Point via e-mail for FREE. It doesn't cost me a cent to send out these "virtual packages."

d. It allows me to send detailed proposals. No one wants to talk for hours on the phone. Who has the time? Good luck with trying to contact a total stranger on the phone, get them on the line, then take an hour of their time. At best, they'll want a sixty-second sound bite before they hang up. But if I lay out a detailed proposal on a Microsoft Word doc in an e-mail *and* attach a video, the important decision-maker who receives it can read it at their leisure. E-mail gives you this opportunity.

E-mail is the perfect platform for your relentless "hunting, hounding, and hammering" strategy. It is also the ideal delivery system for your videos. I thank God every day for the invention of the internet and e-mail. My educated guess is that something new will replace e-mail in the next few years. That's the nature of this high-tech world we live in. But there is no going back. We will only move forward. Whatever the new communication system is, it will make it even easier to relentlessly reach out and touch your future clients, customers, business associates, and partners. For now, the internet is your perfect relentless "delivery system."

RELENTLESS FOLLOW-UP

Now that I've taught you about using the amazing internet and e-mails to expand your day, it's time to learn to use the most important hyphenated word in the English language: FOLLOW-UP. My middle name is "follow-up." I understand that 90 percent of all sales are achieved in the follow-up phase. Yet almost no one bothers to follow up. How do I know? Because rarely does anyone *ever* follow up with me.

You want to hear an amazing story? I bought my dream car last fall—a Maserati Quattroporte. In the same category for luxury four-door supercars were the Mercedes 550, BMW 700 series, Porsche Panamera, Audi A8, Jaguar XJ, and Tesla Model S. Counting the Maserati, that's seven of the most spectacular cars on the road. And they *should be* spectacular for a cost of over $100,000. You'd think the car salesmen representing each of these cars would be falling all over themselves to make the sale, yes? You'd think they'd be calling me a hundred times to get my $100,000+ check, yes? *You'd be wrong.*

Only the Maserati salesman followed up my visit with enthusiasm. Great job, Mike Schiffman! Mike called me a half dozen times and each time had new and interesting reasons for me to buy. He was persistent and relentless. He was willing to do anything to make the sale, including cut his own commission. In short, Mike Schiffman is the kind of person with whom I want to do business. Why would I reward a salesman who isn't willing to go the extra mile to get the sale? The other salesmen either didn't follow up at all, or made one or two phone calls and left a message. When I didn't return the call, I never heard from them ever again. Amazing.

If you don't follow up, you will *never* get my money. I only reward people that are hungry and relentless. I'm driving my dream Maserati Quattroporte because A) I have the money for it because I spend my life following up ... and B) Mike Schiffman followed up repeatedly with me.

In every industry it seems there is very little follow-up or customer service left in America. If you want the sale, why aren't you calling twenty times until you get the customer on the phone? Why don't you have a dozen great reasons (pre-scripted) for me to buy your product versus your competitors' product? Why am I (the customer) calling *you* to find out more about your product? Why don't you know everything ... and I mean everything ... about your product? It seems like 90 percent of the time when I ask an employee a question about their product, they say "I'll have to get back to you with that answer." Really? You don't know the answer to every potential question about your product? Then why should I buy from you?

If a customer asks a question you can't answer, you're in the wrong business. If you have no passion about your own product, you're in the wrong business. If you can't find the time to follow up as many times as it takes to convince me to buy, you're in the wrong business. If you won't cut the price to get me to buy, even if it means cutting your own commission, you're in the wrong business. That's the kind of dedication, tenacity, energy, relentlessness, and AGGRESSIVE ACTION that it takes to win the sale. Almost no one has it anymore.

So don't blame the bad economy. Blame yourself for not being relentless.

If you take one thing from this book, understand that 90 percent or more of all sales are achieved on the follow-up. If you're not practicing "Relentless Follow-up," you're falling relentlessly behind.

RELENTLESS FACE-TO-FACE CONTACT

You use e-mails to make initial contact; then you use the phone for the follow-up. Now here's the third part of the equation. You must make face-to-face contact to close the deal. No one puts big deals together without "pressing the flesh." You must see and meet the people with whom you are doing business—LIVE AND IN PERSON!

You can't hide from face-to-face contact. Far too many young adults have gotten the wrong impression from technology. They think you can hide from real contact through e-mails and texts. You can't. Nothing will EVER replace physically meeting and talking to your clients, customers, investors, business associates, or partners. Nothing. People only do serious deals, or hire people, or form partnerships, or hand checks to people they meet *in person*. Technology will never replace that.

It's not just closing deals that requires face-to-face contact. It's doing business in general. When someone owes me money and is slow in paying they want to either hide, or answer only in e-mails and texts. They won't take calls. They won't meet in person to discuss the problem.

But if I owe *them*, WOW. They call 24/7 until they get their check. Business is a two-way street. If you treat people like that, eventually you will wear out your welcome.

Face your clients. Press the flesh. Be willing to hear negatives and complaints. Be willing to face problems. Do it all face to face. Your clients or customers need to see you "up-close and personal" even more when things are going wrong than when things are going right. This is how you build customer loyalty and lifelong relationships.

How important is face-to-face contact? Don't you tip waiters and bartenders well? But you don't tip the chef. Why? Because you never see him. You never meet him face to face. You only tip the people you see on a face-to-face basis. The dirty little secret in the hotel business is that very few people tip the maid.[10] Why? You don't see her. You can leave without making eye contact. But the same person who doesn't tip the maid would never even *think* of stiffing the waiter—because you can't leave the restaurant without seeing the waiter. Face-to-face contact is that important. Your clients, customers, partners, employees all need to see you face to face on a regular basis. Be a person who practices "Relentless Face-to-Face Contact."

Bonus Principle of RELENTLESS: Relentless ENERGY, CONTAGIOUS ENTHUSIASM, AND NEVER-ENDING OPTIMISM

....

"Nothing great was ever achieved without enthusiasm."
—Ralph Waldo Emerson

So now you know everything you need to succeed beyond your wildest dreams. All it takes is Relentless HEART, CHUTZPAH, AMBITION AND GOAL-SETTING, PREPARATION, BRANDING, STORYTELLING, and AGGRESSIVE ACTION!

But wait just a minute. Does it make you tired just to think about pouring that much RELENTLESS energy into your career or business—day in, day out, ten hours a day, six or even seven days a week? Are you daunted by the number of pitches I make before 9:00 a.m. and after 10:00 p.m.? I can almost hear you saying, "Wayne may be the Energizer Bunny, but I'm not. Maybe The Power of Relentless is not for me."

In this bonus chapter I'm going to tell you the secret of my Relentless ENERGY, CONTAGIOUS ENTHUSIASM, and NEVER-ENDING OPTIMISM—complete with the recipe for the twelve POSITIVE ADDICTIONS I rely on every day to build and maintain the energy I need to be RELENTLESS.

But first let's look at why ENERGY, ENTHUSIASM, AND OPTIMISM are the necessary fuel for your Relentless career.

ENERGY AND ENTHUSIASM ARE THE BRANDS OF SUCCESS

My success is due to energy and enthusiasm. That's my brand. And I'm not alone. The top producers and rainmakers in virtually every business, industry, or field are high-energy, high-enthusiasm individuals. To get people to buy what you're selling, you need to get them excited.

The top TV infomercial salespeople are always about energy, excitement, enthusiasm, waking people up, and stopping them from punching the remote control. That holds true for every profession.

Find me a great high-powered lawyer—I'll show you energy and enthusiasm. Find me a successful politician—I'll show you energy and enthusiasm. Show me a successful small business owner—I'll show you energy and enthusiasm. Show me a great actor—I'll show you energy and enthusiasm. Show me a great business speaker—I'll show you energy and enthusiasm. It even works with government employees. The best teachers make learning exciting. The best cops use their energy and enthusiasm to take control of a neighborhood and befriend the kids before they get lured into gangs. We all need energy and enthusiasm. We all need something that makes us stand out from the crowd, in order to sell ourselves, our talents, or our products.

Let me give you two very different examples, one from sports and one from religion.

TIM TEBOW

First, let's look at Tim Tebow, an amazing example of enthusiasm creating success even when things *don't* work out perfectly. Tebow was a great college football player. He led his team to two national championships and was the youngest-ever winner of the Heisman Trophy.[1]

His brand was incredible energy and enthusiasm. But, his critics claimed that would never work in the NFL. Tebow was maligned as an inferior and awkward NFL quarterback. Yet in 2011 he took over as starting quarterback for the Denver Broncos. The team was 1–4 when he took over. Suddenly, with his world-class energy and enthusiasm leading the way, amazing things started to happen. Denver won six games in the last two minutes or overtime, the most in history. Against Miami they became the first team in NFL history to win a game when trailing by fifteen points or more with three minutes to play. Under Tebow, Denver became only the fifth team in NFL history to make the playoffs after a 2–5 start. They won their first playoff game since 2005, also in overtime, on Tim Tebow's eighty-yard touchdown pass—the longest game-winning overtime pass in NFL history!

That playoff victory was filled with Tebow miracles. John 3:16 is Tim Tebow's favorite Bible verse, and he wore that 3:16 number under his eyes throughout his collegiate career. In this miraculous playoff victory, Tebow passed for exactly 316 yards. He set the all-time NFL record for yards per completion, 31.6 yards per completion. The fourth-quarter TV ratings were the highest in 25 years—a 31.6 share nationally.[2]

Now enthusiasm alone doesn't guarantee everything will go perfectly, and not every story has a happy ending. Despite all that amazing success, Tebow finished 2011 with the lowest quarterback rating in the NFL. While his energy, enthusiasm, and leadership pulled his team to victory week after week, his actual statistics were terrible. After the season he was traded to the New York Jets where he was reduced to playing punt protector. It was an embarrassing detour for his NFL career. Most NFL experts call Tim Tebow's NFL career a failure.

WRONG.

First, as an evangelical Christian, Tebow doesn't play for fame, he plays for God. His goal is to introduce as many fans as possible to Jesus Christ. After his amazing NFL Playoff win with the 316 passing yards, 31.6 yards per pass, and 31.6 TV ratings, the three most searched terms in the world over the next twenty-four hours were John 3:16, Tebow, and Tim Tebow. Ninety-five million people googled John 3:16.[3]

Yes, his NFL career fizzled. But look at what he accomplished:

- His jersey was the #2 seller of all NFL merchandise, behind only Super Bowl champion quarterback Aaron Rodgers.
- His book spent twenty-four weeks on the *New York Times* bestseller list. It was named both the Bestselling Sports Book *and* Bestselling Religious Book of the Year in 2011.
- By 2012 he was voted the #1 most popular athlete in America, ahead of Kobe Bryant. It took Kobe eleven years to make the list. Tim Tebow jumped to #1 in fifteen weeks!
- *Forbes* rated him as the second most influential athlete in the world.
- *Time* magazine rated him as one of the "Hundred Most Influential People in the World."

All of this happened while Tebow was a third-string back-up quarterback and special teams punt protector. How can you explain this?

The answer is simple: relentless energy and contagious enthusiasm. In the end, that's what being a leader is all about. It isn't your talent, or your IQ, or your college degree, or the strength of your passing arm; it's whether you can inspire people. To do that, you need to be relentless. Tebow's record-setting come-from-behind victories prove that. You need faith and optimism. Tebow has a rock-ribbed, unshakeable faith in God and himself.

Is Tim Tebow's NFL career over? Maybe, maybe not. As I wrote this book, he was signed for another try at quarterback by the Philadelphia Eagles.[4]

The jury is still out on his NFL career. But Tim Tebow's energy and contagious enthusiasm might very well push him to greatness in other arenas such as politics or religion. Someday Tim Tebow might be known as "President Tebow." Or "the Reverend Tim Tebow" could become the most watched televangelist in the world. It's up to him. I know he has the chutzpah, energy, and enthusiasm to be either, or BOTH!

BILLY GRAHAM

Contagious enthusiasm works not only in TV infomercials, business, entertainment and sports. This combo works to create mega success in any field. Take religion, for example.

Billy Graham is one of my heroes and role models. He is one of the greatest preachers in world history and a friend and counselor to every president in modern history. But let's go back to 1957. Graham had led evangelical crusades all over the world to great success. But he'd always wanted to take on the biggest challenge of all—New York City.

Media critics and naysayers laughed at Graham. They predicted an "empty house." They said no one would come see a "country bumpkin" preach Jesus in a town filled with atheists and skeptics.

So Graham rented Madison Square Garden for three nights—but stayed for *sixteen weeks.* Over two million cynical, skeptical New Yorkers came to see Graham's brand of contagious enthusiasm! How impressive was Billy Graham? NBC television executives came to see Billy preach and offered him $5 million (in 1957 dollars) to host his own variety show.[5]

Can you imagine a Christian minister today being offered $15 to $20 million (in today's dollars) to become the host of a show like *America's Got Talent* or *American Idol*? That's the kind of energy and contagious enthusiasm Billy Graham projected. He turned even cynical TV executives into *believers!*

In Graham's career he conducted over 400 crusades in 138 countries, with over 2.2 billion people watching him preach the gospel. Graham has appeared on Gallup's list of "Most Admired People in the World" fifty-five times since 1955, more than any other individual in world history. I think it's safe to say his enthusiasm is highly contagious![6]

THE POWER OF OPTIMISM

Optimism goes hand in hand with energy and enthusiasm. It's tough … no, it's impossible to be have the ENERGY and ENTHUSIASM to be Relentless day in and day out without a positive mindset. Two of the most important and eye-opening studies on optimism come from Duke's Fuqua School of Business.

Researchers there studied three thousand CEOs from companies across the globe to identify what they have in common. The number one trait is *optimism*.[7]

Not just simple old-fashioned "optimism," but rather great big over-the-top, through-the-roof optimism! Eighty percent of the CEOs graded out as "very optimistic."[8]

Study co-author Professor Manju Puri said, "Finance executives go so far as to say their CEOs are more optimistic about almost *everything* in life … even beyond their outlook on business prospects."

Co-author Professor Campbell Harvey, said, "CEOs are a vastly different breed than the average person."

A second study by Duke Business School researchers reported MBA graduates with optimistic attitudes have better career prospects. They spend less time searching for jobs and receive offers faster than their fellow MBA grads.[9]

Does that winning streak continue once they are in the workforce? You bet it does. The more optimistic MBA grads are more likely to be promoted within the first two years!

These two studies are perfectly synergistic. My educated guess is the MBA grads from one study are on track to *become* the CEOs from the other study. Optimism works!

There was one more very important trait the Duke researchers found. The optimistic MBA grads were more willing to disengage from a plan when it wasn't working and adapt to a new one. That is a critical "Power of Relentless" trait. I've changed course a thousand times. I've found ways over, under, around and through obstacles. I've smashed through brick walls and glass ceilings. The key to my success is a willingness to change course and plans as often as some people change socks. My winning business plan is to attack ... and if not successful, change plans. Then attack again ... and if not successful, change plans again. Then keep attacking and changing plans until I find one that eventually works.

A positive mindset and The Power of RELENTLESS go together like motherhood and apple pie. Optimistic people are less likely to worry about failure or rejection, take it personally, or become wedded to a plan. Optimistic and relentless people are focused on reaching their goals by taking any steps necessary to get there. That's how you turn what looks to "normal" people like failure ... into a shocking come-from-behind victory.

ALWAYS SAY "YES!"

Optimism and a positive mindset is why I keep saying "YES" to opportunities. The media knows me as "*The Yes Man*." That's because when the media calls, I always say "YES!" I've given media interviews at the top of a ski slope. I've given interviews on the beach in Maui. I've given interviews poolside. I've given interviews to Fox News at 3:00 a.m. in the morning Pacific Time for the 6:00 a.m. East Coast show *Fox & Friends*. I've given Skype television interviews from my hotel room, with my family asleep in the bed behind me. I've given interviews during dinner with my family at restaurants. I've given interviews in my car. Some days start with a 6:00 a.m. radio interview and then end with an 11:00 p.m. interview.

Why? Because I try to say "YES" to everyone, not just the media. If you say "NO," nothing good can happen. Good comes from the word "YES." Opportunity, wealth, or fame can never come from a deal you didn't do. "YES" doesn't guarantee success, but it does make it possible that magic will happen. There is always hope this time will be the home run. With "YES" there is possibility. With "NO" there is zero possibility.

You just never know which deal you turn down was fated to be "the one" that would have changed your life, that would have made your dreams come true. So I try to say "YES" to everyone.

But in particular, I always say, "YES" to the media. The media brands you as successful. The media gives you exposure and reach. The media gives you celebrity. The media gives you millions of dollars in free publicity. Much of my success is due to people seeing or hearing or reading about me in the media.

Here's a great example of why I always say "YES" to the media. I participated in a media prank twenty-five years ago. During an interview, a well-known Chicago radio host lost an on-air wager to me and agreed to host his show live in his pink polka dot underwear, outside in the freezing cold winter. As part of the bet I co-hosted his show that day. Pretty silly, right? *Wrong.* In the audience watching that day was the president of NBC Radio Network. He'd never heard of me in his life—until that day. But he hired me the next day as host on 130 NBC Source Radio stations from coast to coast. My life changed dramatically because of that one media appearance. That's why I always say, "YES!"

I don't know when my next big break will happen. But sometime in the near future, maybe during a media appearance promoting this book, a stranger will see, or hear, or read about me, for the first time—and my life will change.

That's the Relentless OPTIMISM you need to seize every opportunity that could change your life.

But it's not just the media to whom I say "YES." I may meet that important person or once-in-a-lifetime opportunity at a speech. That's why I always say "YES." In that audience may be a political kingmaker. I may meet that kingmaker at a meeting. So I always say "YES" to requests for meetings. The person that could change my life may see or hear me for the first time in one of my TV or radio advertising campaigns. That's why I always say "YES" to every spokesman or TV pitchman opportunity.

Smart businesspeople look for ways to say "YES!" But the rest of society looks for reasons to say "NO." Are you one of those? You may not realize it, but you may have closed the door to the deal, or opportunity, or job, or partnership that would have changed your life. All you had to do was say "YES." After reading this book, I certainly hope you won't make that mistake again!

Here's where you say, "YES, Wayne!"

RISK-TAKERS AND RIVERBOAT GAMBLERS

It isn't just optimism that successful executives had in common in that Duke Business School study. It was also a willingness to take risks. It turns out the greatest super-achievers of our society are riverboat gamblers. It appears their optimism and boundless enthusiasm gives them faith that their gamble will turn out a winner ... which makes them more willing to take the gamble in the first place.

Risk is vitally important to your success. Remember the "Relentless Tribe"—the Jews of Israel? They're the greatest risk-taking entrepreneurs the world has ever seen.

Think of each of my ten miracle achievements. Without risk, the life I've achieved never happens. Without risk, I'm still sitting home in the New York suburbs living an unhappy life. Without risk, I never would have become the host of five shows at CNBC. Without risk, I would have never replaced my boyhood idol Jimmy "The Greek." Without risk, Grandpa Norm would have died without ever experiencing one minute of fame. Without being trained to take risks to be successful, my daughter Dakota would have played it safe, stayed home, and attended community college. She would never have even applied to Harvard. Without risk, you're not reading this book, for two reasons: First, because if I wasn't a risk-taker, this book would not exist. What publisher would have bought it? Second, if I hadn't taken all those risks and succeeded, you wouldn't have bought my book either.

Without the massive risks I've taken again and again throughout my life, I'm watching my own version of *It's a Wonderful Life*. I'm seeing a glimpse of what my life would be like if I'd played it safe. It's a sad and depressing picture. You may be living that life right now. But you picked up this book to change all that. Now you just need the energy, enthusiasm, and optimism to start taking risks. To find the courage and chutzpah to go after your dreams. To stop settling, or playing it safe. It's time to become daring. It's time to become a gunslinger and riverboat gambler. But where will you get the ENERGY, CONTAGIOUS ENTHUSIASM, and NEVER-ENDING OPTIMISM to be a risk-taker? I've developed the perfect program to give you that courage, confidence, chutzpah, energy and enthusiasm. It's called "Positive Addictions" to build up a Relentless Body, Mind, Spirit, and Soul.

THE PARADOX OF RELENTLESS ENERGY

My "Positive Addictions" program will shock many of you. At first glance the program I'm recommending here appears to be the opposite of the power of RELENTLESS. That's the unique paradox of Relentless ENERGY.

Wayne Allyn Root spells W.A.R. Those initials were tailor-made for me—I'm combative, aggressive, action-oriented, always playing offense (on the attack), always living life on the edge, taking risks, confident and tenacious. I'm a Wild West gunslinger and riverboat gambler. In short, I am the definition (and the father) of the power of RELENTLESS.

The guts of this book are about all of that—as you already know—because you just read my crucial SEVEN PRINCIPLES OF RELENTLESS. All of them require a tough-as-nails, indestructible "Terminator" kind of attitude, crossed with the mindset of a Marine Drill Sergeant.

Yes, those are the "guts" of my book. But you are about to read the "heart" of my book. It's the part of my book that would make my mother

Stella Root proud, because she was all HEART. Her story proved that what matters above all else is heart. Well, here it is. What you are about to read and experience is actually the foundation that makes The Power of RELENTLESS possible.

What few ever suspect is that to become this kind of relentless business warrior and super-achiever, you first need to master your inner self. You first need to master mindfulness. You first need to master your body, mind, spirit, and soul. To successfully make war, you need to first make peace.

Relentless may be my mindset (and, of course, my brand). But my foundation is positive and spiritual habits that nourish my body, mind, spirit and soul. I call them "Positive Addictions."

If your goal is wealth, success, and financial freedom, you must first create a perfectly balanced you. That's the real "secret" of this book— without mastering your inner self, you can't master anyone or anything else. Without mastering spirituality, you can never truly master money (or anything else). So ironically, the power of spirituality is the heart of the power of RELENTLESS.

This program has already been battle-tested. First, by me and those around me. Then it was adopted by thousands of others. I've presented it in hundreds of speeches to thundering standing ovations and long lines of hard-edged businessmen telling me I've changed their lives. Once they understood the secret that you must master your inner self before you can master others, that you must master peace before you can wage war, then rough, tough, macho Marine Drill Sergeant types suddenly embraced their body, mind, spirit, and soul. The light bulb went off during my presentation. Lives were dramatically changed.

That's the paradox of The Power of RELENTLESS. This philosophy, mindset, and program combine to create a perfect blend of the saint and the sinner. You might say this program is all about the synergy of Mike Tyson and Mother Teresa!

Buckle up. This is going to be a real eye opener.

POSITIVE ADDICTIONS

Since you have read this far, I'm sure you've decided you want to live the rest of your life with The Power of RELENTLESS. The next obvious questions are ...

"Wayne, how do I develop the same energy level, positive attitude, and relentless mindset as you? How do I stay positive? How do I stay enthusiastic? How do I stay confident? How do I stay focused? How do I keep world-class energy in the face of stress, challenge, and adversity? HOW DO I BECOME AND REMAIN RELENTLESS?"

The answer to those questions is where the rubber meets the road. My mentor Doug Miller taught me one of life's great truisms: "Everything is easy when you know what to do." To know what to do usually means paying your dues, to gain the necessary "experience." Most of the time we learn what to do by first making mistakes and doing it the wrong way. That's why it is often said, "Overnight success takes twenty years of failure, mistakes, and pain."

Here's the great news. This book can cut your twenty-year process by nineteen years. This program is your shortcut. I've already paid the dues, done the research, gone through the trial and error, and endured the failures to gain that experience. So you don't have to go through the same process, so you don't have to "pay your own dues."

I'm going to share with you, step by step, exactly what to do. I bought and paid for it with my hard-earned time, money, and pain. This program is your shortcut. Follow this program and it will take nineteen years (at least) off your twenty-year journey. Remember that Picasso quote from Steve Jobs? *"Good artists copy, great artists steal."*

Keep reading for the blueprint. Then *steal it.* Make it yours.

So, what is the answer as to how to become and remain *Relentless?* It is POSITVE ADDICTIONS—a relentless devotion to your body, mind, spirit, and soul.

Most people are controlled by their negative habits and addictions—such as drinking and eating too much; eating junk food that kills your energy; smoking; drugs; late-night partying; lack of exercise; and negative thoughts—to name a few. And, when times get rough and stress levels rise, they turn to these negative habits even more than in the good times. It is a downward spiral.

Negative habits kill energy and destroy positive thinking. But the "Positive Addictions" you will learn in the remainder of this book not only create a positive and relentless mindset, they supercharge your energy.

By embracing these twelve POSITIVE ADDICTIONS, you will take control of your life. Just like everyone else, you will encounter setbacks, roadblocks, failure, rejection, and the word "NO." That never ends. But rather than succumbing to negative habits when you encounter challenge and adversity, you will now turn to your positive, healthy habits. I can assure you your life will improve more dramatically than you ever imagined.

POSITIVE ADDICTION #1: RELENTLESS EARLY MORNINGS

If you are one of those who believe the saying "The early bird catches the worm" simply means the worm should have slept longer, it is time to change that belief.

I get up at 6:00 a.m. every day...including weekends. It is quiet time...time to think and plan.

It probably won't surprise you that there is a growing body of scientific research that shows the benefits of rising early:

- Morning people are more proactive and positive, therefore, more likely to succeed.
- Morning people accomplish more. They don't just promise, they actually do it.
- Morning people receive better grades, go to better colleges, and get better job opportunities, all leading to better relationships throughout life.

- These are not flukes or coincidences. Morning has been proven by researchers to be the time people are the most full of hope and optimism, therefore the best time to make good decisions.[1]

If you are not already a morning person, let me give you some advice on how to change and incorporate Positive Addiction number one into your personal life:

1. Do it slowly. If you normally get up at 7:30 a.m.... set your alarm one minute earlier every day for three months. If you normally get up at 8:00, set your alarm one minute earlier every day for four months. Easy.

2. Cut back on your TV time and go to bed earlier. Studies show that watching television for long periods of time not only damages your chances of success, but also cuts five years off your life.[2]

   The other reason to cut back on TV time, especially late-night TV, is that it features negative and depressing shows about violent and dysfunctional people and it's filled with advertisements about ambulance-chasing lawyers, bad credit, bankruptcy, and drugs. I call this late night TV wasteland "junk food for the mind" because watching these depressing shows and advertisements has about the same effect as putting junk food into your body. It is poison. The last images you watch at night will be the images you dream about all night long. This is the exact opposite of the positive way I want to wake up each morning.

3. Do you have trouble sleeping? Don't worry. As you read on and adopt several of the Positive Addictions that follow, you will be ensured of sleeping soundly, without drugs. If you need another energy boost during the day, although it is

something I have never needed or done, new research has shown that a short power nap boosts immunity, reduces stress, and repairs damage from a lack of sleep.[3]

Once you're getting up early, what's the first thing you should do in the morning? Take relentless early morning walks!

Here are a few words of wisdom about walking from great thinkers of history:

- "Walking is man's best medicine."—Hippocrates
- "Of all exercises walking is the best."—Thomas Jefferson
- "All truly great thoughts are conceived by walking." —Friedrich Nietzsche
- "An early-morning walk is a blessing for the whole day." —Henry David Thoreau
- "No city should be too large for a man to walk out of it in a morning."—Cyril Connolly
- "My father considered a walk among the mountains as the equivalent of churchgoing."—Aldous Huxley
- "The sum of the whole is this: walk and be happy; walk and be healthy. The best way to lengthen out our days is to walk steadily and with a purpose."—Charles Dickens
- "It is not talking but walking that will bring us to heaven."— Matthew Henry
- "In the morning a man walks with his whole body; in the evening, only with his legs."—Ralph Waldo Emerson
- "In every walk with nature one receives far more than he seeks."—John Muir
- "Take a two-mile walk every morning before breakfast." —Harry Truman *(advice on how to live to be 80 on his 80th birthday)*
- "It is solved by walking."—Ancient Latin Proverb

- "A journey of a thousand miles begins with one step."
  —Chinese Proverb
- "If you are seeking creative ideas, go out walking. Angels
  whisper to a man when he goes for a walk."—Raymond
  Inmon

Clearly I can't take credit for being the first to see the benefit of a morning walk. And with all these testimonials, I doubt any of you can question
the benefits. Let me tell you why a morning walk is so important to
me…and why it will be to you also.

- Starting my day with exercise is a perfect way to set the tone
  for the day—positive and action-oriented.
- Just being outside walking and looking at nature provides
  me mental relaxation and reduces stress.
- Sunshine produces Vitamin D and releases positive endorphins in my body.
- Being alone and communing with nature, I have time to
  pray and express my gratitude to God.
- I earn my breakfast by exercising before I eat.

Perhaps the most important thing I do on my morning walk is "think."
Because I'm outdoors amongst nature and fresh air…in a positive mood
because my skin is soaking up Vitamin D and my body is in motion…many
great ideas come to me while I'm out walking in the morning. During my
morning walks at my homes in Las Vegas and Park City, Utah, I have had
many of my greatest inspirations.

On a macro scale, my walks have been where I've come up with the
ideas for books to write, television shows to produce, and new businesses
to launch.

The benefits of a walk, just like the benefits of sleep, have been shown
by scientific research. But for all you gym rats, did you know that

researchers at Glasgow University have reported jogging or walking outdoors is TWICE as good as a workout in the gym for mental health?[4]

Research also shows:

- A jog in the forest or walk in the park helps depression and anxiety.
- Being around trees and grass lowers brain stress level.
- Activities in a natural outdoor environment were the only ones shown to be associated with a lower risk of poor mental health.
- Exercise in a gym is good for your physical health, but it does NOT lift depression.

There are a host of other health benefits to be gained from walking—starting with weight loss, reduction in your chances of cancer (in particular breast cancer), dramatically lower mortality rates from diabetes, reduction in high cholesterol, and lower rates of dementia.[5]

To succeed in this competitive world, you need every edge you can get. Waking up early is a real edge. So are my other Positive Addictions—all of which are quite naturally done in the early morning, at a time when your brain is most positive, creative, and receptive to new ideas.

POSITIVE ADDICTION #2: RELENTLESS HOME AND FAMILY

Everyone has a different purpose and passion. *To each their own*. But if you picked up this book, and have read this far, it's clear you (like me) are passionate about achieving wealth, financial success, and financial freedom.

I recognized early that my passion was to be financially successful in a broad range of businesses and careers, while staying close to my home and family. That's why my careers have included being a professional sports handicapper; media personality; author and speaker; TV creator, producer, and host; CEO and entrepreneur; and spokesman/pitchman for companies across the globe.

Each of those careers has allowed me to work from home. Very few hours of my life have been spent in a traditional office. And working at home has given me an extra two to four hours per day in time saved ... that has allowed me to "expand my day" and therefore pursue multiple careers. *Synergy*.

While everyone must find their own passion, let me tell you about mine and how that has fueled my success ... and can fuel yours as well.

I work fourteen to sixteen hours per day, six to seven days per week (even I'm human—I put in only half a day on both Saturday and Sunday). How do I do it? How do I spur creativity? How do I find the extra hours?

Well, it all starts with my addiction to "Home Sweet Home." I have been able to structure all my businesses so I can work from home. One of the major benefits is that it allows me to stretch my day:

- With a home office I walk twenty feet from my bed to my office. That shaves one to two hours per day off the usual commute of most Americans. I use those extra hours to take a morning walk and then exercise in my home gym for sixty to ninety minutes.

- I also save time all throughout the day by taking a shower ... then walking twenty feet to my desk ... eating lunch, then walking twenty feet to my desk ... working out at my home gym ... then walking twenty feet to my desk. All day long I'm gaining back time.

- Exercising in my home gym also saves me time. I'm able to work while exercising—I often surf the internet and answer e-mails while on the bike or treadmill. I also answer my phones and texts while working out.

Why not? It's my gym. My friends call it "The Root Ritz." It's bigger than most hotel gyms. There's no one there to tell me to be quiet. And since I'm in my own home, I can stop working out whenever I want to take a call ... then get back to the workout. I make all the decisions. Having a gym at home means there are no excuses to *ever* miss a workout.

Home is my favorite place in world. It is a beautiful place to work and makes me happy. Why would I want to spend my day at an office away from the things and people I love? Home ensures my happiness, reduces stress, and spurs creativity!

The artwork that I love is at home. The furniture I love is at home. The family and dog I love are at home. The food I love is at home. So why would I want to leave my favorite space on earth to go to a drab office every day?

As so many people discover, it is virtually impossible to work fourteen-to-sixteen-hour days away from home and retain a fulfilling relationship with your family. Now, when I say I work sixteen-hour days, that doesn't mean sixteen hours straight. No one can do that all day, every day, seven days per week.

But I do work long hours. I am never "off." I work over a sixteen-hour period every day. My typical workday starts at 6:15 a.m. (just minutes after I hop out of bed) and ends at 10 to 11:00 p.m. So my "work footprint" is sixteen hours on a typical day. Yes, I'm always "on call" during that long day—I take calls and e-mails from morning to night. But I do have some fun and take breaks throughout the day. That's what makes it all doable and pleasurable—I call those breaks my "Positive Distractions." Those frequent short breaks give me the energy, creativity, and constant motion that I need to be at my best. When I say "motion" that means I move around—a lot! You'll read more about my "RELENTLESS MOTION" below.

POSITIVE DISTRACTIONS

Without the need to be at an office at any specific time or commute back and forth, I can schedule family time all day long. Family. Kids. Dog. Exercise. Walks. Swimming, Jacuzzi. Meditation. Yoga. Football with my sons. Watch parts of a football game. Eat breakfast and lunch with my family. These are all "Positive Distractions" that create a daily change of pace and nurture a state of mind that makes me even more creative and productive.

I credit my success to all of these positive distractions. I'm ADD (as many successful people are—my mind never stops working). I need a constant change of pace to keep me focused. I can't do one thing for hours at a time. My body and my mind both need to be in constant motion. My workday is filled with "controlled chaos." This is what makes my sixteen-hour workdays doable and enjoyable.

On a personal note, and knowing that everyone will not have the option of working from home (unless that is your passion and you pursue a plan to do so), let me leave you with a few highlights that I have been blessed to receive because I worked from home. Hopefully they will encourage those of you so inclined to do the same:

Being at home 24/7, I have not missed many important moments in my children's lives.

We are able to homeschool our children—giving me a direct influence on what they learn and how they are taught. Because of this my oldest daughter read the *Wall Street Journal* along with Dr. Seuss ... and played entrepreneur, as well as dolls. You already know the result: Dakota recently graduated magna cum laude from Harvard University.

Even if you are unable to work at home, I want to strongly advise you to be active and involved in your children's lives. Research shows the positive benefits are overwhelming:

- A University of Minnesota study showed that parents' presence at key times, especially dinner, reduced drug use, sex, violence, and emotional distress.[1]
- A University of North Carolina study of 12,000 teens showed the most significant factor protecting teens from risky behavior was "parental connectedness," feeling loved and protected.[2]
- A fifteen-year study at the University of Nebraska looking at Generation Xers showed the best predictor of kids' wellbeing was the quality of their parents' marriage. The

number two predictor was how often children were showered with affection and how close children felt to their parents.[3]

- A study by Cornell economists of 27,000 students found that 50 percent of American college students, but only 10 percent of Ivy League students, came from divorced families. The study also showed that divorce and parental bickering resulted in lower grades, lower SAT scores, and a lower attention span.[4]

(Then there's one benefit to society too. Because I work at home I rarely use my car. My car is used for only three reasons—to drive to business meetings; to drive to lunch or dinner business meetings; and to drive to the airport for business flights. What that means is I use very little gas or oil … I don't pollute the environment … and I don't put wear and tear on the roads. My choice of the work-at-home lifestyle is good for our planet. Perhaps we could name it the "Green Workstyle"—because it produces a greener planet and produces plenty of green in my pockets too!)

Working from home allows me to bestow all these benefits on my family. It is the secret weapon of my business success. It is the secret to my children's remarkable academic performance, as well as my personal happiness. This "Positive Addiction" to my home and my family is one of the primary factors contributing to my energy, enthusiasm, and positive mindset. Working from home has allowed me to turn my vocation into a lifelong vacation.

POSITIVE ADDICTION #3: RELENTLESS MINDFULNESS

As you might imagine, I am often in situations of intense stress and pressure. But then, aren't we all? Meditation is my lifesaver. Meditation keeps me sane. It is not something I just believe implicitly. It is something obvious to everyone around me. My friends, family, and business associates can tell *instantly* if I did not meditate. When I skip meditation I'm a different person. I yell. I'm negative. I'm more harsh. I'm more scattered, less focused. I'm quick to stress out.

I meditate while on airplanes, before speeches, before TV or media appearances, before (and often while) writing the pages of this book. Meditation will clear, refresh, and supercharge your mind, thereby significantly increasing your creativity and ability to focus.

So, how do you meditate? It is so simple. Let me give you the Cliffs-Notes version:

- Set your alarm for fifteen minutes.

145

- If possible put on calming music, or simply do your best to ignore outside distractions.
- Breathe in…breathe out.
- Feel your breath in, feel your breath out.
- Think only of the single breath you are breathing.
- It's natural to get distracted and think of something else. No problem. Just drop the thought and go back to breathing in and out and concentrating on that single breath as you do it.

That's it. Do it once in the morning, then once or twice more during the day when you're under stress, or feeling exhausted. Meditation keeps your energy high, keeps you focused like a laser, and creates massive levels of enthusiasm, creativity, and a positive mindset no matter what you face.

Again, you don't need to just take my word for it. The benefits of meditation have been proven by scientific research.

A Harvard study shows meditation literally changes your body and your brain. It reduces stress and boosts the immune system.[1]

A study by a Nobel Prize-winning scientist at UCLA proved that just twelve minutes per day of meditation slows the cellular aging process and extends lifespan. It literally increases the length of your telomeres. So meditation is the real-life "Fountain of Youth"![2]

Studies show meditation lowers your healthcare bill, lowers depression, changes the brain to protect against mental illness, reduces the severity of colds, improves grades for kids in college, improves the performance of troops in the military, helps you lose weight, and helps you sleep better. (All the better to implement Positive Addiction #1 and wake up earlier.)[3]

Psychology Today reported on studies showing that meditation boosts productivity, boosts health, increases immunity, decreases pain, decreases anxiety and stress, increases intelligence by boosting the cortical thickness of your brain (in the area related to paying attention), improves memory, improves focus, and boosts your ability to multi-task, be creative, and think outside box. That explains me (and soon you!).[4]

The UCLA Brain Mapping Center studied gray matter loss due to aging. In doing so they recruited fifty people who don't meditate as a control group and fifty who do. Then the scientists compared their brain scans with high-resolution magnetic resonance imaging. Each group of fifty was comprised of twenty-eight men and twenty-two women ranging in age from twenty to seventy-seven. Those who meditated had been doing so for at least four years and up to forty-six years, with an average of twenty years. Although all the older subjects, both meditators and non-meditators, showed signs of diminishing gray matter, large parts of the gray matter in the brains of those who meditated appeared better preserved.

As a matter of fact, according to Dr. Florian Kurth, a co-author of the study and postdoctoral fellow at the UCLA Brain Mapping Center, the researchers were surprised by the magnitude of the difference.

"We expected rather small and distinct effects located in some of the regions that had previously been associated with meditating," he said. *"Instead, what we actually observed was a widespread effect of meditation that encompassed regions throughout the entire brain."*

Meditation not only appears to slow brain cell loss, but also appears to help the immune system by allowing recovery from "fight or flight" hormones, especially cortisol, which builds up with even minor chronic anxiety and worry to the point of inviting, rather than warding off, more illness. Reducing chronic cortisol reduces inflammation, and inflammation is the root of much disease. Therefore, physical as well as mental health is enhanced by meditation.[5]

The best news of all about meditation is you don't have to become a monk and devote your life to it to gain the benefits. You don't even need to meditate an hour or longer. Short doses, as little as twelve minutes a day, work just fine. Even if I (and all this scientific research) can't convince you of the benefits... just try it out for twelve to fifteen minutes once a day for two weeks. I'm betting you'll feel a remarkable difference and become hooked on this positive habit for life.

POSITIVE ADDICTION #4: RELENTLESS PRAYER, GRATITUDE, AND FORGIVENESS

saiah 40:30-31 is my favorite Bible passage. It gives me great comfort. It gives me faith. But most importantly, it gives me energy:

> Even the youths shall faint and be weary,
> And the young men shall utterly fall,
> But those who wait on the Lord
> Shall renew their strength;
> They shall mount up with wings like eagles,
> They shall run and not be weary,
> They shall walk and not faint.
> —Isaiah 40:30–31, New Living Translation

Whenever I'm feeling down, I read that passage. Even youths are weary, but with God's strength, anyone can run like the wind! Then I stand up to my challenges, mount up with wings like eagles, and run through any obstacle or roadblock standing in my way. This verse is the power of RELENTLESS *personified*.

That's the whole point of this specific "Positive Addiction." No man is superman. No human is superhuman. We all need help. We all need a boost of energy and faith now and then.

We all need a team to support us. I am a firm believer that God is that team. God gives us each the horsepower of a Ferrari! When we need strong shoulders to hold our problems and stress, God gives us the shoulders of ten thousand bodybuilders. Faith is the foundation of success.

I'm here to tell you how important prayer and gratitude are to my success and how I use both to improve my wellbeing. But if you are an atheist or nonbeliever, don't fear. Don't skip this section. I was born Jewish and became a born-again Christian. But that's my personal faith. I'm not here to preach any one faith—although I can testify about the strength, energy, and passion I've enjoyed since taking Jesus Christ as my savior.

But I find much inspiration in the writings of many different religious leaders throughout time. I want every reader of this book to enjoy the power of faith—no matter your religion. In the end, faith and prayer are both really an extension of positive thinking.

Prayer is really (at its simplest) meditation (with God). It is affirmation and visualization. It is exercise (of your mind and your faith). It is the perfect holistic, organic diet (of positive thought). It is perfection. It is team-building. It is a synergistic combination of everything in my "Positive Addictions" ... and everything I believe in.

Read on.

Prayer is about faith in something greater than yourself. Gratitude—or thanksgiving, if you like—is about thanks and acknowledgement to God for the blessings in your life.

As we are told in **1 Thessalonians 5:16–18** ... Few things can change our lives more than turning our complaining into thanksgiving: "Rejoice always; pray without ceasing; in everything give thanks; for this is God's will for you...."

Sounds like the Bible has much in common with the section of this book where I preach "hitting and pitching ... instead of bitching!"

The key words here are "in everything give thanks." Prayer is my anchor. It is the root (excuse the pun) of my passion, energy, enthusiasm, positive attitude, confidence, tenacity ... and of course, it is my power of RELENTLESS.

My personal faith in God inspires me and motivates me. It gives me confidence in knowing I'm not alone. My shoulders simply could NOT carry the weight all by themselves.

How do I know this for a fact? Because all the truly great things in my life happened only after I developed a deep faith in God. A whole new world was opened to me. My faith inspires me to believe in miracles; to make the impossible, *possible*; to move mountains; and to ignore critics and the limitations set by naysayers.

I firmly believe no man is an island. We all need support and help. If two heads are better than one, having God on your team is ... *INFINITY*.

A faith in God reduces stress and fear, and with fear out of the way, creativity comes alive.

Perhaps most of all, prayer makes me happy. It is the ultimate extension of positive thinking (a.k.a. RELENTLESS OPTIMISM). No matter how low my mood, prayer lifts it. That's why for me, spiritual wealth has led to material wealth.

But that was all opinion. Now I will interject scientific studies that prove the power of prayer. Prayer does more than lift your spirits. It heals your body and keeps you healthy—and I can prove it.

A 2012 Duke University study by the Center for Spirituality, Theology, and Health found a strong spiritual belief led to a healthier, happier, longer life.[1]

The researchers examined 1500 medical studies and found that prayer not only prevents sickness, but also promotes faster healing. Those stating they were faithful believers were found to have stronger immune systems and lower blood pressure than the general population.

A 2006 University of Texas study showed the more you go to church, the longer you live.[2] And not just a little. The study found a seven-year difference between those who never attended and those who were weekly church-goers.

Dozens of scientific studies connect faith in God and regular church attendance with success; stability in marriage, family, and parental responsibilities; and societal well-being.[3]

Here's where you might say, *"Okay Wayne, you've convinced me. How do I incorporate this specific "Positive Addiction" into my everyday schedule and life?"*

Again, it is very simple, easy, and straightforward:

PRAYER: I pray daily, not for specific things (although I have been known to do that), but for continued good health, happiness and blessings for myself and my family, and then simply for God to inspire me to make the right decisions and be the best person I can possibly be. To make sure I do it, I make prayer part of my morning TRIAD. That way it is "scheduled" each and every day.

GRATITUDE: Every morning, usually on my walk, I think of five to ten blessings in my life to be grateful for and thank God for them. Just the act of coming up with all these wonderful blessings puts me in a fabulous positive mood to start the day. Who wouldn't be positive when focusing your energy on the great blessings in your life?

FORGIVENESS: Forgiveness goes hand-in-hand with gratitude. Several times a week, usually on my walk, I think of people who have wronged me, or disrespected me, or offended me; people who have caused me pain; people who have cheated me; people who I harbor anger or ill feelings towards; and I forgive them unconditionally.

This breakthrough in my life was triggered by the incredible book *Unbroken* about the life of legendary World War II prisoner-of-war Louis Zamperini. It was later made into a hit movie, also called *Unbroken*.

Zamperini's story was so remarkable … the pain, torture and near-death experiences he suffered so tragic … yet he eventually chose to forgive his Japanese tormentors. That forgiveness allowed Zamperini to go onto live a wonderful, blessed life and live to the ripe old age of ninety-seven. We all need to learn to forgive. When I forgive the people that wrong me, I feel the weight of the world lift off my shoulders. Forgiveness produces *freedom*.

THOUGHTFULNESS: I keep notes and at least once or twice a week I send cards, notes with photos, personal thanks, wisdom, or great sayings to brighten someone's day.

There's even a fantastic company that allows anyone to do that with ease. It's my wife Debra Root's business, and it's called SENDOUTCARDS. They do all the work for you. They have cards for any and every occasion in your personal life. Plus cards for every business occasion (or any other reason you can think of). They even have cards created for each profession—cards just for doctors, lawyers, dentists, realtors, stockbrokers, etc. You go online, produce the card in minutes, they stamp it, address it and send it out from their facility. What a great idea!

But I haven't told you the best part. SENDOUTCARDS not only does all the work, they make it remarkably inexpensive. I send out thousands of cards at a fraction of the cost if I did it myself. Each Christmas or holiday I simply create one card, press a key on my computer, and over 1,000 cards go out all at once. It's that easy. I never stuff them, close them, or stamp them.

How successful is SENDOUTCARDS? This company is now the #1 customer of the U.S. Postal Service in the world. The U.S.P.S. has its own annex inside the corporate offices of SENDOUTCARDS! Kudos to Debra Root. I guess RELENTLESS runs in the family.

This is the perfect way to congratulate, thank, and show gratitude and appreciation to all your business associates, clients, and partners (not to mention friends and family). SENDOUTCARDS is a valuable business tool in my success arsenal.

You can register for SENDOUTCARDS here: new.sendoutcards. com/147164.

BIBLE READING: I read Bible passages anytime I need a boost of energy, faith, or confidence. Some people drink booze … some do drugs … some reach for a cup of coffee. I reach for prayer, or a Bible passage. I highly recommend it.

TITHING: I tithe—as God asks us all to do. I donate a generous portion of my income to good causes. My favorite charities and their contact information can be found in "POSITIVE ADDICTION #9: RELENTLESS CHARITY."

As I end this section I want to share one more of my favorite prayers. I read it aloud every morning, and it has given me great peace, strength, faith, energy and of course, the power of RELENTLESS:

> And I am convinced that nothing can ever separate us from God's love. Neither death nor life, neither angels nor demons, neither our fears for today nor our worries about tomorrow— not even the powers of hell can separate us from God's love. No power in the sky above or in the earth below—indeed, nothing in all creation will ever be able to separate us from the love of God that is revealed in Christ Jesus our Lord.
> —Romans 8:38–39, New Living Translation

POSITIVE ADDICTION #5: RELENTLESS AFFIRMATION AND VISUALIZATION

Positive affirmations are used to bring positive change to your thinking. The idea is to change your subconscious thought patterns from negative to positive. This is accomplished by repeating positive self-statements out loud, as if they are factual and have already happened.

If repeated daily and with passion and conviction, it is believed that positive affirmations can alter your thought patterns and belief in yourself and your ability to achieve success. The key is that you start to believe deep down in your subconscious that these statements are true, thereby changing how you feel about yourself and how you see yourself. Suddenly you walk with more confidence, you feel great when you wake up, you believe it's not only possible to live the life of your dreams, in your mind it has already happened.

The power of affirmations begins with believing. If you believe, all things are possible. Therefore the biggest obstacle you need to overcome is yourself. To overcome the negative conditioning most of us have developed over the years, we must first get rid of all the negative self-talk.

As the international best-selling book *The Secret* pointed out, an affirmation needs to be said out loud in the past tense as if it has already happened. If you do this regularly, you can convince your own subconscious to accept the affirmation as true and to block out the doubt and negativity.

Again, this is confirmed by scientific studies.[1] Research from a team led by Carnegie Mellon University's David Creswell found that college students can boost their ability to solve problems under pressure and boost academic grade point averages by using self-affirmation.[2]

Scientific research supports the importance of positive self-talk. The psychologist Martin Seligman studied insurance agents at MetLife and found that optimistic salespeople outsold their pessimistic peers by an average of 37 percent. When these salespeople were turned down by clients, they reacted differently. The ones who thought of themselves in the most positive light didn't sit around and mope, instead they made more phone calls and never took it personally.[3]

"That all sounds reasonable," you might say. *"But give me specific examples on the right way to do affirmation, so I know how to do it."*

The following is the best advice I can give and a few examples that you can follow. It is important to remember that vague affirmations are useless. The more detailed, specific, and goal-oriented the affirmation, the more likely it is to be effective.

Here are four examples:

WEIGHT LOSS

The simple affirmation, *"I will lose weight"* is no good and not worth your time saying it. Why? First, it is not in the past tense. And second, it does not have any specific actions and reinforcements in it. Much better is the affirmation:

"I have been losing weight each and every day because I am eating a salad at lunch every day. It tastes great. I feel great."

Now, repeat that—out loud—several times a day and you will soon find yourself eating a healthy, great-tasting salad for lunch, losing weight, and feeling great.

MAKING MONEY

The affirmation *"I will make $1,000,000 this year"* will not get you far. Why? Again, it is not in the past tense and lacks specifics. Much better is the affirmation:

"I made $1,000,000 this year by selling my unique software to Apple."

Now, repeat that—out loud–several times a day. It will keep you focused, and you may just make it come true—assuming you have software to sell Apple. Obviously fill in those same spaces with whatever your product or talent is ... and the company you want to sell it to.

PROFESSIONAL GOAL

The affirmation *"I will be the #1 salesman at my firm this year"* will not take you far. Again, for the same reasons—it's not in the past tense and lacks specifics. Much better is the affirmation:

"I became the #1 salesman at my firm because of my amazing follow-up skills. I followed up every call a hundred times to make the sale. I never accepted NO for an answer. No one can compete with me. I am a machine!"

THE POWER OF RELENTLESS

The affirmation *"I will be a success because I will be relentless"* does not make the grade. It's not in the past tense and it's not detailed or specific enough. Try this one:

"It's been a great year because I am relentless, full of energy and enthusiasm, and have attracted many new clients. I have dramatically improved my income because I relentlessly applied Wayne Root's Seven Principles of Relentless and Twelve Positive Addictions to my life every day, in every way."

If you repeat that affirmation out loud several times a day your sub-conscious will soon ensure you act on it and you will be amazed at how quickly you can turn your dreams into reality.

Past tense. Specific. Detailed. Goal-oriented.

Now here's my knock on affirmations.

Affirmations aren't magic. I believe "God helps those who help themselves." You have to put in the time to succeed. Words alone will never do the trick. Otherwise everyone would simply avoid hard work and talk or pray about success. If that was all that was needed, who would actually put in the effort?

Affirmations won't work unless they are realistic. They won't work unless they fit your purpose (passion) in life. They won't work unless you are doing the homework. They won't work unless you are taking action. They won't work unless you have already harnessed the power of RELENTLESS.

The problem with affirmations is you can get the impression you can say, "I am the world's greatest concert pianist" and it will happen. Well, it will … *if* you're practicing on the piano eight to twelve hours per day … and if you have the finest piano teacher in the world who has a proven track record of coaching many students to the top of your profession … if you already have the talent … and if you've already won hundreds of piano competitions.

What I'm saying is, if you're on your way to greatness, or already at a level that puts you in competition with the best pianists in the world, then affirmations or visualizations may very well be your "winning edge." They might put you over the top.

But if you haven't even taken a serious lesson yet, or you hate playing piano, or you have a third-rate teacher, or you refuse to practice even a few minutes per day ... well, then all the affirmations in the world won't help (even if they are in the past tense). Affirmations are activated and super-charged by action. Not just any action—although even a few steps in the right direction is always a great start. Then add in the power of RELENTLESS.

No one tells you this. This is the real world. It's brutal. No amount of affirmations will give you an edge without motion, AGGRESSIVE ACTION, and a commitment to do the homework. If you're not out-working and out-hustling your competition, you will fail (affirmations or not).

If you repeat affirmations out loud (in the past tense) designed to make you into the #1 racecar driver in Formula One or NASCAR, *great!* I love hunger, drive, and ambition. But affirmations will only work if you are already driving racecars and within striking distance of winning major races. Then affirmations or visualizations can provide the winning edge.

But if you're riding a bike around town and have never driven a car, that affirmation is a waste of time. You have to be on the path ... headed in the right direction ... have the talent ... have the passion ... and be will-ing to do the homework. There are no shortcuts. But all things being equal, if you have the talent ... have already put in a decade of hard work ... and you're right at the precipice of winning the Indy 500, then affirmations may very well put you over the top.

If you repeat affirmations out loud designed to make you into the CEO of the company you work for, great! I love hunger, drive, and ambition. But they'll only work if you already have a college degree and MBA, you have put in fifteen years in executive management, your division led the company in sales, and you are already in contention for the CEO job.

But if you're a janitor earning minimum wage, with no college degree, and don't know a single soul in the executive management ranks, all the affirmations in the world won't help you become CEO.

Affirmations do work. They can provide that slight edge you need to beat the competition. But they have to be applied correctly. Otherwise you are doomed to fail and then lose faith in affirmations—when it isn't the affirmations that failed, *it's you.*

If your heart isn't in the goal, if you aren't willing to do the homework, if you don't already have the qualifications, if you aren't willing to follow up your goals relentlessly ... nothing can help you. Don't blame the affirmations. The problem is you.

Affirmations work—if applied to the correct, reasonable, do-able goal ... not to a pie-in-the-sky Pollyanna dream that is impossible to achieve, given your resume and experience. But I have seen affirmations inspire students of mine to go get the right education, experience, and resume. I've seen affirmations inspire people to achieve great things they always dreamed about. Affirmations are a winning edge. They are an important part of your "tool box."

Still ...

The hard and raw truth is you must put in the hard work and have the talent in the first place, plus a love and passion for what you're doing, in order for affirmations to work their magic.

Visualization is an adjunct and extension to affirmation. "Seeing is believing." Every great athlete uses visualization. Think of champion golfers Tiger Woods and Phil Mickelson. Before they hit a great shot, they've been taught by swing coaches and sports psychologists to see it, feel it, taste it, and touch it. It must seem real ... you must believe it ... in order to achieve it. The same belief in success holds true for every great athlete-whether he's hitting a homerun, swooshing a three-point jump shot, racing a Ferrari in Formula One, or racing in the hundred-yard dash at the Olympics.

Practice your Affirmations and Visualizations for five to ten minutes every day ... to convince your own subconscious.

Does visualization work?

In 1979 my high school classmates were asked to include our favorite saying on our personal page in our high school graduation yearbook. My page says:

"Anything the mind can conceive, you can achieve."

My belief in a positive and relentless mindset obviously started early.

My first fancy business brochure, created in 1985 said, *"Meet the Next Jimmy The Greek."* Only four years later I would become Jimmy The Greek's partner on national TV. What are the odds?

When I created that powerful video at a sports anchor desk and played the part of a TV sportscaster, I had never been a TV sportscaster one day in my life. But it led to interviews with CNN and Fox Television, then to my landing the job at Financial News Network (now CNBC) as a host of five shows.

My business card in late 1986 read:

Wayne Allyn Root
Author—Speaker—TV personality

When I created that business card, I was only three years out of college. I had never given a paid speech in my life, I had never written a book in my life (my first book deal would come three years later in 1989) ... and I had never been on TV.

Today those titles accurately describe my life. Visualization clearly helped to turn my dream into a reality. I had to see my future clearly on that business card in order to make it happen.

Many of the successes in my life came directly from my "future vision." In a 1997 radio interview on the *Connecting Point* radio show in Los Angeles, I talked about my then five-year old daughter Dakota going to Stanford or Harvard in thirteen years.[4]

I continued to talk about it and write about it in several of my books. In 2010 she was accepted to both Harvard and Stanford.

You must see it and feel it before you can achieve it.

But again, you can't be lazy with visualizations and expect results. Just like affirmations, your visualizations must be specific, detailed, and goal-oriented.

And they must be the *right kind* of visualizations. Studies prove that just visualizing the end result does not work. You must visualize the entire journey—starting with the hard work, the college admissions interview, studying for SATs, you must clearly see the entire process necessary to get accepted by Stanford. Just seeing yourself sitting in a classroom at Stanford isn't enough.[5]

The purpose of this type of specific visualization is to constantly remind you of the hard work required and obstacles you must overcome to reach the goal you are visualizing. By clearly seeing the hard work, you'll be more likely to actually do it. And by also seeing the obstacles and road-blocks in your visualizations, you'll be ready for them, less stressed, more prepared, calm, and have solutions in mind when they happen. And trust me—*they will happen.*

So don't visualize yourself sitting in the CEO chair. It will do you no good. Have a plan on how you are going to get there and clearly visualize the specific, detailed steps you'll take along the way. Then also see yourself overcoming the obstacles along the way.

That's how you turn visualization into a Positive Addiction!

POSITIVE ADDICTION #6: RELENTLESS PHYSICAL FITNESS

Few of you doubt that physical fitness (exercise) is a key element in a long and healthy life. But more importantly, it is also a vital element in the relentless pursuit of *success*. Exercise is at the center of every bit of business and financial success in my life. My hope is that the knowledge of the role of exercise in making you both healthy *and* wealthy will motivate you to make daily exercise one of the foundations of your life.

Most people know the truth about the importance of exercise deep down. They just never act on it. For those of you who repeatedly tell yourself, "I'll start tomorrow, I promise" please allow Marine Drill Sergeant Root to give you a swift, relentless kick in the butt and tell you to "START TODAY!"

Just look at the latest research. It is mind-blowing how important exercise is:

- A lack of daily exercise kills more people than obesity![1]

- Even if you're active and exercise every day … long periods
  of sitting SHORTEN YOUR LIFE and erode your health![2]

And Harvard Medical School makes it clear there's a correlation between exercise versus watching television and disease and death. Harvard reports on several studies—including studies by the CDC (Center for Disease Control) and the Nurses Health Study (following 50,000 middle-aged women for six years). The results are the same. First, your life depends on exercise. Second, America's economy depends on your willingness to exercise regularly. If Americans exercised regularly it would cut medical bills in the U.S. by $70 billion annually.[3]

The same Harvard study concludes that television is like poison to your health and aging. The more television that women in the Nurses Study watched, the higher their rate of obesity and diabetes. Even two hours of watching television greatly increased the odds of disease.

Other studies confirm that long hours sitting doing *anything*— watching television, talking on the phone, working on the computer, attending meetings at work—changes your metabolism to promote disease and obesity.[4]

The point of all this new research is to get your body moving—not just for an hour at the gym, but **all day long.**

Exercise is so good for you that new studies confirm it's better than … *medicine!* Harvard and Stanford Medical School researchers found that exercise is more effective at keeping heart attack and stroke patients alive than drugs.[5]

Exercise is supposed to be about improving your physique. But in reality (just like yoga) it's really just as much about improving your brain. Studies prove aerobic exercise creates new brain cells.[6] And improves overall brain performance.[7] Exercise even wards off the degeneration, memory failure, and learning loss of Alzheimer's Disease and dementia.[8]

Exercise even has a positive effect on your children's developing brains. The American Academy of Pediatrics Council on Sports Medicine and

Fitness credits exercise with producing better moods, better health, better grades, better concentration, more confidence.[9] Funny how that's exactly the point of this entire book. My goals for adults who want to increase their income are exactly the same as the proven results of exercise upon children. We all need a positive mindset, better health, better concentration (focus), and more confidence.

Think and Grow Rich never mentioned exercise (because it was written in the 1930s), but you can't think and grow rich without constant exercise for your body, mind, spirit, and soul.

I will grant you that working from home definitely makes it easier for me to get in my daily exercise. It is also a great argument for why, if at all possible, your life plan should include the ability to work from home, sooner rather than later. I constantly get up from my office chair to exercise, take a walk, walk the dog, practice yoga, swim, and play sports with my kids.

But even if you are stuck in an office, you can still stand, walk around, and be in motion as much as possible. Don't just sit at your desk. Even better, fitness equipment manufacturers now make treadmill desks.[10]

Get yourself a treadmill desk for your office, even if you have to buy it yourself (knowing that long periods of sitting at your desk, or typing on your computer, shortens your life). Can you imagine the difference if you replace sitting all day doing your work ... with walking all day doing the exact same work on a treadmill! You shouldn't wait for your boss to buy a treadmill desk for you (you might be waiting forever). That purchase is an investment in your health and lifespan.

When I say I exercise every day, I mean *every day*. And you must, too. Your body requires motion every day, 365 days per year. That includes birthdays, holidays, and even vacations. It is actually easier to exercise on those days, because your workload is not as heavy. It's all about attitude— a positive, relentless mindset. Is the glass half empty, or half full?

You have a choice. You can say, "It's the weekend. I'm off work. I'm not going to ruin a perfectly good day by exercising." Or you can say,

"Wow. How lucky am I? It's the weekend. I have an extra eight hours for myself today. No work 9 to 5 today. Those eight hours are mine. So I can work out two hours and still have six extra hours left to enjoy myself. What a bonus. What a GREAT day!" The choice is yours.

You know by now which attitude I choose. I choose 60 minutes of aerobic exercise (treadmill, bike, elliptical, rower); 30 minutes of weight training; a 45-minute walk; plus 15 minutes of yoga. That's 2 hours and 30 minutes of exercise on weekends, holidays, or vacation days. Does that sound like a lot to you? I work 12 to 16 hours on a normal workday. So that leaves me with 9.5 to 13.5 hours of *extra* time on my hands on weekends, holidays, or vacation days! That's 9.5 to 13.5 hours of pure freedom and fun. Do I really need to goof off the entire time? I believe some part of every day needs to be dedicated to relentless body, mind, spirit, and soul.

Once you get in the habit of daily exercise you will find both your body and your mind crave it. For those of you who are not already regular daily exercise addicts, I can assure you that once you have broken through the first couple of weeks of mental (more than physical) resistance, you will look forward to regular daily exercise for the rest of your life.

One of my heroes is Jack LaLanne. Jack was the first famous exercise guru on television in the 50s and 60s. I had the great pleasure of meeting and interviewing Jack for a magazine article when he was in his mid-eighties. That led to me interviewing Jack for an entire one-hour TV show on Financial News Network (now CNBC). I asked Jack about his current level of physical fitness. He looked at me and smiled. Then he grasped the arms of the chair he was sitting in and lifted his body from the chair. Then, holding his legs straight out like you see a gymnast do on the parallel bars, he swung them effortlessly to the left and right a couple of times before easing himself back into his chair.

"I used to be able to do that," he said with a sly smile. "But, of course, at my age I can't do it any longer."

How can anyone not fall in love with a man with that kind of spirit? Jack stayed relentlessly committed to exercise and keeping his body in great shape for his entire life. Of course that didn't just lead to a better quality of life. Jack proved physical fitness leads to financial success too. His TV infomercials earned hundreds of millions of dollars—with Jack as host between eighty and ninety years old. That's The Power of RELENTLESS.

I feel different on days when I don't exercise. Scientific research has proven why. Psychiatrist John Ratey from Harvard Medical School has reported that daily exercise reverses the detrimental effects of stress. According to his studies, exercise works on a cellular level to reverse stress's acceleration of the aging process and lifts depression as effectively as anti-depressants. Dr. Ratey proved exercise also makes you happier and smarter.[11]

Mounds of scientific research now prove that exercise results in the release of endorphins in the body, thereby making you feel happy and think positive. This used to be called a "runner's high." Today it is scientifically proven that exercise leaves you feeling euphoric.[12]

Many other positive effects of exercise have been shown, including increased self-esteem and body image (you simply feel good about yourself). But the most amazing news of all is that exercise creates new brain cells and improves learning skills. It literally makes your brain bigger![13]

In other words, exercise makes you smarter. The old stereotype about the "dumb jock" is absolutely false. My old friend Jack LaLanne was right in preaching the amazing benefits of exercise. The reality is those who don't exercise are the dumb ones! Exercise gives you a shot at growing smarter as you grow older.

From my personal experience, I can assure you regular exercise is a key component to my being relentless and achieving success in business and life. Exercise gives you the confidence to go beyond mental as well as physical pain, beyond the place where most people give up. That's the benefit you'll never find in these medical or scientific studies. Every day I struggle with weights, or jogging on the treadmill. I want to quit. My mind screams at me to quit. But I don't. I force myself to go beyond the pain, beyond the will to give up. That success gives me the confidence to be relentless in the business world, to work longer hours, to stay positive and keep going after I hear "NO." What I'm saying is, exercise fuels The Power of RELENTLESS.

One last thing important to remember about physical exercise is to combine both aerobic exercise (like running) with weightlifting. Another Harvard study showed that while weight training was surprisingly more effective for weight loss and keeping your stomach trim than running or cycling, combining *both* is best.[14]

If you are not already a daily exerciser, start today. Tomorrow may be too late ... for your health ... for your length of life ... for your confidence ... for your brainpower ... for your ability to push beyond the comfort zone in business ... for your relentlessness.

I exercise daily, including weekends, holidays, and even vacations. I'm always in motion. Naturally, working from home makes this easier. Not only do I have a home gym, but I also schedule my day to specifically include time to do my morning walk, walk the dog throughout the day, play football with my boys, and practice yoga. I know that I feel different on those few days in the year when my travel and schedule prevents me from getting in all the exercise I normally do throughout each day.

If you are unable to work at home, or fit a full-scale home gym there, you can still have a piece or two of exercise equipment positioned in front of the TV. Better yet, get yourself a treadmill desk at the office. It doesn't matter how you do it—as Nike says, *JUST DO IT!*

While I believe it is important to include both weight and aerobic training in your exercise schedule (I'll report on studies involving both below), I am also a firm believer in yoga. Yoga takes you beyond exercise. Yoga is a kind of *out-of-body* experience.

Yoga is an ancient mind-body discipline that originated in India over four thousand years ago. I've been practicing it since I graduated college. That means I've been doing yoga for over thirty years!

Yoga brings together physical and mental discipline to achieve peace of body *and* mind. This form of exercise helps you to manage stress and anxiety. What was once a niche practice has now become mainstream in America: according to a survey in 2008 by *Yoga Journal*, more than 15 million U.S. adults practice yoga.[15]

Not surprisingly, there is serious scientific research supporting yoga's physical benefits as well.

The American Psychological Association reports that studies show the practice of yoga—which combines stretching and other exercises with deep breathing and meditation—can improve overall physical fitness, strength, flexibility and lung capacity, while reducing heart rate, blood pressure and back pain.[16]

What is perhaps unknown to those who consider yoga "just another form of exercise" is that there is a growing body of research documenting yoga's psychological benefits.

Several recent studies suggest that yoga may help strengthen "social attachments" (meaning it helps you build better relationships); reduce stress; and relieve anxiety, depression, and insomnia.[17]

Researchers arc also starting to see proof that yoga is crucial in helping both active-duty military and military veterans relieve the symptoms of Post Traumatic Stress Disorder. A combined Harvard–Brigham Young study showed that yoga eases PTSD symptoms in combat veterans.[18]

Now to my personal testimony.

I started doing yoga in 1983. By the following year I was involved in the most stressful business deal of my young life (to this day it's one of the top five most stressful ever). The stress and anxiety were overwhelming. Yoga saved the day for me. I not only survived under intense pressure, I actually *thrived*. I never felt better in my life. I credit yoga with saving me from emotional ruin.

That started a pattern. I've used yoga, as well as meditation, prayer, morning walks, and intense daily workouts in the gym to get me through even the worst of stress and doubt (as well as to instantly reverse depression). Yoga has saved me again and again for over thirty years. Yes, it's physical exercise. Yet for me, its best results are mental. After I do yoga, I feel like I can take on the world. Bad news and negative thoughts are erased and I'm in a great mood. Worry and fear are neutralized. Depression is eradicated. Yoga is like sunshine for me. No matter how bad or negative or depressed I feel when I start, yoga releases endorphins and quickly leaves me feeling like a million bucks!

If you are going to be RELENTLESS, you must be in top physical and mental condition. Physical fitness, including yoga, is a key component to maintaining your "peak fighting condition."

POSITIVE ADDICTION #7: RELENTLESS HEALTHY DIET

Back in the hippie days of the 1960s the saying was born, "Your body is your temple." It turns out the hippies were right! What you put into your body doesn't just sustain your physical body, it also feeds your mind, spirit, and soul. So a healthy, holistic, nutritious diet is the "Positive Addiction" that *feeds* your success.

The latest "World Cancer Report" issued by the World Health Organization predicts a cancer EPIDEMIC. It predicts cancer will rise by 57% worldwide over the next two decades. The WHO calls this "an imminent human disaster."[1]

There are two components to this disaster. The first is the number of sick and dying. What a terrible waste of human life. What terrible unnecessary suffering.

The second component is the cost to society and governments around the world. This cancer epidemic is simply unaffordable. It threatens to bankrupt economies across the globe. As of 2010 (the latest figures) the cost of cancer treatments worldwide was $1.16 trillion per year. You can bet by this year that number is over $1.5 trillion. Now add in a 57 percent increase in cancers and the runaway inflation of healthcare costs. My educated guess is soon the world will be spending $2 to $3 trillion annually to deal with cancer alone. This is a budget buster.

Yet the report also contains good news: half of all cancers are preventable. The World Health Organization says, "We cannot treat our way out of this problem." The WHO reports four simple changes can dramatically prevent and reduce cancer:

- Improved Diet
- Increased Exercise
- Quit Smoking
- Reduce Alcohol Consumption

All are part of my "Positive Addictions" program. It's that simple. Put good things into your body, exercise your body, eliminate the bad things … and like a computer, what goes in, will come out. Program a computer with good information, good results come out. Put good stuff into your body, nourish your body, and your mind will produce positive thought and creative ideas. That's how you "Think and grow rich."

Unfortunately, cancer is not the only epidemic we are facing. Diabetes and obesity caused by sugar may be just as costly. Let's look at the latest research.

Scientific studies report that soda is even worse for your health than *cigarettes*.[2] Obesity caused by junk food and sugar is a worse threat to kids than cigarettes.[3]

Limiting sugar is the key to anti-aging and disease prevention. Researchers are coming to the conclusion that sugar is pure poison. It's like pouring sugar into your car engine. Bad stuff in, bad results. Your car won't run on sugar. Except in this case, the human body is so amazing it continues to run. However, you get sicker and sicker. Your mind gets foggy. Your energy dissipates. Your health breaks down.[4]

Drinking soda dramatically accelerates aging, according to scientists at University of San Francisco. Over five thousand people were studied. Less than two cans of soda per day increases aging by 4.6 years.[5]

Researchers are also warning that pesticides in our food are a major health threat. Skyrocketing depression rates are linked to the pesticides in our food.[6]

So the answers are pretty simple. Stop smoking and drinking, cut out soda, reduce sugar dramatically, eliminate junk and fast food, and eat organic (to avoid pesticides) whenever possible. Your odds of living a long, healthy, and prosperous life just increased dramatically!

The bonus is, if you look and feel healthy and have lots of energy, focus, and confidence, you'll find it much easier to be relentless and successful in your business and financial life.

It is not just important that you adopt these "Positive Addictions" for yourself. It is just as important that you ensure your entire family adopts a healthy diet and lifestyle. Again, more proven studies and facts:

A new UK study of over 11,000 fifth- and eighth-grade students indicates eating junk food reduces IQ. The more junk food children eat, the lower their IQ goes. Once again, bad stuff in, bad results.[7] A new Ohio State study reported the more junk food kids ate the lower their test scores go. It showed a 20 percent reduction in grades for those who ate the highest levels of junk food.[8]

THINK. If junk food reduces IQ and performance for children, what does it do to you? What is it doing to your career? Your looks? Your energy? Your ability to project confidence and charisma? Your sex life? Your ability to be relentless in the face of challenge and adversity?

As always, I have my own personal dietary success to share with you. I'm not a MD or scientist. I'm not advising you what to eat. I'm merely sharing a way of eating and living that has worked wonders for me. My diet is divided into "home and away."

DIET AT HOME

My diet at home is a high-protein, low-carb, gluten-free, ketogenic diet.[9] It is often called a paleo or caveman diet. Look it up. It is rich in protein (meat, chicken, turkey, fish) combined with brown rice, beans, vegetables, and fruit.

But there is a catch. When it comes to meat, although I eat about 80 percent chicken and turkey, the 20 percent that is red meat is a particular kind of red meat ...

I eat 100 percent grass-fed beef. Cattle raised on grass is completely different from the grain-fed beef you buy at the local supermarket. It is even far superior to organic meats. Grass-fed beef is now carried nation-wide at every Whole Foods supermarket.[10] You can also find grass-fed meat at gourmet markets or butcher stores. Or you can buy it online at a grass-fed beef monthly buyers club.[11]

The flavor and texture of grass-fed beef is far superior; it's as tender as butter. But most importantly, grass-fed beef is dramatically higher in Omega 3s and CLA (Conjugated Linoleic Acid). When cattle feed on grass-only diets, CLA levels are three to five times higher than grain-fed diets.[12] These Omega 3s and CLA have health benefits such as enhancing the immune system, increasing good cholesterol, lowering bad cholesterol and triglycerides, reducing inflammation, lowering insulin resistance, and lowering blood pressure. But here's the really amazing part: grass-fed beef lowers body fat and increases lean muscle tissue.[13]

A study published in the *American Journal of Clinical Nutrition* found that people who ingested 3.2 grams of CLA a day lost about 0.2 pounds of body fat per week (about one pound a month). No exercise was involved.[14]

That's a loss of twelve pounds per year just by eating delicious high-protein, grass-fed meat, WITHOUT exercising! So I guess you could say my body is a high-protein, grass-fed temple!

And like beef labeled as "organic," most grass-fed cattle are raised "free-range" on grasslands with limited pesticides, fertilizers, antibiotics, hormones, or growth stimulants, and will never see the inside of a feedlot.

MY DIET WHEN EATING OUT

I'm not a monk. I'm a businessman. I live in the real world. So it's impossible to live a perfect life. I am forced to eat out constantly for business lunches and dinners. So I had to figure out a way to eat healthy while dining out. When I eat out at restaurants, my body is more like an "Asian Temple." My away-from-home diet is primarily Asian food: Chinese, Thai, Vietnamese, or sushi. Just chicken, beef, or raw fish with veggies and occasional brown rice or rice noodles (all non-gluten).

Rarely do you see an obese Asian person...not in Japan...not in Thailand...not in Vietnam...not in China. Also, did you know that the instance of diabetes, cancer, and heart disease is much lower in Asian countries...at least until an American diet is introduced? Once Asians start eating fast food, junk food, and fried food, their levels of obesity and diabetes skyrocket (just like in America).[15]

It's not the quantity of food, it's the *quality*. Like me, do you like to eat a lot of food? I like to eat! Then eat a primarily protein-based, non-gluten diet (very little bread, cakes, donuts, pasta, or pizza), combined with an Asian diet with very few grains or carbs.

The latest science agrees that this is the way to dramatically reduce the odds of disease and death. But my motives are more financial than health-related.

This book isn't a health book. It's a success and wealth book. You're reading this book because you want to achieve wealth and financial freedom. The diet I just described above will leave you lighter, healthier, and high-energy from morning to night. I'm literally never tired. I never "lose steam." And I rarely ever get sick. When I do catch a cold, it's so minor I've never missed a full day of work because of illness in my life.

Health leads to wealth. Feeling positive and having perfect health are central to The Power of RELENTLESS. You can't be relentless if you're sick. You can't be relentless if you're overweight. You can't be relentless if you're low-energy. You can't be relentless if you're negative and lacking in confidence.

So in fact your body is your temple. Put a healthy holistic diet into your body... you'll get prosperity and positivity out! This is how you "Eat and grow rich."

POSITIVE ADDICTION #8: RELENTLESS VITAMINS AND NUTRITION

Now let me turn to one of the most important aspects of good nutrition: vitamin supplementation. My brand—what I'm known for—is ENERGY. If you've ever heard me speak you'll know why. "Time Management" is a concept of the 1980s. Today, I believe the key to success is "Energy Management."

I speak about energy management all over the world. Energy is the most valuable commodity of the business world! Everyone wants energy. If you have it, everyone wants to do business with you. They want to befriend you. They want to become your business partner. They even want to date you. They want to plug their electric cord into your electrical socket! Everyone wants what you have!

I express it the following way. I call it "Root's Theorem For Success."

Energy Makes Things Happen.

Energy Gets You Noticed and Makes You Stand Out in a Crowd.

Energy = Friends and Relationships.

Energy = People Want to Be Around You.

Energy = Others Want What You Have.

Energy = Opportunity and Success.

People born with the genetic energy level required to reach mega success are few and far between. But it can be taught. And even if you think you are one of those rare high-energy individuals, I am here to teach you how to have even more energy than you've ever experienced before in your life. The way to start generating that energy is to have the perfect combination of vitamins, minerals, herbs, essential fatty acids, and excellent nutrition.

I promised to be detailed and specific in how to implement these "Positive Addictions" into your life. That said, the following list below is the combination of vitamins and nutrients (the core of my health regimen) that I believe is responsible for my world-class levels of energy.

Note that everybody is different. I'm not an MD, and I and don't claim to be. I'm not prescribing vitamins. I'm a "Human Energizer Bunny" who is merely showing you the exact vitamin regimen that has worked fantastically for me. Everywhere I go in the world, I am asked the same question: "Where do you get that amazing energy, enthusiasm, health, and vitality? I want whatever you are taking. Please tell me!"

My answer is this regimen of vitamins and nutrients below. The rest is up to you. You may want to (slowly over time) try all of these vitamins and nutrients, to find out what works for you. You may want to take only a few. Or you may find only one that is right for you. If you add just one vitamin and dramatically improve your health and energy level, I've done my job!

You should consult your doctor if you have any diseases, or health concerns, or take any prescription drugs. I'm leaving the decisions up to you. But I am giving you the exact vitamin regimen that changed my life. It took me thirty years to find the perfect combination and the right brands. I'm giving all of that to you right here—for free. *This alone is worth the price of admission!*

FOR ANTI-AGING (IF YOU WANT TO MAKE MONEY, YOU BETTER STAY YOUNG!):

- Finiti—from Jeunesse
- AM & PM Essentials—from Jeunesse
- Reserve Antioxident Gel—from Jeunesse
- Luminesce—from Jeunesse

FOR PERFECT HEALTH AND IMMUNE BOOST:

- MultiVitamin Formula—this is very important. I use one specific brand: "Six Daily Advanced" by DrVita.com
- Vitamin C with quercetin and bioflavonoids (my favorite brand is Ester C)
- Vitamin D3
- Omega 3 Fish Oil
- Coenzyme Q10
- Turmeric (found at Costco.com under Nature's Lab brand—created by DrVita)
- Vitamin E
- Selenium
- Multi-Probiotic
- Garlic (the brand I take is Kyolic)
- Zinc
- Collodial Silver (immune, anti-viral)
- Aloe Vera Juice (supports digestion)
- Green Tea standardized for 45–50 percent EGCG (the equivalent of 5–7 cups is in "Six Daily Advanced" by DrVita)
- Biocell Collagen with MSM (Found at Costco.com under the Nature's Lab brand—created by DrVita)

FOR THE BRAIN:

- Magtein (magnesium for maximum brain absorption)

FOR ENERGY:

- Chlorella—single-cell green algae (the brand I take is Sun Chlorella A)
- Max One Riboceine (found at Max.com)
- Ginseng (Sibergin—the most effective brand of Siberian Ginseng)
- R-Alpha Lipoic Acid
- L Acetyl Cysteine
- Resveratrol Plus (foung at Costco.com under Trunature brand—created by DrVita)
- Octacosanol
- 7-Keto (for healthy hormone support and weight loss via burning fat while maintaining muscle)
- Olive Leaf extract (immune, anti-viral)

I've been practicing a vitamin supplementation regimen my entire adult life. I start every day with a walk in the sunshine (thereby filling my body with natural Vitamin D); eat a natural, holistic, and whenever possible organic diet; supplement with the right vitamins (including mega doses of Vitamin C); exercise 1 to 2 hours every day (7 days per week), don't smoke, don't drink, don't use drugs, and don't eat junk food or fast food.

Now add in the other POSITIVE ADDICTIONS that you are just now reading about in this section of my book: meditation, prayer, yoga, affirmation, visualization, and positive thinking; and the result is that I'm rarely ever sick; have never been seriously ill in my life; have never missed a full day of work because of illness in my life; have incredible levels of energy from morning until night; put in 16-hour days; run multiple businesses; give speeches all over the world; do 20 to 30 media interviews per week; write books; write 2 to 3 commentaries every week; produce TV shows; serve on multiple boards of directors; serve as spokesman for multiple national and international companies; and co-manage a family of four children ranging in age from seven to twenty-three.

I owe my success to my personal "fountain of youth"—***vitamins!***

Vitamins changed my life. Without vitamins, I would not be the success authority I am today. Without vitamins, you wouldn't be reading this book.

MY PERSONAL STORY: HOW VITAMINS SAVED AND CHANGED MY LIFE

I started out the pale skinny kid with glasses, braces, and acne, who was beaten up ten times a day at my rough inner city high school. I was chased home from school by bullies almost every day. I ran for my life. And these were no idle threats. Kids carried knives and guns at my rough urban high school. Kids were beaten, robbed, mugged, assaulted, and threatened every day. I was so scared, I didn't even want to go to school anymore.

One summer I changed all that. I read up on vitamins, nutrition, and healthy diet. I changed my eating habits, started taking mega doses of vitamins, bought a weight set, lifted weights all summer, and took boxing lessons. I tanned in the sun every day. I replaced my glasses with contact lenses. With my healthy diet in place, my acne disappeared. My braces came off. I felt like a million bucks.

I walked into my high school in September a new man. No one—not even my closest friends—recognized me. I had to tell them it was me. No one could believe it was me. I walked through the same halls I had cowered in before, with total confidence. No one ever picked on me again.

Author's Note: I did wind up in one more fight. It was a fight for my life. But I wasn't picked on. I became so confident, I went from a wimp being beaten up every day to a marshal (on the school police force). I caught a kid cutting class and using drugs. I told him he was coming with me to the principal's office. He spun out of my grasp and pulled a machete on me. I contend vitamins, exercise, and my faith in God kept me alive that day!

My life changed so dramatically, it was like a story out of a movie. I was elected class vice president. I took a gorgeous blonde college girl to my eleventh-grade dance. I became the coolest kid in the school. The nerdy kids came to me to ask me to protect *them* from the bullies. I relished this role. My love affair with vitamins and the way they made me feel began that summer—and it's never gone away.

Other kids smoked, drank, and took drugs. They ruined their lives. I took mega doses of vitamins and MADE my life. I've never looked back!

Energy became the brand I was known for—for the rest of my life. That energy led to successful careers in television, politics, business, books, speeches, and entrepreneurship. Always my energy (fueled by my vitamins) was at the center of my confidence and success.

I am known as the "Human Energizer Bunny." Energy is the foundation of all of my success. Everyone wants to be around people with energy. They want to plug into your energy source. Energy is one of the most valuable commodities in the world.

Where do I get my energy? While it's a synergistic effect of my entire healthy "Positive Addictions" program, the single most important piece of the puzzle is nutrition and vitamin supplementation. I plead guilty as charged—"*I am a vitamin addict!*"

I daily consume mega doses of vitamins and anti-aging nutrients. My energy comes naturally, from the vitamins and the nutrition that fuel my enthusiasm, vitality, and robust health.

I have a recommendation here:

I take anti-aging nutrients from a specific company called Jeunesse. I have become hooked on the cutting-edge, breakthrough anti-aging,

DNA-repair, and telomere support nutrients found at Jeunesse. Let me tell you about the company.

Jeunesse is a global leader in anti-aging, health, longevity, and cell renewal. This product-driven direct-selling company is devoted to encouraging its distributors and customers to look and feel younger, earn more, and enjoy life. Company research focuses on adult stem cell technology, telomere support, DNA repair, and nutrigenomics. Products are made in the USA and are exclusively formulated for Jeunesse.

With multi-lingual customer service, a back office support team, global enrollment system, and in-house programming already in place, the company is fully operational in thirty-two offices around the world. Its distribution channels extend to over 100 countries.

NutriGen™ means Nutrition in the Genomic level. Jeunesse nutritional products are not just ordinary supplements. They work both outside and inside of our cells to maximize the rejuvenating effect. These innovative products have been endorsed by world-renowned doctors and scientists such as Dr. Vincent Giampapa (regarded as the father of anti-aging medicine) and Dr. Michael Nobel, co-inventor and developer of the Magnetic Resonance Imaging (MRI) device and a co-founder and former president of the Nobel Charitable Trust.

Jeunesse products target DNA Repair and telomere maintenance and protect cells from free-radical damage.

To learn more about Jeunesse and their unique anti-aging products contact:

Website: RelentlessHealth.jeunesseglobal.com

E-mail: RelentlessHealth@Yahoo.com

PH: (888) 444-7668

Outside of Jeunesse, I buy all of my remaining key vitamin supplements from DrVita.com—the only other vitamin company I trust (because they manufacture every vitamin at their own state-of-the-art facility in Las Vegas). The founder of DrVita, Wayne Gorsek, is the most knowledgeable vitamin authority in America. I call him "Dr.

Vitamin." (And he's also known to my friends and readers as "the other Wayne.")

The DrVita website offers the highest quality vitamins in America today, at a fraction of the cost of any retail vitamin store or health food supermarket. So you're getting healthy for about half the cost!

Here is how to reach DrVita for your vitamin and nutritional needs:
PH: (800) 211-4188
Website: www.drvita.com/WAR
Due to our great friendship, Wayne Gorsek has graciously agreed to personally answer any of your nutrition questions. You can e-mail "the other Wayne" at: wayne@drvita.com

Author's Note: At the time of the writing of this book, I use the vitamins of Jeunesse and DrVita and recommend them wherever I go. Since I am the best darn product spokesman in America and I am so passionate about the value of their products, I have entered into and am in discussion to enter into further business relationships with these companies.

POSITIVE ADDICTION #9: RELENTLESS CHARITY

I may be a small businessman, but I'm a mega-successful one. And the reason why I'm successful is simple. Remember the line Steve Jobs quoted from Pablo Picasso? "Good artists copy, great artists steal." I've spent my life studying billionaires and billion-dollar multi-national corporations and how they operate. Then I try to replicate.

Here is what I discovered: The richest men and women in the world donate millions of dollars to charity as a way of life...and the biggest corporations donate to charity as a way of doing business. Charity is literally built into the DNA and the business plans of the richest people and companies.

Why? Because "doing good" is good for your community and your business too. Everyone wins. When you give away millions of dollars to charity, something amazing happens—tens of millions, or hundreds of millions of dollars come back to you! *Charity has a boomerang effect.* It makes you feel good, which gives you purpose, which gives you happiness, which gives you energy and enthusiasm, which makes you or your products attractive to others. That's why when you give, it comes back to you times ten, or one hundred, or one thousand.

Trust me, corporations—especially billion-dollar ones—first and foremost care about themselves and their bottom line. Most public CEOs would sell out their mother for a more profitable quarter to report to stockholders. So if they are giving millions of dollars to charity, you can bet it's good for business; it's good for employee morale; it's good for their brand; and it's good for profits. If it wasn't, they wouldn't do it.

The NFL is a multi-billion dollar brand—one of the world's most valuable. Branding is all about image. That's why this macho sports league ties their name to "Breast Cancer Awareness Month" for one month each year and orders NFL players to wear pink.[1]

The NFL wears pink for one simple reason—because charity is good for the bottom line. Is this about greed or doing good? Who cares? Everyone wins. If the cause of breast cancer prevention and treatment winds up with an extra $250 million, does it matter why? If 10,000 women live because this money extended their lives, does it matter why the NFL raised the money?

How about the National Hockey League? Here in Las Vegas, as I write this book, a billionaire named Bill Foley is trying to bring an NHL franchise to Las Vegas. It looks like he'll be successful. But as I write this book, it's still only a goal…a wish list. No team has been approved by the NHL yet. But charity is so important to this deal, billionaire Foley has already tied his future team (that doesn't exist yet) to a Las Vegas charity called "Opportunity Village."[2]

To get the new franchise approved by the NHL, Foley needs to get 10,000 season tickets sold. That's the requirement the NHL set. Well, Foley has agreed to donate $1 for each ticket sold in the team's first year to "Opportunity Village," a charity for people with intellectual disabilities. In the interest of disclosure, "Opportunity Village" is a favorite local charity of mine too. I wrote a $5,000 check to them last year.

But this story proves how important charity is to brilliant billionaire businessmen like Bill Foley. Las Vegas doesn't even have a team yet, but the charity is already in place. Why? Because image is everything in business. Companies want to create "goodwill" in the community. That makes people like you. That makes people feel positive when they see or hear your company's name. And if they like you, they'll buy what you're selling.

Is the charity tie-in good for Foley's new team? Sure. First the announcement of his charity donation made news headlines. That positive publicity will make more people buy season tickets. "Opportunity Village" even agreed to help promote ticket sales to its donors and friends. So Foley got free promotion in the media, as well as community goodwill. But Opportunity Village stands to make $717,500 the first year of this deal (and quite possibly that much or more money every year moving forward). Everyone wins.

What other major companies give to charity? *All of them do.* Here are just a few examples from publicly listed information. Kroger supermarket chain gave away over $60 million to charity (in the last year of public disclosure). Safeway supermarkets gave over $70 million. Macy's department store gave over $40 million (plus they throw one heck of a Thanksgiving parade for kids). Morgan Stanley gave over $50 million. Bank of America gave over $200 million. So did Wells Fargo. So did ExxonMobil. Goldman Sachs gave over $350 million. And Walmart gave over half a billion in a two-year period.[3]

Other companies donating collectively billions to charity through their charitable foundations include Coca-Cola, GE, Intel, Johnson & Johnson, UPS, MetLife, Merck, Verizon, Google, Pepsi, IBM, and 3M.[4]

Why do these billion-dollar multi-national companies choose to give millions of dollars away to charity? Because charity is good for image, branding, media promotion, and "goodwill." And it's also tax deductible. In other words, charitable giving is good for business *and* healthy for the bottom line.

Trust me, nothing Bill Gates, Warren Buffett, or Richard Branson does is just for charity. There's always a profit motive. But who cares? As long as charities receive billions, the world is a better place. *Everyone wins.*

Small business owners and independent contractors (like you) should follow the same business model. You need to tie your business, career, and product to charity too. If Coca-Cola does it, you <u>know</u> it's smart.

If you want to be successful, do as the "big boys" do. Promote your tie-ins and donations to the media—just like Coca-Cola does. Tie your donation into your promotion of products—just like Coca-Cola does. Send out promotions to your database trumpeting your favorite charity and how much you've raised for the cause. Put it on your business cards and advertisements. Your brand should become synonymous with charity.

There are three ways to donate to charity. The first way is simple: write a check. The second is to volunteer time to a good cause. The third is to influence and inspire others to do the same—your friends, clients, customers, employees, business partners.

I'm sure cynics will say how awful it is that I'm recommending publicizing your good deeds. They are wrong. First, times have changed. This is 2015. No one is afraid to toot their own horn. Billion-dollar companies all scream from the highest rooftops about their charitable giving, why shouldn't you? Everyone at the highest levels of business understands that if a tree falls in the forest and no one witnessed it falling, *it never fell.*

Secondly, promoting your good deeds is not only good for your business or career, it's also good for the charity you are helping. If you donate in silence, no one else would be inspired or "guilted" into doing the same. The more people who find out about your charitable good deeds...the more others will be inspired to do the same...the more ultra-competitive people will be inspired to give even more than you...the more the charity will benefit...and the more people in need will be helped. As you promote your good deeds, the charity is branded.

Finally, let's say that by bragging about your charitable giving, your business dramatically increases (which it will). If you tithe (donate 10 percent of your income) then charity benefits! Your personal giving will *double*. So you personally give the charity $50,000 instead of $25,000. So tell me again why I should be shy and humble about my good deeds?

Everyone wins when you use your business to help charity. Donating to charity is the definition of the saying, "It's a win-win." That's why RELENTLESS CHARITY is one of my daily Positive Addictions.

Two charities that are of special significance to me are listed below. I hope if you enjoy this book, you'll make a contribution to my favorite charities:

Camp Soaring Eagle in Sedona, Arizona. This charity provides the healing power of laughter to thousands of seriously ill children by giving them the opportunity to go to a medically supervised camp at no cost to the campers and their families.

You can donate at:

www.CampSoaringEagle.org

The Rainbow Centre in Burundi, Africa. This charity is a Christian ministry in Burundi, Africa, whose mission is to provide care, treatment and safe keeping of orphaned, abandoned, and HIV positive babies. The ministry was started in 2001 and continues to grow and expand as God blesses and leads.

You can donate at:

http://www.rainbowcentre.net

POSITIVE ADDICTION #10: RELENTLESS INSPIRATION AND EMPOWERMENT

No matter how positive or relentless you are, we all need inspiration now and then. We all need a kick in the pants. We all need a spark, a burst of energy. We all need to supercharge our vision of success. You must set aside time to read and watch and listen to inspiring stories. It's just a necessary part of doing business. We all need to put fuel in the tank from time to time—otherwise we're running on empty.

We all must set aside time to improve ourselves, educate ourselves, empower ourselves, and inspire ourselves. How do you do that? By reading, listening to, or watching stories of great people who made their dreams come true.

Read. I recommend reading books or listening to audio books about great business, political, and military leaders. These stories will inspire and motivate you to do great things. They will also keep you motivated, committed, and relentless when the going gets tough. They'll inspire you to be creative when facing failure—and give you ideas for turning lemons into lemonade.

Read Bios. I credit the biography of a great Hollywood movie tycoon with giving me the courage and kick in the pants to leave a dream job at Financial News Network to start my own business. That was the scariest decision of my life, and when I look back I still can't believe I did it! If I hadn't read that book, I never would have found the courage.

Don't give me the excuse that you have no time to read books. That's nonsense. I'm one of the busiest men in the world and I still find time to read five to ten books per year—mostly while on airplanes.

Read *Forbes* and the *Wall Street Journal*. I also read business publications on a regular basis. I'd recommend two in particular: *Forbes* and the *Wall Street Journal*. I read *Forbes* every month and the *Wall Street Journal* every day. They are the Bibles of business. The ideas in the *WSJ* and *Forbes* aren't just valuable, they are *priceless*. On a side note, Steve Forbes has become a friend of mine. When you meet a brilliant and fine human being like Steve, you suddenly understand why his magazine is the #1 arbiter of "success" in the world. He is among the smartest and classiest CEOs I've ever met in my life. Steve Forbes defines more than success and wealth. *He defines class.*

When it comes to *Forbes* and the *Wall Street Journal*, you're either staying up to date with business trends, or you're being left behind.

As far as politics (the love and passion of my life), most of my best political and economic ideas and opinions have been formed from reading the editorial page of the *Wall Street Journal* for the past thirty plus years. I met a wealthy CEO when I was in college. He gave me one piece of advice. He said, "For the rest of your life, be sure you read the editorial page of the *Wall Street Journal* every single day. Make those opinions your opinions. Follow those opinions and you will attain wealth and success." As President Calvin Coolidge once said, "The business of America is business."

Attend. I recommend attending business events dedicated to success and motivation several times per year. Yes, some might seem a bit on the "hokey" side. But you need the excitement and motivation these events produce. You will return home inspired, with a refreshed outlook on life and a kick in the pants. I'd choose an overly enthusiastic employee every time over one who is too intellectual and cynical to get excited about what we're selling.

Watch. I recommend watching DVDs and webinars dedicated to teaching you traits and skills that lead to success. We can all learn something new every day.

Surf. I recommend surfing websites dedicated to success, and taking online education courses.

The *Robb*. Finally, I recommend one specific monthly magazine—the *Robb Report*. The *Robb* is *the* magazine for the super wealthy and successful people of the world—and more importantly, for those who want to become super wealthy. It features articles, stories, bios, and advertisements that will inspire you to greatness. Almost every single photo I have cut out to paste in my "dream book" photo album for the past thirty years has come from *The Robb*. This amazing magazine has been my inspiration since I was a kid without two cents to my name.

The point of this "Positive Addiction" is nonstop immersion in success…positivity…inspiring stories…and creative ideas that you can use to empower your career or business. As long as you live, you can and should aim to relentlessly educate, empower, improve, and inspire.

If you do stop, and your competition keeps learning new tricks, you've just lost the battle.

Here are just a few of my favorite books of all time—that will inspire, empower, and motivate you to greater heights:

Think and Grow Rich by Napoleon Hill
The Law of Success by Napoleon Hill
The Power of Positive Thinking by Norman Vincent Peale
Enthusiasm Makes the Difference by Norman Vincent Peale
The Secret by Rhonda Byrne
Billy Graham: Just As I Am by Billy Graham

Billy Graham: His Life and Influence by David Aikman

My Journey: From an Iowa Farm to a Cathedral of Dreams by the Reverend Robert H. Schuller

If It's Going to Be, It's Up to Me: The Eight Proven Principles of Possibility Thinking by the Reverend Robert H. Schuller

How to Win Friends and Influence People by Dale Carnegie

The Conscience of a Conservative by Barry Goldwater

Jesus, CEO: Using Ancient Wisdom for Visionary Leadership by Laurie Beth Jones

Moses on Management: 50 Leadership Lessons from the Greatest Manager of All Time by David Baron

The Art of War by Sun Tzu

Fighter Boys: Saving Britain 1940 by David Bishop

Joshua Chamberlain—A Hero's Life and Legacy by John J. Pullen

The Real Custer: From Boy General to Tragic Hero by James S. Robbins

General Patton's Principles for Life and Leadership by Porter B. Williamson

Robert E. Lee on Leadership by H.W. Crocker III

Cavalryman of the Lost Cause: A Biography of J.E.B. Stuart by Jeffry D. Wert

The Magic of Thinking Big by David Schwartz

Reinventing You: The 10 Best Ways to Launch Your Dream Career by Lisa Lockwood

The Secrets of Closing the Sale by Zig Ziglar

The Greatest Salesman in the World by Og Mandino

An American Life: Ronald Reagan by Ronald Reagan

Reagan on Leadership: Executive Lessons from the Great Communicator by James M. Strock

Benedict Arnold, Revolutionary Hero: An American Warrior Reconsidered by James Martin

Washington's Crossing by David Hackett Fischer

Churchill: A Biography by Roy Jenkins

Churchill on Leadership by Steven Hayward

Long Walk to Freedom: The Autobiography of Nelson Mandela by Nelson Mandela

Running Scared: The Life and Treacherous Times of Las Vegas Casino King Steve Wynn by John L. Smith

Unbroken by Laura Hillenbrand

Money: Master the Game by Tony Robbins

One shameless plug...

The Murder of the Middle Class and *The Ultimate Obama Survival Guide* by Wayne Allyn Root (yours truly)

And of course...

The Holy Bible

POSITIVE ADDICTION #11: RELENTLESS SMILING AND SAYING YES

Smiling wins political elections. Smiling is also the foundation of communication in general. No matter what you're selling, a smile sells it better! A study from Penn State University showed that when you're smiling, other people see you as more "likeable, courteous and competent."[1]

If you're giving a speech, it will be received better if you're smiling. If you're selling real estate or insurance, a smile will help close the deal. If you're a high school teacher, a smile will help you sell American history or algebra. If you own a plumbing company, a smile will help you sell a new commercial client. If you're a cop, a smile might diffuse a bad situation. If you're a mom, a smile will make you a better parent.

And a smile will also help you find and master your inner self. A smile versus a frown tells your brain that you are happy. The latest research shows that smiling re-wires your brain to be more positive and optimistic.[2]

It also tells the person you are communicating with that you are a nice person. That makes them like you. The latest research shows that it's hard for others to frown when looking at a person smiling. So by smiling, you are making other people happy too, which in turn makes you happier and more secure. A nice smile changes your attitude…changes the attitude of the people you're doing business with…and changes your day for the better. It's all about SYNERGY.

So smiling is an important addiction.

And smiling goes hand in hand with one word: "YES!"

I have already told you how I always say yes whenever humanly possible.

One "YES" has the power to change your life. To find that one "YES," start by being a "YES" person yourself.

Just like a smile, saying "YES" makes other people's day. "YES" makes them happy. "YES" makes them smile. "YES" makes them like you.

A "YES PERSON" will be the last one fired in a bad economy. A "YES PERSON" will close on more deals as a salesman—whether selling aluminum siding, cars, stocks, or $10 million mansions.

Opportunity often comes with many unknowns—the risk of failure, or additional time and work. The easy thing to do, the low-risk thing, is to say "No." "YES" can get you in trouble (if things go terribly wrong). But there's no risk of losing your job for saying "NO." That's why most people take the easy way out, by always saying "NO." That's why most lawyers say "NO" to every deal they are presented. They see no downside to saying "NO." Nothing bad can happen if you don't take a risk, right? You are avoiding disaster.

Wrong! That's why I decided against going to law school. Being a lawyer depressed me. I knew I wanted to be a positive person. A cheerleader. A "YES MAN!" The people who say "YES" get the job…keep the job…get the date…get the marriage proposal…get the partnership…win the election…land the CEO suite.

By always saying "YES" you are keeping yourself in a position to take advantage of opportunities that may only come along once. The truth is that more billions of dollars have been lost through missed opportunities because of "NO" than any other word in the world. "NO" shuts you out of the ballgame. The truth is there is zero chance of success by saying "NO." The only chance is to say "YES." Opportunity is tied to the word "YES."

"YES" is all about taking a risk. And risk-takers are respected and rewarded in life. When you say "YES," other people (who are too frightened to take the risks necessary to succeed) see you as a swashbuckler, a riverboat gambler, a gunslinger, a Wild West hero. You're like the sheriff facing down the bad guys at "the OK Corral." Everyone wishes they could be that guy. Everyone wishes they had that kind of courage. Everyone wishes they could be the hero. And the hero always wins the beautiful girl!

If you smile and say "YES" at every available opportunity, I can assure you that your life will change dramatically for the better. So screw the lawyers and their favorite word "NO." The world would be a better place without the negativity and fear of lawyers. The world needs a few heroes. So say "YES" with me now. "YES!"

And for the rest of your life always ask yourself an important question every time you are presented an opportunity and are about to say "NO." Instead ask yourself "How could I say YES to this offer? There has to be a creative way to say 'YES' and turn this into a win-win situation." And of course, smile while you are asking yourself that question.

POSITIVE ADDICTION #12: RELENTLESS MOTION

My entire Positive Addictions Program is dedicated to turning you into a super-achiever. What defeats and destroys success and achievement for most people? Four things:

- Doubt
- Fear
- Stress
- Depression

Not coincidently, those are the same four things that destroy positive thinking. And of course, as we've already hammered home again and again, positive thinking is the foundation of all success and achievement.

Not coincidently, those are the same four things that kill confidence. And of course, confidence (a.k.a. faith) is absolutely necessary to harness The Power of RELENTLESS when you get smashed in the face.

So what is the antidote to doubt, fear, stress, and depression? MOTION.

And not just any motion, but rather something specific: RELENTLESS MOTION.

In a nutshell, that's what this entire book is about. Whether it's **mental motion** (prayer, meditation, affirmation, visualization, goals, etc.) ...

Or **physical motion** (morning walk, yoga, fitness training, weight training, etc.) ...

Or **financial motion** (hunting, hitting, pitching, hooking, hammering, hounding, filling your pipeline, following up, etc).

The point is that the way to counter stress, negativity, doubt, fear and depression is to always be in RELENTLESS MOTION! Sometimes it's mental motion, sometimes it's physical motion, sometimes it's financial motion, but the point is ... *you gotta keep moving to win!*

Each of my seven PRINCIPLES OF RELENTLESS and twelve POSITIVE ADDICTIONS is crucial to your success. It is the synergy of all of them together that is so powerful. I could not subtract one of them. They each have a crucial role. But this "addiction" is the final and crowning one for a reason. I always save the best for last. In the end everything I teach comes down to motion. Each of these twelve Positive Addictions comes down to motion. The Power of RELENTLESS comes down to motion.

If you're sleeping, *you're losing ground.* Sleep after you're dead. There's plenty of time for that.

If you're sitting, *you're losing ground.*

If you're on the couch watching TV, *you're losing ground.*

If you're wasting time slouching off, *you're losing ground.*

If you're not in action, in motion, risking, attacking, taking the offense, *you're losing ground.*

If you're not up early relentlessly hunting, hitting, pitching, and hooking, *you're losing ground.*

RELENTLESS MOTION equals confidence. It equals progress. It always results in a step forward, never backward.

You will be tested. You will be attacked. You will get smashed in the face. And when you do—Mike Tyson was right—for most normal people, their plan goes out the window. But the proper response to being punched is RELENTLESS MOTION.

I'm human. Just like everyone else, I have good days and bad days. Other people respond to a bad day with Prozac, a late-night TV binge, or drugs and alcohol. I respond with motion. And it works every time (without the side effects of drugs or alcohol).

One of the best examples of this in my life happened during the writing of this book. Not just the book, but more specifically during the writing of this section of the book you're now reading. One of the companies I'm a spokesman for called to say they were ending our relationship. Because of the poor economy, they could no longer afford to keep paying me. During the same three-day period, not one, not two, not three, but four deals I was working on—deals I thought were done, or as close to done as you can get without signed contracts—all fell through. So I lost important income, plus four potential new deals at the same time. WOW. *Crushing.*

What was my response? Well, of course, as always, I responded with mental and physical MOTION. I prayed, meditated, affirmed, visualized, practiced yoga, took my morning walks, exercised hard, ate healthy and organic, etc.

But more importantly, I responded with *financial motion.* I tossed and turned all night. I couldn't sleep. So I got up at 5:00 a.m. after all of this happened. And I got on my computer and phone and started ATTACK-ING...hard, aggressively, with an "enthusiasm unknown to mankind."

I contacted new potential clients, and also followed up with people and deals that I had heard nothing about for months, that I had forgotten about, that I had given up for dead. I e-mailed...I called...I e-mailed some more...I called some more. Then I followed up some more. There was no time for depression, doubt, or fear. I attacked like a cornered wolverine. I took AGGRESSIVE ACTION. I was a man in MOTION. I relentlessly made something happen.

In forty-eight hours I had four new deals and four new income streams. Outside of magicians David Copperfield, David Blaine, or Criss Angel, not too many people can do what I did. I created magic…out of nothing. That's what motion does. It creates magic. It creates poetry. It creates beautiful music. It creates positivity. Good things are attracted to people in motion.

Negativity, complaining, blaming, sitting or lying around in shock saying "woe is me" are dream killers. Motion is a dream fulfiller.

But motion is more than good. It fights evil too. It is a doubt-, fear-, stress-, and depression-killer! Tens of millions of Americans live on pills for depression. But it's action and motion that effectively kill depression (without side effects). That's how you respond to a punch in the face…or in this case, to a flurry of smashes to my face and gut. I didn't retreat. I didn't hide. I didn't rest. I took the offense. I smashed back and won.

RELENTLESS mental, physical, and financial motion is the answer to doubt, fear, stress, and depression. Motion is a "natural born killer." But motion kills more than just your own personal depression. Motion is also the antidote to a national economic depression as well. Motion is a double-edged depression killer.

In the first Great Depression, from 1929 to 1941, more self-made millionaires were created than any other time in history. How? While 99 percent of the population was suffering in despair and poverty and feeling bad for themselves, a tiny few were in constant relentless motion and taking aggressive action. There are always deals, jobs, customers, and clients for a man or woman in motion.

In the end you have to find a way to beat depression, or negativity, or even the seeds of doubt. Any crack in your confidence can destroy everything you've worked so hard to build. RELENTLESS MOTION is one addiction you can't live without.

BONUS CHAPTER: RELENTLESS WEALTH PROTECTION AND APPRECIATION

I've saved something important for last. Because if you follow all my rules, you may very well become wealthy, famous and successful. That's great news, right? You may even become a legend in your field. But it's all for nothing, if you don't figure out how to protect "what's yours." All the income and assets you acquire are for nothing if you can't protect them, if you can't save them and your family from economic crisis. Getting rich is one thing. Staying rich is even harder! Here is how you stay rich.

In all my years in school and college, no one ever taught me this lesson. I wish I could go back in time and learn, at the start of my career, about the two most relentless investments in the world. These two unique investments relentlessly protect "what's yours" against all forms of economic crisis. And they relentlessly appreciate in good times and bad like no other investment or asset. These two amazing relentless investments are Precious Metals (gold and silver) and Rare Fancy Color Diamonds.

I'll tell you more in a moment. But first let's take a detailed look at the current economy and why I believe every reader of this book needs to quickly move to protect their income, assets, and fortune just as *relentlessly* as they earned it.

This country (and most of the world) is in serious economic trouble. Debt is exploding and getting worse every day. Governments are desperate to spend more money, print more money, as well as add to the debt, in order to try to keep the economy afloat. Yes, stock markets are dramatically higher, but that too is based on debt (printing fake money), which you and your children owe back.

The same exact debt that "saves" our economy short term, will destroy it long term. No nation in world history has ever recovered from a debt-to-GDP ratio of 100 percent or higher. America is now over that 100 percent threshold (much higher, according to some economists).[1]

But this is not a uniquely American problem. Global debt is almost three times larger than the entire world economy.[2]

We are heading for a cataclysmic event—debt crisis, dollar crisis, currency war, world war, stock market implosion, or widespread economic collapse.

Before I get to the personal solution for each of us, allow me to paint a picture of how bad the debt situation really is.

SOBERING FACTS ABOUT THE DEBT

Obama is on track to add $12 trillion to the national debt—a staggering three times more than Bush added in his eight years as president:[3] the "marketable debt" of the U.S. government has increased by 106 percent under Obama, increasing from $5.749 trillion at the end of January 2009 to $11.825 trillion at the end of January 2014, according to the U.S. Treasury.[4]

If the U.S. debt was stacked in dollar bills, it would stretch 1.1 million miles into space, five times the distance from the moon to the earth.[5] The national debt now exceeds the entire output of the U.S. economy.[6] The dangerous debt-to-GDP ratio is now over 100 percent.[7] The national debt jumped $328 billion in one day under Obama, more than the entire budget deficit for the year 2007 under President George W. Bush.[8]

Total public and private debt in advanced economies across the globe is 30 percent higher now than before the Lehman Brothers financial crisis in 2008.[9] Student loans are on track in two to three years to be DOUBLE that of credit card debt.[10]

Because of all of this debt, the U.S. credit rating has been downgraded for the first time in history. Expect many more downgrades to come.[11]

The worst news of all—interest rates are being kept artificially low. They are the lowest in history. Any increase in interest rates in the future would result in just interest on the debt exploding to levels that would eat up the entire budget and send the U.S. economy into a death spiral.

- In January 2001, when President George W. Bush took office, the Treasury was paying an average interest rate of 6.620 percent on its marketable debt.
- In January 2009, when Obama took office, the Treasury was paying an average interest rate of 3.116 percent on its marketable debt.
- In January 2014, according to the Treasury, the U.S. paid an average interest rate of only 1.998 percent on its marketable debt.[12]

Do a little basic math. That means that the average interest rate on the U.S. government's marketable debt is now less than a third of the interest rate we were paying in 2001, when our marketable debt was only about 25 percent of what we owe now. If interest rates were to rise up from the historically low rates they are at now, our economy would be destroyed; the assets that you've worked for your entire life would become worthless; and our children's future would be doomed.

So what's the solution?

PART I: PRECIOUS METALS

It's time to introduce you to the antidote to debt: the *relentless* protection and appreciation of your money. We start with Precious Metals (gold and silver). Precious Metals are the perfect financial instrument for a book called *The Power of RELENTLESS*. Because gold and silver are quite simply the most relentless forms of currency in world history.

Nothing has ever stopped the relentless appreciation of gold—not presidents, or entire countries, or central banks, or the world's most powerful banking families, or the experts on CNBC (who slander gold at every opportunity), or even deceptive billionaires with an agenda like Warren Buffett (who also slanders gold at every opportunity). In the end, gold always wins. That's The Power of RELENTLESS *squared*.

There are many reasons to lose sleep at night. Our country is headed in the wrong direction. The things that have destroyed every country in world history are big government, big spending, big taxes, big entitlements, and big debt. That last one (debt) is the poison of all poisons. I've already laid out the debt tsunami that America is facing.

Over the past 100+ years (since 1913 when the Fed was founded), if you kept your money in dollars, $1,000,000 in cash is now worth **$20,000** (in today's buying power, as of the writing of this book). The dollar has declined in value by about 98 percent during that period.

But if you had kept your assets in gold, $1,000,000 today would be worth about **$60,000,000**.

I don't know about you, but my math says $60 million beats $20,000 every time!

Think of the difference in what you'd leave your family on the day you die. $20,000 is basically worthless—it doesn't even provide a down payment for a cheap condo. But leave your family $60 million and they're set for *generations* to come. Your grandchildren's grandchildren will still be thanking you one hundred years from now.

If you'd prefer a more short-term outlook, let's look at the year 2000. If you kept your money in dollars since the year 2000, $1,000,000 cash is worth about $660,000 (in today's buying power, as of the writing of this book) versus over **$4,000,000** if you had converted paper dollars into physical gold (as of the writing of this book).

Gold is the best long-term asset to hold in the twenty-first century:

- "Gold is up 3500% since 1970!"—*London Telegraph*[13]
- "Gold has DOUBLED versus stocks since 1967!"—*Seeking Alpha*[14]
- "Gold has outperformed stocks for 40 years!"—*Zero Hedge*[15]

Why the forty-year demarcation line? Because up until 1967 gold was pegged to world currencies. Once France dropped ended that in 1967, gold has outperformed stocks over almost every period in the past forty-seven years, except for the tech bubble (from 1997 to 2000). Overall since 1967, stocks were up 18.45 percent versus gold's rise of 37.43 percent.[16]

From January 1, 2000, to Dec 31, 2013 (fourteen years), gold outperformed every other asset class by a mile. Gold beat stocks, bonds, real estate, and even inflation. By how much? The NASDAQ was up over those fourteen years by 16.40 percent. The S&P 500 was up by 56.50 percent. Gold bullion was up by 446 percent.[17]

Now since 2013 gold has been down. But as my investing hero Benjamin Graham said, "Buy low, sell high." Buying gold or silver each time they dip is my definition of a bargain.

What accounts for this over-the-top success for such a long period of time? It's actually pretty simple. Gold is more than an investment, or a form of currency. It's "wealth insurance."

You don't expect to die today, yet you pay for life insurance. You don't expect to be sick today, yet you pay for health insurance. You don't expect to wreck your car, yet you wouldn't even think of getting into your car without auto insurance. Insurance protects you from disaster (an unexpected event that could wipe you out).

Well, buying gold is "wealth insurance"—it protects you from overall economic disaster. There are many forms of economic disaster. There are the obvious kinds (war, tragedy, terrorism). But far worse over time is a more subtle form of economic disaster—reckless, irresponsible, spendthrift, and corrupt politicians and governments. The more they spend, the more debt they create. That debt destroys economies and creates economic crises that erode the value of paper money (the dollar) and eventually leads to the collapse of dominant empires (think of the Greek and Roman Empires).

Gold is your hedge. While paper money issued by reckless governments declines in value, gold holds its value. That's what has happened since 1913, since 1967 and since 2000. But that's all short-term thinking. Gold has served as wealth insurance for thousands of years. It has successfully held its value during major wars, economic collapses, debt crises, hyper-inflation and unrest in the streets.

While the typical investor has slowed their purchase of gold since 2013 (the first down year since 2000), the smartest, most sophisticated investors in the world have *increased* their gold buying—central banks.

Central banks around the world bought more than $3 trillion of physical gold in 2013.[18] All that buying by central banks in 2013 followed a record buying spree in 2012 that saw central banks buy more gold that year than in all the years since 1964 *combined*.[19] In 2014 central banks did it again—they went on a gold-buying spree. They bought 477 tonnes of gold, 17 percent more than in 2013 and the second most gold bought in a year in the past half century (topped only by 2012).[20]

So why isn't any of this in the news? Why isn't it a headline at CNBC? Why does no one teach you about gold in high school...or college...or even business school?

Why does no one mention that the antidote to a debt crisis is gold?

Here's the most important question of all: If gold rose over 400 percent from 2000 to 2013 because of the massive debt being accumulated by the U.S. government (with its out-of-control spending), why wouldn't gold be an even better investment now that debt is dramatically higher both in America and around the world?

If you understand math... and you've read history... you have to understand that this won't end well. History repeats, and we are on a collision course with tragic history.

All the "Principles of Relentless" are worthless if the economy implodes; your assets are destroyed or devalued to almost nothing; and you and your family are left helpless. All your relentless work, relentless energy, relentless optimism, relentless risk, relentless branding, and relentless YESes will have been for nothing.

But I come bearing gifts! I have the solution. This is the powerful one-two punch that protects "what's yours" from crisis and disaster, while relentlessly appreciating in good times and bad.

The first half of my arsenal is precious metals (gold and silver). I call it "wealth insurance." I could not sleep at night without owning gold and silver as my insurance policy.

Here are just a few crises that would keep me up late at night if I didn't own "wealth insurance." I own gold and silver just in case...

In case the over-priced stock market suffers a 1929-like crash, or a long steady decline...

In case of a debt crisis, or economic collapse...

In case of massive hyper-inflation combined with a dollar crisis...

In case World War III breaks out with ISIS in the Middle East...

In case World War III breaks out between the U.S. and Russia over Ukraine...

In case World War III breaks out between the U.S. and China over Taiwan...

In case World War III breaks out over an Iranian nuclear attack on Israel...

In case of unrest in the streets of America…or bank runs…or capital controls…

In case of a massive terrorist attack on U.S. soil…

In case of an EMP (Electro-Magnetic Pulse) attack on America's power grid that would shut down the internet, banks, businesses, credit cards, electricity, pumps at gas stations, etc.…

In case of a massive overdue earthquake in California that will make the costs of repairing New Orleans after Hurricane Katrina look "dirt cheap" in comparison…

In case of a health crisis in this country like Ebola, or a deadly flu pandemic that shuts down commerce, tourism, travel, and strains the healthcare system to the breaking point.

In case any of these "Black Swan" events happens, then owning even as little as 5 to 10 percent of your assets in gold and silver could save your entire life savings (by replacing the value of your falling stocks, bonds, and real estate assets).

Knowing how many bad things could happen, the ownership of precious metals should be a crucial part of any portfolio. Keep in mind that U.S. tax law now allows you to own precious metals inside your IRA accounts.

Gold and silver are about safety and security. Gold and silver give me "staying power" in case of disaster or tragedy. Gold and silver protect my family, income, and assets. Gold and silver help me sleep at night. Gold and silver often appreciate while other forms of investment are in decline or collapse. And that's the very definition of The Power of RELENTLESS.

For more information on how to purchase precious metals (gold and silver), contact THE authority that I trust:

Swiss America

Website: www.RelentlessGOLD.com

PH: 800 519-6270

Dean Heskin is the President of Swiss America

Dean's personal e-mail: Heskin@SwissAmerica.com

RELENTLESS PROTECTION AND APPRECIATION, PART II: RARE FANCY COLOR DIAMONDS

But I'm not done yet. There's a Part Deux to wealth protection and appreciation. Precious metals have a "kissing cousin." I'm talking about diamonds. Not just any diamonds. We all know that traditional diamonds—like a wedding ring—generally go down in value after you walk out of the showroom (kind of like a car).

But Rare Fancy Color Diamonds are a unique asset class all their own—some have called them "indestructible wealth." Because of their rarity, much like rare collectible coins or rare works of art they have proven to hold their value or dramatically appreciate during times of great economic crisis, instability, and uncertainty.

History shows that fancy color diamonds have been one of the best-performing assets during periods of inflation and currency devaluation. Since formal records began in the 1970s, prices for the highest grades of color diamonds have increased in value by an average of between 10 and 15 percent per year (with rarer colors and higher grades enjoying the greatest appreciation).[21]

Perhaps more importantly, the appreciation of fancy color diamonds has no direct correlation to stock market or bond prices—thereby giving investors true diversification.

"Rare" is the key. Regular coins that your child keeps in his piggy bank—pennies, nickels, dimes, quarters—never go up in value. A nickel is worth exactly five cents. Nickels don't go up in value. But rare collectible coins are a very different breed. Just one rare coin from the late 1787 sold at auction in 2014 for $4.58 million. The coin contained 26.66 grams of gold, worth about $400. That's the importance and value of "rarity."[22]

In 2013, a 1794 silver dollar sold for $10 million at auction. An ordinary dollar (the kind you keep in your wallet) may not go very far anymore, but a rare collectible dollar has *ten million times* the value![23] Don't you wish in all your years of schooling, someone, anyone had taught you about the value of rare collectible assets?

Well, it's not too late. That kind of rare value and appreciation is offered by Rare Fancy Color Diamonds here and now. In fact eight of the eleven most expensive diamonds ever sold at auction (at famous auction houses like Sotheby's and Christie's) are fancy natural rare color diamonds.[24]

In late 2014 the "Fancy Color Diamond Index" showed a 167 percent appreciation of Rare Fancy Color Diamonds since January of 2005. This compared to a 58 percent increase in the Dow Jones Industrial Average, 63 percent in the S&P 500, and an 82.1 percent increase in London real estate prices. Pink diamonds showed the greatest appreciation—up 360 percent over the past nine years—clearly a hard asset that you can appreciate, while it is appreciating![25]

Since 2007, over fifteen price records have been broken—such as "highest price per carat ever paid at auction" and "highest price paid for any diamond and any jewel sold at auction"—all by Fancy Color Diamonds.[26]

Rare Color Diamonds are on fire, with record prices being achieved. For example twenty years ago a fancy intense pink color diamond sold for approximately $70,000 per carat. Today that same diamond is worth $500,000 per carat. The highest price ever paid for a color diamond was achieved at Sotheby's in 2013 when a pink color diamond sold for $83.2 million.[27]

Bloomberg, FOX Business News, CNBC, and media across the globe are all talking about the growing trend of investing in Rare Fancy Color Diamonds.[28]

The head auctioneer of Christie's, Rahul Kadakia, says, "Anyone who bought diamonds in 2004, by 2014 noticed 200 percent appreciation."[29]

Leviev Executive V.P. Lisa Klein reported on Fox Business, "Rare Color Diamonds have averaged 15% per year for the last decade."[30]

Naval Bhandari of Sotheby's Diamonds stated that Rare Color Diamonds have averaged about 10 to 15 percent appreciation per year since record keeping began in the mid-1970s.[31]

When anyone acquires Rare Fancy Color Diamonds they should come graded and certified with GIA grading papers and accompanied by a GIA graduate gemologist appraisal.[32]

If you are looking for a non-correlated inflation hedge product that offers Privacy, Performance, Portability, Stored Wealth, Legacy Transfer and Long-Term Growth, then this is the place to be.

One tiny Fancy Color Diamond, about the size of a button, fits in your shirt pocket. It has a weight that is virtually undetectable. You can fit literally millions of dollars of fancy rare color diamonds in an envelope that weighs about two ounces.

Rare Fancy Color Diamonds are a one-of-a-kind portable "wealth insurance" policy. Combined with precious metals (gold and silver), it's the most *relentless* one-two knockout punch in the investing world.

For more information on how to purchase rare fancy color diamonds now, contact THE only authority that I trust:

The Diamond Market
PH: 1-877-432-6291
Website: www.thediamondmarket.com/vault
Adam J. Lowe is the President of The Diamond Market and Adam's direct e-mail is: CEO@TheDiamondMarket.com

Author's Note: I am so sold on the importance of Precious Metals and Rare Fancy Color Diamonds, and more specifically the quality and credibility of Swiss America and The Diamond Market, that I became a paid spokesman for both companies. I cannot recommend them highly enough.

Be Relentless, and you will see all your dreams come true.

God Bless & Best Wishes,

WAR
Wayne Allyn Root
April 29, 2015

Contacting Wayne

Wayne is a spokesman for many companies (both big and small). He is the face, voice, and host of their TV, radio, and internet advertising campaigns. He is always looking for unique new companies to brand and represent. If you'd like to engage Wayne as your spokesman, please contact Wayne at the phone number or e-mail below.

Wayne also hosts and produces spokesman videos for small businesses, professionals (lawyers, doctors, dentists, stockbrokers, real estate brokers, insurance brokers, architects, etc.), and independent contractors. If you'd like Wayne to brand you, your business, or product in a one-time endorsement video, please contact Wayne at the phone number or e-mail below.

Wayne speaks at business conferences, success and personal development events, multi-level marketing events, and corporate conventions, as well as presenting all-day branding, marketing, and sales seminars across the globe. If you'd like to engage Wayne as a speaker for your next event, please contact Wayne at the phone number or e-mail below.

Wayne Allyn Root
WEBSITE: WayneRoot.com
PHONE: 702 407-5548
Toll Free (888) 444-ROOT
E-MAIL: Wayne@WayneRootforAmerica.com
ADDRESS:
Wayne Allyn Root
Cool Hand Root LLC
2505 Anthem Village Drive Ste 318
Henderson, NV 89052

Notes

The 2nd Principle of RELENTLESS: Relentless CHUTZPAH

1. Daniel Holloway, "Travel Channel Tells Ghost Stories to Young, Female Audience," August 29, 2014, *Broadcasting & Cable*, http://www.broadcastingcable.com/blog/bc-beat/travel-channel-tells-ghost-stories-young-female-audience/133557.

2. Arian Eunjung Cha, "Jewish 'success' sells big in China / Boom in books purporting to reveal business secrets," SF Gate, February 9, 2007, http://www.sfgate.com/news/article/Jewish-success-sells-big-in-China-Boom-in-2618613.php.

3. Brett Arends, "It's official: America is now No. 2," MarketWatch, December 4, 2014, http://www.marketwatch.com/story/its-official-america-is-now-no-2-2014-12-04.

4. StandWithUs, "Quick Facts," AskIsrael, http://www.askisrael.org/facts/qpt.asp?fid=5; "Israel," Wikipedia, https://en.wikipedia.org/wiki/Israel.

The 5th Principle of RELENTLESS: Relentless BRANDING

1.   Chris Isadore, "Mayweather vs. Pacquiao: Biggest Payday in Sports," CNN, February 23, 2015, http://money.cnn.com/2015/02/23/news/companies/mayweather-pacquiao-purse/.

2.   Jeff Powell, "Floyd Mayweather vs Manny Pacquiao Purse Could Hit $300m with Pay-per-View Buys Expected to Double 2.4m Record," *Daily Mail*, March 2, 2015, http://www.dailymail.co.uk/sport/boxing/article-2976047/Floyd-Mayweather-vs-Manny-Pacquiao-purse-hit-300m-pay-view-buys-expected-double-2-4m-record.html.

3.   Chris Isadore and Katie Lobosco, "Only High-Rollers Get Ringside Seats for Mayweather-Pacquiao," CNN, February 24, 2015, http://money.cnn.com/2015/02/24/news/companies/mayweather-pacquiao-ringside/index.html?iid=EL.

4.   Mariah Summers, "Vegas Is Almost Entirely Booked Out for the Mayweather-Pacquiao Fight," BuzzFeed, April 8, 2015, http://www.buzzfeed.com/mariah-summers/mayweatherpacquiao-helps-create-perfect-storm-in-vegas#.vkmj7P96K.

5.   "Joe Namath," Pro-Football-Reference, http://www.pro-football-reference.com/players/N/NamaJo00.htm.

6.   "Joe Namath," Wikipedia, http://en.wikipedia.org/wiki/Joe_Namath.

7.   Rheana Murray, "Joe Namath's Fur Coat Steals the Show during Super Bowl XLVIII," *New York Daily News*, February 3, 2014, http://www.nydailynews.com/life-style/fashion/joe-namath-fur-coat-steals-show-article-1.1600358.

8.   "Quarterback Joe Namath Seduces in Pantyhose," *Los Angeles Times*, http://www.latimes.com/business/la-fi-mo-strangest-business-sponsorships-20121-005-photo.html.

9.   "Joe Namath Net Worth," Celebs Net Worth, http://getnetworth.net/joe-namath-net-worth/.

10.   "Facts & Stats," Las Vegas Convention and Visitors Authority, http://www.lvcva.com/stats-and-facts.

11. "Nevada Gaming Revenues 1984–2014," UNLV Center for Gaming Research, February 2015, http://gaming.unlv.edu/reports/NV_1984_present.pdf.

12. "Nevada Sees First Drop in Population since 1910–20," *Las Vegas Review-Journal*, December 31, 2009, http://www.reviewjournal.com/news/nevada-sees-first-drop-population-1910-20.

13. Paula Hendrickson, "More Reality Show Producers Gamble on Las Vegas," *Variety*, June 11, 2014, http://variety.com/2014/tv/awards/more-reality-show-producers-gamble-on-las-vegas-1201217913.

14. Doug Elfman, "Vegas Clubs Are Drowning in Money, As a Nation Comes to Binge Drink and Hook Up," *Las Vegas Review-Journal*, February 14, 2015, http://www.reviewjournal.com/columns-blogs/doug-elfman/vegas-clubs-are-drowning-money-nation-comes-binge-drink-and-hook.

15. Ed Vogel, "Gambling, Quickie Divorces Rescued Nevada's Economy," *Las Vegas Journal-Review*, April 19, 2014, http://www.reviewjournal.com/nevada-150/gambling-quickie-divorces-rescued-nevada-s-economy.

16. Wills Robinson, "Wall Street Intern, 23, Who Quit Her Job to Become a Porn Star Lands Six-Figure Deal to Star in Adult Movies … and Insists Her Boyfriend Is Supportive," *Daily Mail*, January 31, 2015, http://www.dailymail.co.uk/news/article-2934344/Wall-Street-intern-23-quit-job-porn-star-lands-six-figure-deal-star-adult-movie-insists-boyfriend-supportive.html.

17. Veronica Vain, "This Is Why I Left Wall Street for Porn," *New York Post*, February 25, 2015, http://nypost.com/2015/02/25/i-am-the-wall-street-porn-star/.

18. "Lionel Richie Net Worth," Celebs Net Worth, http://getnetworth.net/lionel-richie-net-worth/.

19. Chris O'Shea, "V.A. Musetto, Man behind Iconic 'Headless Body in Topless Bar' Headline, Fired by *NY Post*," Adweek, August 15, 2013, http://www.adweek.com/fishbowlny/v-a-musetto-man-behind-iconic-headless-body-in-topless-bar-headline-fired-by-ny-post/92745.

20. "Headline of the Year: Tiger Puts Balls in Wrong Place Again," ColdHardFacts, April 14, 2013, http://www.coldhardfootballfacts.com/cold-hard-football-facts-blog/headline-the-year-tiger-puts-balls-wrong-place-again/22204/.

21.   John Lehmann, "Mobster Sleeps with the Swishes," *New York Post*, May 1, 2003, http://nypost.com/2003/05/01/mobster-sleeps-with-the-swishes/.

22.   Eric Goldschein, "The *New York Post* Got a Little Carried Away with Their Cover This Morning," Sports Grid, April 21, 2012, http://www.sportsgrid.com/mlb/new-york-post-100-years-cover/.

23.   "Drudgereport Network," QuantCast, https://www.quantcast.com/drudge report.com.

24.   Lauren Indvik, "Study Says Drudge Report Drives More Traffic Than Facebook and Twitter Combined," Mashable, August 10, 2011, http://mashable.com/2011/08/10/news-traffic-referral-study/.

25.   "How Much Is Drudgereport.com Worth?," Worth of Web, http://www.worth ofweb.com/website-value/drudgereport.com.

The 6th Principle of RELENTLESS: Relentless STORYTELLING

1.   "List of Best-Selling Books," Wikipedia, http://en.wikipedia.org/wiki/List_of_best-selling_books.

2.   "The Secret (Book)," Wikipedia, http://en.wikipedia.org/wiki/The_Secret_(book).

3.   "The Secret (2006 Film)," Wikipedia, http://en.wikipedia.org/wiki/The_Secret_(2006_film).

4.   Gail Mitchell, "Exclusive: How Michael Jackson's 'Thriller' Changed the Music Business," *Billboard*, July 3, 2009, http://www.billboard.com/articles/news/268212/exclusive-how-michael-jacksons-thriller-changed-the-music-business.

5.   "List of Best-Selling Albums," Wikipedia, http://en.wikipedia.org/wiki/List_of_best-selling_albums; Bill Wyman, "Did 'Thriller' Really Sell a Hundred Million Copies?," New Yorker, January 4, 2013, http://www.newyorker.com/culture/culture-desk/did-thriller-really-sell-a-hundred-million-copies.

6.   "Thriller (Michael Jackson Album)," Wikipedia, http://en.wikipedia.org/wiki/Thriller_(Michael_Jackson_album).

7. Tyler Durden, "'Peak Dream,': The Death of the Young American Entrepreneur," Zero Hedge, January 3, 2015, http://www.zerohedge.com/news/2015-01-03/peak-dream-death-young-american-entrepreneur.

8. Guy Benson, "Obama to Voters: Hell Yes, My Agenda Is on the Ballot This Fall," Townhall, October 3, 2014, http://townhall.com/tipsheet/guybenson/2014/10/03/obama-to-voters-my-agenda-is-on-the-ballot-this-fall-n1900146.

9. Steve Straub, "The Massive GOP Landslide of 2014 That Nobody's Talking About," Federalist Papers Project, http://www.thefederalistpapers.org/us/the-massive-gop-landslide-of-2014-that-nobodys-talking-about.

The 7ᵗʰ Principle of RELENTLESS: Relentless AGGRESSIVE ACTION

1. Lane DeGregory, "More than 10,000 Families Want to Adopt Orphan Davion Only," *Tampa Bay Times*, October 25, 2013, http://www.tampabay.com/features/humaninterest/more-than-10000-families-want-to-adopt-orphan-davion-only/2149190.

2. Annie Karni, "Real Estate GI Swings Manhattan Property Deals from Afghanistan," *New York Post*, August 5, 2012, http://nypost.com/2012/08/05/real-estate-gi-swings-manhattan-property-deals-from-afghanistan/.

3. "Rachel Martin," LinkedIn, https://www.linkedin.com/pub/rachel-martin/13/330/201.

4. Paul Gatling, "Top Residential Realtors Sell $1.08 Billion in 2011," NWABusinessJournal, March 19, 2013, http://www.nwabusinessjournal.com/11502/top-residential-realtors-sell-108-billion-in-2011.

5. "Meza Harris," Lindsey & Associates, http://www.lindsey.com/agents/index.asp?id=17812.

6. George Waldon, "NWA Residential Firms Endure Market Fallout in '07," *Arkansas Business*, June 23, 2008, http://www.arkansasbusiness.com/article/42405/nwa-residential-firms-endure-market-fallout-in-07?page=all.

7. "The List," http://melaniegabel.com/Portals/210/TopRealtorsofNWA.pdf.

8. "The List," http://www.pageturnpro.com/Gray-Matters,-LLC/57006-Top-Producing-Realtors-2014/index.html#1.

9.   "Top Infomercial Stars of All Time," Daily Finance, http://www.dailyfinance. com/photos/profiles-of-tv-product-pitchmen/#!fullscreen&slide=988992.

10.   Bill Chappell, "Marriott's New Envelope for Room Tips Stirs Debate," National Public Radio, September 16, 2014, http://www.npr.org/blogs/thetwo-way /2014/09/16/348961485/marriott-s-new-envelopes-for-room-tips-stirs-debate.

Bonus Principle of RELENTLESS

1.   "Tim Tebow," Wikipedia, http://en.wikipedia.org/wiki/Tim_Tebow.

2.   Ibid.

3.   Ibid.

4.   Frank Schwab, "Eagles VP of Personnel Explains Why They Signed Tim Tebow," Yahoo!, April 23, 2015, http://sports.yahoo.com/blogs/nfl-shutdown-corner/eagles-vp-of-player-personnel-explains-why-they-signed-tim-tebow-211405324.html.

5.   "Billy Graham," Wikipedia, http://en.wikipedia.org/wiki/Billy_Graham.

6.   Ibid.

7.   Susan Adams, "Optimists Become CEOs, Study Finds," *Forbes*, November 15, 2012, http://www.forbes.com/sites/susanadams/2012/11/15/optimists-become-ceos-study-finds/.

8.   Duke: The Fuqua School of Business, "News Release: Study: CEOs Are More Optimistic, More Open to Risk," November 5, 2012.

9.   "Study: Optimistic MBA Grads Have Better Career Prospects Than Pessimists," Duke Today, January 31, 2011, https://today.duke.edu/2011/01/optimistic_ mba.html.

POSITIVE ADDICTION #1: Relentless EARLY MORNINGS

1.   Philip Delves Broughton, "Why Morning People Rule the World," *London Evening Standard*, July 5, 2010, http://www.standard.co.uk/lifestyle/why-morning-people-rule-the-world-6488205.html.

2.   Jenny Hope, "Is Your TV Killing You? Every Hour of Viewing Takes 22 Minutes Off Your Life, Couch Potatoes Are Warned," *Daily Mail*, August 16, 2011, http://

www.dailymail.co.uk/health/article-2026380/TV-watching-Every-hour-takes-22-minutes-life.html.

3.   Lizzie Parry, "Power Napping Really IS Good for You: A 30-Minute Snooze Can Repair the Damage Caused by a Lack of Sleep," *Daily Mail*, February 10, 2015, http://www.dailymail.co.uk/health/article-2947999/Power-napping-really-good-Just-half-hour-snooze-repair-damage-caused-lack-sleep-study-finds.html.

4.   Auslan Cramb, "Jogging in Forest Twice as Good as Trip to Gym for Mental Health," *Telegraph*, June 20, 2012, http://www.telegraph.co.uk/news/health/news/9344129/Jogging-in-forest-twice-as-good-as-trip-to-gym-for-mental-health.html.

5.   Joanna Hall, "Walk This Way...and Lose 10Lb in Four Weeks! How Simply Putting One Foot in Front of the Other Can Beat the Bulge," *Daily Mail*, May 18, 2013, http://www.dailymail.co.uk/health/article-2326637/Walk-way—lose-10lb-weeks-How-simply-putting-foot-beat-bulge.html.

POSITIVE ADDICTION #2: Relentless HOME AND FAMILY

1.   Sue Shellenbarger, "Family Togetherness Goes beyond Dinner Chat," *Wall Street Journal*, July 29, 1998, http://www.wsj.com/articles/SB901666 141713796500.

2.   "Parenting," Christ United Methodist Church, http://www.cumcmemphis.org/assets/1549/internet1-parenting.pdf.

3.   Randal D. Day, et al., "Marital Quality and Outcomes for Children and Adolescents: A Review of the Family Process Literature," U.S. Department of Health and Human Services, May 2009, http://aspe.hhs.gov/hsp/08/relationshipstrengths/LitRev/.

4.   Katie Moisse, "Two Minus One: Divorce Drops Kids' Math Scores," ABC News, June 2, 2011, http://abcnews.go.com/Health/w_ParentingResource/divorce-impacts-kids-school-performance/story?id=13735021; Brittany Odenweller, "Does Parental Divorce Have an Affect on a Child's Education?," Virtual

Commons—Bridgewater State University, April 25, 2014, http://vc.bridgew. edu/cgi/viewcontent.cgi?article=1056&context=honors_proj.

POSITIVE ADDICTION #3: Relentless MINDFULNESS

1. Makiko Kitamura, "Harvard Yoga Scientists Find Proof of Meditation Benefit," Bloomberg, November 21, 2013, http://www.bloomberg.com/news/articles /2013-11-22/harvard-yoga-scientists-find-proof-of-meditation-benefit.

2. Ibid.

3. Amanda L. Chan, "Mindfulness Meditation Benefits: 20 Reasons Why It's Good for Your Mental and Physical Health," Huffington Post, April 8, 2013, http://www.huffingtonpost.com/2013/04/08/mindfulness-meditation- benefits-health_n_3016045.html.

4. Emma M. Seppälä, "20 Scientific Reasons to Start Meditating Today: New Research Shows Meditation Boosts Your Health, Happiness, and Success!," *Psychology Today*, September 11, 2013, https://www.psychologytoday.com/blog/ feeling-it/201309/20-scientific-reasons-start-meditating-today.

5. P.F. Louis, "Meditation May Slow Brain Matter Loss Due to Aging," *Natural News*, February 28, 2015, http://www.naturalnews.com/048793_meditation _brain_matter_loss_aging.html.

POSITIVE ADDICTION #4: Relentless PRAYER, GRATITUDE, AND FORGIVENESS

1. Joseph Eron O'Donnell, "The God Solution: Spirituality As a Coping Mecha- nism and Healing Tool for Mental Illness and Addiction," Wesleyan University honors thesis, April 2013, http://wesscholar.wesleyan.edu/cgi/viewcontent. cgi?article=1972&context=etd_hon_theses.

2. Tom Knox, "The Tantalising Proof That Belief in God Makes You Happier and Healthier," *Daily Mail*, February 18, 2011, http://www.dailymail.co.uk/femail/ article-1358421/The-tantalising-proof-belief-God-makes-happier-healthier. html.

3. Patrick F. Fagan, "Why Religion Matters Even More: The Impact of Religious Practice on Social Stability" (Backgrounder #1992 on Religion and Civil Socety

and Civil Society) Heritage Foundation, December 18, 2006, http://www.
heritage.org/research/reports/2006/12/why-religion-matters-even-more-the-
impact-of-religious-practice-on-social-stability.

POSITIVE ADDICTION #5: Relentless AFFIRMATION AND VISUALIZATION

1. J. David Cresswell, et al., "Self-Affirmation Improves Problem-Solving under Stress," Plos One, May 1, 2013, http://journals.plos.org/plosone/article ?id=10.1371/journal.pone.0062593.
2. "Benefits of Self-Affirmation," Carnegie Mellon University, summer 2013, http://www.cmu.edu/homepage/health/2013/summer/benefits-of-self-affirmation.shtml.
3. Vince Favilla, "Do Positive Affirmations Work?," SoonIWill.Be, http://sooniwill.be/happier/do-affirmations-work-the-truth-about-positive-affirmations/.
4. Wayne Allyn Root, "Failing Your Way to Success," Connecting Point, http://connectingpointdigital.com/uncategorized/wayne-allyn-root-failing-your-way-to-success.
5. David DiSalvo, "Visualize Success If You Want to Fail," *Forbes*, June 8, 2011, http://www.forbes.com/sites/daviddisalvo/2011/06/08/visualize-success-if-you-want-to-fail; Jeremy Dean, "The Right Kind of Visualisation," Psyblog, March 16, 2011, http://www.spring.org.uk/2011/03/the-right-kind-of-visualisation.php.

POSITIVE ADDICTION #6: Relentless PHYSICAL FITNESS

1. "Study: Lack of Exercise Causes Twice As Many Deaths As Obesity," CBS Atlanta, January 15, 2015, http://atlanta.cbslocal.com/2015/01/15/study-lack-of-exercise-causes-twice-as-many-deaths-as-obesity/.
2. Joseph Mercola, "Even if You Exercise, Sitting Eight Hours a Day Significantly Increases Your Risk of Dying from Any Cause," Peak Fitness, February 6, 2015, http://fitness.mercola.com/sites/fitness/archive/2015/02/06/effects-prolonged-sitting.aspx.

3. "The Benefits of Physical Activity," Harvard T. H. Chan School of Public Heath, http://www.hsph.harvard.edu/nutritionsource/staying-active-full-story/.

4. Ibid.

5. Nancy Hellmich, "Is Exercise the Best Medicine? Studies Show Big Benefit," *USA Today*, October 2, 2013, http://www.usatoday.com/story/news/nation/2013/10/02/exercise-medicine-heart-disease-diabetes/2907853/.

6. E. W. Griffin, et al., "Aerobic Exercise Improves Hippocampal Function and Increases BDNF in the Serum of Young Adult Males," PubMed, U.S. National Library of Medicine, National Institutes of Health, October 24, 2011, http://www.ncbi.nlm.nih.gov/pubmed/21722657.

7. "Aerobic Exercise Is the Critical Variable in an Enriched Environment That Increases Hippocampal Neurogenesis and Water Maze Learning in Male C57BL/6J Mice," PubMed, U.S. National Library of Medicine, National Institutes of Health, September 6, 2012, http://www.ncbi.nlm.nih.gov/pubmed/22698691.

8. Alexandra Sifferlin, "Exercise Trumps Brain Games in Keeping Our Minds Intact," *Time*, October 23, 2012, http://healthland.time.com/2012/10/23/exercise-trumps-brain-games-in-keeping-our-minds-intact/.

9. R. Morgan Griffin, "Your Kid's Brain on Exercise," WebMD, http://www.webmd.com/parenting/raising-fit-kids/move/kid-brain-exercise.

10. "Treadmill Desk," NordicTrak, http://www.nordictrack.com/fitness/en/NordicTrack/Treadmills/nordictrack-desk-treadmill?utm_source=Google Shopping&utm_medium=organic&im_pid=1&im_mid=142&im_channel=GoogleShopping.

11. Deborah Kotz and Angela Haupt, "7 Mind-Blowing Benefits of Exercise: Think Exercise Is All about Toned Abs and Weight Loss? It Also Makes You Happier and Smarter," *U.S. News & World Report*, March 7, 2012, http://health.usnews.com/health-news/diet-fitness/slideshows/7-mind-blowing-benefits-of-exercise.

12. Tom Scheve, "Is There a Link between Exercise and Happiness? Happiness, Exercise, and Endorphins," howstuffworks, http://science.howstuffworks.com/life/exercise-happiness2.htm.

13.   Heidi Godman, "Regular Exercise Changes the Brain to Improve Memory, Thinking Skills," Harvard Health Publications, April 9, 2014, http://www.health.harvard.edu/blog/regular-exercise-changes-brain-improve-memory-thinking-skills-201404097110.

14.   Telegraph Men, "Why Weight Training Is Better for Your Waistline Than Running: A New Harvard Study Has Found That Weight Training Is a Better Way of Keeping the Middle-Aged Spread at Bay Than Aerobic Activity," *Telegraph*, December23, 2014, http://www.telegraph.co.uk/men/active/11310141/Why-weight-training-is-better-for-your-waistline-than-running.html.

15.   Amy Novotney, "Yoga As a Practice Tool: With a Growing Body of Research Supporting Yoga's Mental Health Benefits, Psychologists Are Weaving the Practice into Their Work with Clients," American Psychological Association, vol. 20, no. 10 (November 2009), 38, http://www.apa.org/monitor/2009/11/yoga.aspx.

16.   Ibid.

17.   Maria Popova, "An Antidote to the Age of Anxiety: Alan Watts on Happiness and How to Live with Presence," Williamsburg Yoga Psychotherapy, January 29, 2015, http://www.yogapsychotherapynyc.com/?page_id=1076.

18.   Rachel Zimmerman, "Harvard, Brigham Study: Yoga Eases Veterans PTSD Symptoms," WBUR, December 8, 2010, http://commonhealth.wbur.org/2010/12/harvard-brigham-medical-study-yoga-veterans-ptsd.

POSITIVE ADDICTION #7: Relentless HEALTHY DIET

1.   Tim Hume and Jen Christensen, "WHO: Imminent Global Cancer 'Disaster' Reflects Aging, Lifestyle Factors," CNN, February 4, 2014, http://www.cnn.com/2014/02/04/health/who-world-cancer-report.

2.   Joseph Mercola, "Fructose: Drinking This 'Popular Poison' Is Worse Than Smoking," Mercola, November 21, 2011, http://articles.mercola.com/sites/articles/archive/2011/11/21/soda-linked-to-health-problems.aspx.

3.   Joseph Mercola, "Junk Food: Just As Bad As Cigarettes, and Marketing Tactics Also Rival Those of Big Tobacco," Mercola, June 7, 2014, http://articles.

mencola.com/sites/articles/archive/2014/06/07/junk-food-marketing-children.aspx.

4.   Joseph Mercola, "Avoid Sugar to Help Slow Aging," Mercola, February 22, 2012, http://articles.mercola.com/sites/articles/archive/2012/02/22/how-sugar-accelerates-aging.aspx; Joseph Mercola, "Big Sugar Tips Balance of Scale," Mercola, January 15, 2014, http://articles.mercola.com/sites/articles/archive/2014/01/15/sugary-beverage-obesity.aspx.

5.   "Sugary Soda Drinks Linked to Cell Aging," Medical News Today, October 17, 2014, http://www.medicalnewstoday.com/articles/283994.php.

6.   Carolanne Wright, "Landmark Study Links Pesticides to High Depression Rates," Natural News, February 6, 2015, http://www.naturalnews.com/048529_pesticides_depression_suicide.html.

7.   Joseph Mercola, "Fast Food May Stunt Your Child's Academic Performance," Mercola, January 7, 2015, http://articles.mercola.com/sites/articles/archive/2015/01/07/fast-food-slows-learning.aspx.

8.   "Fast-Food Consumption Linked to Lower Test Score Gains in 8th Graders," Science Daily, December 22, 2014, http://www.sciencedaily.com/releases/2014/12/141222111605.htm.

9.   Kris Gunnars, "10 Proven Health Benefits of Low-Carb and Ketogenic Diets," http://authoritynutrition.com/10-benefits-of-low-carb-ketogenic-diets/.

10.   Theo Weening, "Grass-Fed Beef Now Nationwide," Whole Foods, May 6, 2010, http://www.wholefoodsmarket.com/blog/whole-story/grass-fed-beef-now-nationwide.

11.   "Rain Crow Ranch Buyer's Club," American Grassfed Beef, http://www.americangrassfedbeef.com/monthly-grass-fed-beef.asp.

12.   "The Secret Sauce in Grass-Fed Beef," Mercola, https://www.mercola.com/beef/cla.htm.

13.   Mike Hajoway, "CLA: Conjugated Linoleic Acid Research," Bodybuilding, March 12, 2015, http://www.bodybuilding.com/fun/mike8.htm.

14.   Leah D. Whigham, et al., "Efficacy of Conjugated Linoleic Acid for Reducing Fat Mass: A Meta-Analysis in Humans," *American Journal of Clinical Nutrition*, vol. 85, no. 5 (May 2007), 1203–11, http://ajcn.nutrition.org/content/85/5/1203.full; Joseph Elijah Barrett, "A Comprehensive Guide to Weight Loss," Living a

Healthy Lifestyle, http://www.living-a-healthy-lifestyle.com/support-files/
guide2weightloss.pdf.

15. David Gutierrez, "China Faces Epidemic of Diabetes after Adopting Western
Diet," Natural News, August 4, 2010, http://www.naturalnews.com/029354_
China_epidemic.html.

POSITIVE ADDICTION #9: Relentless CHARITY

1. "A Crucial Catch: Annual Screening Saves Lives," NFL, http://www.nfl.com/
pink.

2. "Prospective NHL Team Owner Strikes Deal with Opportunity Village," *Las
Vegas Review-Journal*, March 3, 2015, http://www.reviewjournal.com/sports/
hockey/prospective-nhl-team-owner-strikes-deal-opportunity-village.

3. Greg Emerson, "The 10 Most Charitable Companies in America," Yahoo!,
December 2, 2011, http://finance.yahoo.com/news/the-10-most-charitable-
companies-in-america.html.

4. "Top Funders: 50 Largest Corporate Foundations by Total Giving," Foundation
Center, April 25, 2015, http://foundationcenter.org/findfunders/topfunders/
top50giving.html.

POSITIVE ADDICTION #11: Relentless SMILING AND SAYING YES

1. Vivian Giang, "How Smiling Changes Your Brain: Putting on a Happy Face
Doesn't Just Make You More Likeable; It Makes You Healthier, Both Good
for Your Career," Fast Company, January 28, 2015, http://www.fastcompany.
com/3041438/how-to-be-a-success-at-everything/how-smiling-changes-
your-brain.

2. Ibid.

BONUS CHAPTER: Relentless WEALTH PROTECTION AND APPRECIATION

1. Tyler Durden, "This Is the Biggest Problem Facing the World Today: 9 Countries Have Debt-to GDP over 300%," Zero Hedge, February 23, 2015, http://

www.zerohedge.com/news/2015-02-23/biggest-problem-facing-world-today-9-countries-have-debt-gdp-over-300.

2.   "Global Debt Is More Than Twice as Big as the World Economy…What Does It Mean?," Washington's Blog, March 3, 2015, http://www.washingtonsblog.com/2015/03/debt.html.

3.   Amy Payne, "Morning Bell: $16,000,000,000,000," Daily Signal, September 5, 2012, http://blog.heritage.org/2012/09/05/morning-bell-16000000000000.

4.   Terence P. Jeffrey, "+106%: Obama Has More Than Doubled Marketable U.S. Debt," CNS News, February 18, 2014, http://cnsnews.com/news/article/terence-p-jeffrey/106-obama-has-more-doubled-marketable-us-debt#sthash.CpAfiM9f.dpuf; "Monthly Statement of the Public Debt of the United States," Treasury Direct, January 31, 2014, http://www.treasurydirect.gov/govt/reports/pd/mspd/2014/opds012014.pdf.

5.   Gregory Gwyn-Williams Jr., "National Debt Stacked in Dollar Bills Would Stretch from Earth to Moon Five Times," CNS News, July 26, 2013, http://cnsnews.com/mrctv-blog/gregory-gwyn-williams-jr/national-debt-stacked-dollar-bills-would-stretch-earth-moon-five.

6.   "U.S. Debt Exceeds Annual Economic Output," CBC News, January 9, 2012, http://www.cbc.ca/news/business/story/2012/01/09/us-gdp-debt.html.

7.   "United States Government Debt to GDP 1940–2015," Trading Economics, http://www.tradingeconomics.com/united-states/government-debt-to-gdp.

8.   Stephen Dinan, "U.S. Debt Jumps a Record $328 Billion—Tops $17 Trillion for the First Time," *Washington Times*, October 18, 2013, http://www.washingtontimes.com/news/2013/oct/18/us-debt-jumps-400-billion-tops-17-trillion-first-t/.

9.   Ambrose Evans-Pritchard, "BIS Veteran Says Global Credit Excess Worse Than Pre-Lehman," *Telegraph*, September 15, 2013, http://www.telegraph.co.uk/finance/10310598/BIS-veteran-says-global-credit-excess-worse-than-pre-Lehman.html.

10. "Student Loans Hit Record $1.08 Trillion; Delinquent Student Debt Rises to All Time High," Bankster News, February 19, 2014, http://news.dethronethebanksters.

com/student-loans-hit-record-1-08-trillion-delinquent-student-debt-rises-to-all-time-high/.

11.   Tracy Withers, "U.S. to Get Downgraded amid Fiscal 'Theater,' Pimco Says," Bloomberg, October 18, 2012, http://www.bloomberg.com/news/2012-10-17/u-s-to-get-downgraded-amid-fiscal-theater-pimco-says.html.

12.   Jeffrey, "+106%."

13.   Kyle Caldwell, "Gold Turns £27,800 into £1m: Gold Has Achieved a Staggering 3,500pc Return since 1970, a New Report Has Found," *Telegraph*, November 13, 2013, http://www.telegraph.co.uk/finance/personalfinance/investing/gold/10445952/Gold-turns-27800-into-1m.html.

14.   "Since Losing the Peg, Gold Has Outperformed Stocks except for the Tech Bubble," Seeking Alpha, October 17, 2013, http://seekingalpha.com/article/1752332-since-losing-the-peg-gold-has-outperformed-stocks-except-for-the-tech-bubble?source=email_rt_mc_related_2.

15.   Phoenix Capital Research, "Gold Beat Stocks except during the Tech Bubble," Zero Hedge, November 23, 2013, http://www.zerohedge.com/contributed/2013-11-23/gold-beat-stocks-except-during-tech-bubble.

16.   Ibid.

17.   "Key Asset Class Returns for 2000–2014," Evanson Asset Management, January 2015, http://www.evansonasset.com/index.cfm?Page=161.

18.   Agustino Fontevecchia, "Central Banks Bought More Than $3B in Gold in 2013: UBS," *Forbes*, March 27, 2013, http://www.forbes.com/sites/afontevecchia/2013/03/27/central-banks-bought-more-than-3-trillion-in-gold-in-2013-ubs/.

19.   Jeff Clark, "Guest Post: Whom to Believe on Gold: Central Banks or Bloomberg?," Zero Hedge, March 26, 2013, http://www.zerohedge.com/news/2013-03-26/guest-post-whom-believe-gold-central-banks-or-bloomberg.

20.   Tyler Durden, "Central Banks Buy the Second Most Gold in 50 Years: A Look at Who's Buying," Zero Hedge, February 12, 2015, http://www.zerohedge.com/news/2015-02-12/central-banks-buy-second-most-gold-50-years-look-whos-buying.

21. "Coloured Diamond Investment Continues to Soar As Elite Gems Sells 10.88ct Pink Diamond," PRWeb, November 18, 2010, http://www.prweb.com/releases/2010/11/prweb4795634.htm.

22. "Brasher Doubloon, the First Coin to Be Minted in US, Fetches More Than U.S. $4.5 Million at Auction," ABC News, January 11, 2014, http://www.abc.net.au/news/2014-01-11/brasher-doubloon-coin-sells-for-us-45-million/5195546.

23. "It's Top Dollar! Rare 1794 Silver Dollar Sells for Record $10 Million at U.S. Auction," *Daily Mail*, January 25, 2013, http://www.dailymail.co.uk/news/article-2268041/Rare-1794-silver-dollar-sells-record-10-million-U-S-auction.html.

24. "Investing in Colored Diamonds," White Coat Investor, June 26, 2013, http://whitecoatinvestor.com/investing-in-colored-diamonds/.

25. "Colored Diamonds Market Report," International Hard Asset Investment, November 12, 2014, http://internationalhardasset.com/reports/IHAI_Report_ColoredDiamonds.pdf.

26. "Colored Diamonds Compared to Other Investment Opportunities," Leibish, December 20, 2012, http://www.leibish.com/colored-diamonds-compared-to-other-investment-opportunities-article-594.

27. Robert Frank, "Most Expensive Diamond Ever Sold Goes for $83.2M," CNBC, November 13, 2013, http://www.cnbc.com/id/101196278.

28. "Are Colored Diamonds an Investor's Best Friend?," Bloomberg, July 19, 2015, http://www.bloomberg.com/news/videos/b/f6858432-d328-41c8-8bb7-cb7c751dc99e.

29. "Why Now Is the Time to Own Diamonds," Bloomberg, June 10, 2015, http://www.bloomberg.com/news/videos/b/1e22707c-89e1-4e02-bce8-34f9a633f894.

30. "The Growing Trend of Colored Diamonds," Fox Business, March 1, 2013, http://video.foxbusiness.com/v/2198322974001/the-growing-trend-of-colored-diamonds/?playlist_id=933116634001.

31. Alison Burwell, "Colored Diamonds: An Insider's Guide," *Departures*, May 5, 2011, Departures Magazine, May/June 2011, by Alison Burwell, www.depatures.com/articles/colored-diamonds-an-insiders-guide.

32. "Guide to Understanding Diamond Quality and GIA Diamond Grading Reports," GIA, http://www.4cs.gia.edu/EN-US/.

Index